The Great Nation of Futurity

OXFORD STUDIES IN SOCIOLINGUISTICS

General Editors:
Brook Bolander
Monash University
Adam Jaworski
University of Hong Kong

RECENTLY PUBLISHED IN THE SERIES:

Stance: Sociolinguistic Perspectives
Edited by Alexandra Jaffe

Investigating Variation: The Effects of Social Organization and Social Setting
Nancy C. Dorian

Television Dramatic Dialogue: A Sociolinguistic Study
Kay Richardson

Language Without Rights
Lionel Wee

Paths to Post-Nationalism
Monica Heller

Language Myths and the History of English
Richard J. Watts

The "War on Terror" Narrative
Adam Hodges

Digital Discourse: Language in the New Media
Edited by Crispin Thurlow and Kristine Mroczek

Leadership, Discourse, and Ethnicity
Janet Holmes, Meredith Marra, and Bernadette Vine

Spanish in New York
Ricardo Otheguy and Ana Celia Zentella

Multilingualism and the Periphery
Sari Pietikäinen and Helen Kelly-Holmes

Discourses in War and Peace
Edited by Adam Hodges

Legal-Lay Communication: Textual Travels in the Law
Edited by Chris Heffer, Frances Rock, and John Conley

Speaking Pittsburghese: The Story of a Dialect
Barbara Johnstone

The Pragmatics of Politeness
Geoffrey Leech

Language and Superdiversity: Indonesians Knowledging at Home and Abroad
Zane Goebel

Sustaining the Nation: The Making and Moving of Language and Nation
Monica Heller, Lindsay A Bell, Michelle Daveluy, Mireille McLaughlin, and
Hubert Noel

Style, Mediation, and Change: Sociolinguistic Perspectives on Talking Media
Janus Mortensen, Nikolaus Coupland, and Jacob Thogersen

Reimagining Rapport
Zane Goebel

Elite Authenticity: Remaking Distinction in Food Discourse
Gwynne Mapes

In Pursuit of English: Language and Subjectivity in Neoliberal South Korea
Joseph Sung-Yul Park

Choreographies of Multilingualism: Writing and Language Ideology in Singapore
Tong King Lee

THE GREAT NATION OF FUTURITY
The Discourse and Temporality of American National Identity

Patricia L. Dunmire

OXFORD
UNIVERSITY PRESS

Oxford University Press is a department of the University of Oxford. It furthers
the University's objective of excellence in research, scholarship, and education
by publishing worldwide. Oxford is a registered trade mark of Oxford University
Press in the UK and certain other countries.

Published in the United States of America by Oxford University Press
198 Madison Avenue, New York, NY 10016, United States of America.

© Oxford University Press 2023

All rights reserved. No part of this publication may be reproduced, stored in
a retrieval system, or transmitted, in any form or by any means, without the
prior permission in writing of Oxford University Press, or as expressly permitted
by law, by license, or under terms agreed with the appropriate reproduction
rights organization. Inquiries concerning reproduction outside the scope of the
above should be sent to the Rights Department, Oxford University Press, at the
address above.

You must not circulate this work in any other form
and you must impose this same condition on any acquirer.

Library of Congress Control Number: 2022950252

ISBN 978–0–19–765822–2

DOI: 10.1093/oso/9780197658222.001.0001

Printed by Integrated Books International, United States of America

I dedicate this book to the memory of my brother Marc Dunmire, to whom I owe my interest in politics and the Cold War, and to the memory of my dear, brilliant friend Kevin Floyd.

CONTENTS

Preface   *ix*

1. Futurity, National Identity, and American Foreign Policy Discourse   1

2. "America's Most Precious Natural Resource": The Temporality of American Exceptionalism   31

3. "Vistas to the Future": Shaping the Postwar Future   51

4. "New Vistas of Opportunity": Modernizing the Other   78

5. "Alerting America": The Committee on the Present Danger and the Re-Securitization of the Soviet Union   101

6. From the American Century to the End of History: An American Future of Democratic Peace   133

7. The Future of American Exceptionalism   156

Notes   *169*
Appendix: Data Bibliography   *175*
References   *181*
Index   *195*

PREFACE

As a critical discourse analyst, I am primarily concerned with the role language plays in creating, mediating, maintaining, and resisting unequal relations of power. My particular line of inquiry examines the intersection of discourse and futurity: the linguistic and discursive means by which projections of the future are constructed within political discourse and the rhetorical and ideological functions those projections serve. In short, I view the future as a discursive construct, rhetorical resource, and domain for the exercise and contest of power. Furthermore, I presume a "critical futures" perspective, which holds that the global future has to a significant extent been dominated and exploited by a Western capitalist conception of modernity in a way that undermines the agency and potentialities that the future offers for social and political transformation (Inayatullah 1999: 130; also see Goode and Godhe 2017, 2018; Sardar 1999).

It is against this critical theoretical backdrop that I examine the role futurity plays in conceptions of American national identity and geopolitical purpose embedded within Cold War foreign policy discourse. Given the symbolic and material significance of the temporal domain of the future to the vitality of sociopolitical life, as well as to movements of resistance and change, the assertion that America has "privileged access to an unknown future" and, thus, a right to "occupy the future" has important ideological implications (Englehardt 2010: 209). Such a claim is inherently hegemonic, as it serves to legitimate an approach to foreign policy that seeks to design the global future in the American image. That is, by claiming, as President Obama put it, a "unique capacity to speak to [other people's] hopes," U.S. foreign policy has, in fact, implicated people in futures not necessarily of their making (USNSC 2010; Grosz 1999). Indeed, the insistence that the United States is the nation of progress and, as such, is uniquely qualified to lead the world to a better future has all too often been used to sanction policies that not only usurp people's claim to their own future but also create futures of misery, want, and destruction.

American post-9/11 "call-to-arms" discourse (Graham et al. 2004; Oddo 2011), for example, grounds arguments for the necessity of military action in idealized, often grandiose, projections of the future that such action will deliver. President George W. Bush's policy of preemptive war promised to "extend the benefits of freedom across the globe" (USNSC 2002: 02). For Iraqis in particular, President Bush unequivocally promised that through military action the oppression of ethnic minorities "will be lifted" and by waging war on Iraq the United States "will give hope to others" and "will secure peace and lead the world to a better day" (Bush 2002). Regarding "the way forward in Afghanistan and Pakistan," President Obama (2009) similarly pledged that military escalation "will lead to a world that is more secure, and a future that represents not the darkest of fears but the highest of hopes." He grounded this pledge in an abiding belief in the purported exceptional role America has played in the history of human progress, insisting that "From the birth of our liberty, America has had faith in the future . . . a belief that where we are going is better than where we have been . . . at each juncture that history has called upon us . . . we have advanced our interests, while contributing to the cause of human progress" (USNSC 2010).

American claims that its geopolitical policies have advanced the progress of humankind have, of course, been subject to criticism and controversy. Most recently with the election and presidency of Donald Trump, the proclaimed faith in the American future—both the belief that the future will be better than the past and present and the conviction that the nation has a special role to play in shaping that future—has come under scrutiny both from within the nation and abroad.[1] What role can the United States play in shaping a global future of democracy and freedom, and warding off challenges to that future, when the shape and character of its own democracy is under siege by some of its own citizens and leaders? What hope for the future does America represent to the world's people when the future of its own citizens is threatened by a range of economic, social, and political crises?

While answering such question requires multiple disciplinary perspectives, a critical examination of the discursive construal and rhetorical deployment of American national identity within foreign policy discourse has a role to play. Critical discourse analysis is concerned, after all, with providing insight into sociopolitical practices and problems by examining their discursive dimensions (Fairclough 2003). As such, it is my hope that the following pages, by interrogating the discursive practice of creating relations of identity and difference and of configuring those relations in temporal terms, have something say about the way America has been identified with respect to the future and the implications of that identification for the capacity of the future to serve as a domain of possibility, potentiality, and change.

CHAPTER 1

Futurity, National Identity, and American Foreign Policy Discourse

INTRODUCTION

Noting the constancy of claims about the future in American media and political discourse in the early years of the 21st century, Lewis Lapham (2011) posits the future to be "America's most precious natural resource, the ground of its being and basis of its economy as well as the focus of its politics" (14). My purpose here is to examine how this resource figured within Cold War foreign policy discourse. The central premise of this book is that conceptions of American national identity and geopolitical purpose embed a crucial temporal element that situates the nation in a privileged position vis-à-vis the future. Specifically, I argue that Cold War foreign policy discourse embeds the claim that America is the exemplar of the future and, as such, has a special right and responsibility to shape the geopolitical future. I further argue that this claim on the future serves rhetorically to legitimate an expansionist and interventionist foreign policy. My goal in the following pages is to provide insight into the discursive means by which the *future*—as a discursive construct, rhetorical resource, and conceptual space—has figured in America's conception of its place and purpose in the world.

I situate my argument within the discourse and ideology of American exceptionalism—the insistence that the United States, as the "exemplary" nation, has "a unique destiny and history" and a "special role to play in human history"—which has undergirded the nation's identity and its geopolitical role throughout its history (Bell 1989: 41; Kammen 1993: 6; McCrisken 2003: 1). My particular tack is to draw out the temporal dimension of the exceptionalist ideology, namely, the construal of America as the "great nation of futurity"

The Great Nation of Futurity. Patricia L. Dunmire, Oxford University Press. © Oxford University Press 2023.
DOI: 10.1093/oso/9780197658222.003.0001

(O'Sullivan 1839), and analyze how this claim on the future has figured in Cold War foreign policy discourse.

My argument is grounded in a critical discourse study of a variety of texts (i.e., speeches, essays, and policy documents) generated at moments during the Cold War when America's geopolitical purpose and role were subject to debate: its formulation in the mid-1940s, enactment in the 1950s and 1960s, reassertion in the 1970s and 1980s, and reformulation in the late 20th century.[1] My analysis demonstrates that assertions of the nation's identity and geopolitical purpose were consistently grounded in the claim that America bears a special relationship to the geopolitical future and, thus, has a right to claim the geopolitical future as a means of protecting and furthering its interests and, thereby, those of global society.

In brief, the onset of the Cold War saw the introduction of a temporal scheme that positioned the United States as uniquely capable of shaping the future of the post–World War II world and leading others to that future. During the "hot" Cold War of the 1950s and 1960s, the battle between East and West was, to a significant extent, deemed a battle over the future of the newly decolonized societies. American policymakers and pundits waged this battle rhetorically by rendering the United States as the true vanguard of the future and the Soviet Union as a false prophet of the future. This phase of the Cold War was followed by an easing of tensions between the United States and the Soviet Union and a foreign policy approach focused on cooperation and mutual interest. The discourse of detente was quickly countered with a discourse of "a clear and present danger" that re-identified the Soviet Union as the nation's radical Other. This discourse employed an "anticipatory regime" (Adams et al. 2009: 249) that constituted the present danger through projections of catastrophic futures. In so doing, it underscored the necessity of the United States having reign over the global future. The reignition of the Cold War was soon followed by its ending in 1989. The demise of the nation's radical Other, nevertheless, raised questions about what America represented and the geopolitical purpose it would serve in the post–Cold War world. Once again, the foreign policy community looked toward the future to reaffirm the ineluctable need for American global leadership. Should the nation shun its role in shaping the post–Cold War future, so the argument went, it would cede that future to the forces of chaos, anarchy, and disorder.

In what follows, I explain the theoretical framework that grounds my argument concerning the temporal nature of American national identity and my analysis of Cold War foreign policy discourse. I begin with an overview of critical conceptions of temporality and futurity and relate them to critical conceptions of national security. I then review the theoretical connections between discourse, national identity, and foreign policy and outline a theory of identity construction as spatiotemporal practice. I conclude this review by linking the ideology of American exceptionalism to foreign policy practice and consider

[2] *The Great Nation of Futurity*

the specific ways in which this ideology positions the United States vis-à-vis the future. In the remainder of the chapter, I outline the analytic framework and data set I use to carry out my study and substantiate my argument.

THEORETICAL FRAMEWORK

Although my theoretical framework draws on well-established theories and concepts, it is novel in that it draws out and foregrounds the politics of temporality and the significance of temporality to foreign policy discourse, construals of identity/difference, and assertions of American national identity. I have constructed a framework that posits foreign policy to be a discursive practice in which and through which temporality, along with spatiality, plays a vital role in differentiating Self and Other in ways that privilege Self and marginalize, even demonize, Other. At the same time, this framework offers a temporal lens for examining American national identity, namely, its future orientation and how that orientation was used as a legitimation strategy within Cold War foreign policy discourse.

The Politics of Temporality and Futurity

My critical examination of the temporality of American national identity understands temporality, generally, and futurity, specifically, to be political phenomena and instruments.[2]

As Fabian (1983) explains, "chronopolitics" is a consequential modality of power that provides the ideological grounding of geopolitics (144). Adams et al. (2009) further note that the political nature of temporality has long been "capitalized and colonized" in the service of the present needs and interests of privileged social actors and institutions (247). In this view, temporal schemes serve to create, sustain, and, ultimately, mystify social orders in ways that prioritize certain social processes, constituencies, and actors over others (Bussey 2007: 53, 56).

As the domain of the possible and potential, the future is a particularly important site of political, ideological, and material contest; as such, examining representations of the future can tell us something about how power is shaped and exercised (Engerman 2012: 1403; Fraser 1975: 54). This view holds that the future is not to be understood as an approaching material reality created by "law bound developments" but as a "quintessential social construct" (Andersson 2019: 2). As a "constitutive category and repertoire of world making," the future, at its core, is a political problem and, as such, warrants critical attention (Andersson 2019: 20, 1, 23). Graham (2019) likewise argues that given the role utopias, that is, "desired future states," play in framing political discourse and shaping collective action, critical attention must be given to how they are constructed, the actions they "incite," and "what they propose to abolish" (1, 4).

Indeed, the history of the future is fundamentally a "political history of power and control," as the people and institutions who hold sway over the future of the modernizing world also hold sway over its politics (Andersson 2012: 1415; Huntington 1968: 461). Exercising this power involves, in part, eliminating or marginalizing options for action to ensure that the "stream of history" flows in a particular direction (Connor 2017: 19; Wæver 1995: 76). Moreover, political practice is fundamentally concerned with gaining public support for proposals for future actions and policies (Edelman 1988: 8). Such proposals are grounded in projections of "fields of imaginable possibilities" that prime the public's view of the future and, thereby, influence behaviors and commitments (Cruz 2000: 311; Edelman 1988: 8). For Galtung and Jungk (1969), the ability to create the future is the very essence of power, as the social actor who is able to claim foreknowledge of the future is also able to claim control over the present (368).

The temporal domain of the future, then, is a consequential site in which and through which social actors wage battle over prevailing social orders. Since the early 20th century, images of the future have served as a "social technology" for controlling the future and, thereby, controlling social reality (Loye 1978: 18). Andersson's (2019) history of futures research reveals how expert prediction in the post–World War II era served as a sociopolitical technology of "future making and world crafting" and, thereby, as a means of "control and management of the present" (6, 215).[3] These futures technologies are marked by an elitism, as the authority to predict and control the future has typically been granted to a scientifically minded Western elite that has deemed itself the guardian and conveyor of "the wisdom of the ages" (Wells 1985; Polak 1973). Through its "scientification of the future," expert prediction undermines the potentiality inherent in the future, its capacity to serve as a "territory of freedom," in order to dominate public imagination, suppress collective action, and maintain the status quo (Andersson 2019: 19; Heller 1999: 7). Those who claim to possess knowledge of the future participate, Connor (2017) contends, in a "temporal imperialism" whereby realis projections of the future marginalize alternative projections that are deemed unrealistic, even dangerous (19). The disciplining work of this "anticipatory governance" involves future-oriented techniques for exploiting time as a resource of power and control (Aradau and Blanke 2017: 374, 377). The result is an ossified future that does not admit alternative ways of being, socioeconomic arrangements, values, or interests (Connor 2017: 19).

Graham (2019) argues that the institutions that govern contemporary life focus "almost exclusively" on regulating expectations of the future

[4]   *The Great Nation of Futurity*

through relentless acts of prophesy and anticipation (2; see also Andersson 2019: 221). Such acts, he insists, have led to the "enclosing [of] the future" and the loss of the ability, even desire, to imagine and enact alternative futures (Graham 2019: 2, 7; see also Graham 2001, 2017; Graham and Luke 2003). Goode and Godhe (2017) similarly note that what has been identified as the "Future Industries" exercises tremendous power in "agenda-setting, horizon-setting and problem defining," which allows them to shape society's ideas and discussions about the future (110; Inayatullah 1999). Guided by an ethos of unchallengeable expertise, the Future Industries have undermined a democratic vision of the future by colonizing and exploiting the future in service of present-day interests and concerns (Goode and Godhe 2017: 112; Godhe and Goode 2018: 153). The modern era, consequently, has seen the privileging of "today-centered realism" at the expense of "future-centered idealism" and the rendering of the future as a "flat, ahistorical, non-philosophical accumulation of computer printouts" (De Jouvenal 1965: 195; Dolbeare and Dolbeare 1976: 214). This "corporatization" of thinking about the future, in turn, has situated America as the site of the future (Sardar 1999: 13; emphasis added).

As numerous scholars have noted, the modernist future has an obvious geographical character. In Rasmussen's view (2002), the distinguishing characteristic of Western society has been its role as "the driving force" of the global future (334). The privileged status of Western futurism derives from its exploitation of a double anxiety: a fear of the unknown and a suspicion that the affluence enjoyed by some states and people isn't sustainable (Udayakumar 1999: 98; Connolly 1991: 23). This anxiety, in turn, sanctions the use of political and military power both to maintain global order and foment continuous geopolitical hostilities (Udayakumar 1999: 98; Connolly 1991: 23). As Lapham (2011) argues, "fear of the future" is a boon to the Western state, which "extorts" it for "the payment of the protection money" (14). Within this Western paradigm, projections of the future have produced and reproduced images that represent a "grotesquely mindless celebration of Pax Americana" and largely ignore images produced by non-Western people and organizations (Inayatullah 1996: 509; Davies 1999: 243, 240; see also Adam 1995: 116). In short, the exercise of Western hegemony has involved forcing the course of history in a particular direction whereby the present of the West is understood to be the future of the non-West (Inayatullah 1999: 52; Nandy 1999: 233).

The political and contested nature of the future and its importance to geopolitics undergirds the analysis comprising this book. Indeed, as I discuss in the following section, the particular trajectory of the postwar future was very much at stake during key junctions of the Cold War, as the global future was the site of the battle between "East" and "West."

The Futurology of Security in the Postwar Era

Like all policy proposals,[4] arguments over security policy are grounded in projections of alternative future scenarios: "What will happen if we do not take 'security action,' and what will happen if we do?" (Connor 2017: 19; Buzan et al. 1998: 32). As such, it is not surprising that security statements bear the mark of futurity, as they call for defense against some future threat (C.A.S.E. 2006: 469; Buzan 1997: 24). Given its future orientation, security discourse constitutes an "anticipatory discourse," as it is concerned with predicting which security threats will or will not arise and shaping the security environment in relation to those threats (Scollon and Scollon 2000). Indeed, security practice functions as an "anticipatory regime" in that it brings possible negative futures into the present by projecting "a future that may or may not arrive, is always uncertain yet is necessarily coming and so therefore always demands a response" (Adams et al. 2009: 248–249). Even ostensibly descriptive statements concerning present actions and conditions point to the future, as they are often used rhetorically to presage a perilous future (Dunmire 2005: 490).

Anticipatory security practice, although being one step removed from potential danger, is nevertheless real because of the consequences projections of the future have on security decisions made in the present (van Munster 2004: 147). Anticipatory security, moreover, is not conceived in Manichean terms—secure, not secure—but, rather, as an amorphous "future state of being" focused on "our enduring vulnerabilities" (Cavelty and Mauer 2010: 4; van Munster 2004: 147). This tendency has been traced to the prevalence of risk management discourse within the security establishment, which seeks to discern and evaluate future threats in order to govern "potentialities" and "tame" contingency and uncertainty (C.A.S.E. 2006: 468; van Munster 2004: 147; Aradau and Blanke 2017: 378). By embracing a risk management approach, security professionals focus policy and practice on, in Giddens' (1994) words, "bringing the future under control" (58).

Competing conceptions of the future become particularly salient at moments of significant geopolitical change as partisans seek to sustain and/or challenge the existing global order by managing that change. The aftermath of World War II was one such moment, as the future became the focus of postwar "political imaginaries" embedded within security discourses (Andersson and Rindzeviciute 2015: 4). During this period, the future became the domain of struggle and conflicting claims over how the Cold War world "could be shaped and reshaped," controlled, or transformed (Andersson 2019: 2, 3, 20). It served as a space onto which hopes and fears concerning the shape of the postwar world were projected (Andersson 2019: 17). The future, in sum, was a construct of the postwar moment, the domain and product of contesting

[6]   *The Great Nation of Futurity*

"universalizing ambitions" and competing efforts to create the modern world order (Andersson 2019: 22).

Postwar geopolitical changes brought about by decolonization and the idea of "temporal pluralism," Fabian (1983) argues, threatened the political and economic security of the West and its conception of modernity and, thus, posed particular problems for the postwar international order (144). The response to these threats, and to the broader need of sustaining the geopolitical primacy of the West, took shape as an "objective, transcultural temporal medium for theories of *change*" that came to dominate the social sciences (Fabian 1983: 144–145, emphasis in original; also see Andersson 2019). Within this scheme, the consequential role of the future stemmed from its dual role of amassing power and control while also rallying dissension and calls for change (Andersson and Rindzeviciute 2015: 1; Andersson 2019: 26). Mitigating the potential danger of an open and ill-defined postwar future, consequently, was deemed essential if the West was to stave off challenges to the capitalist order by its two Others, the newly decolonized nations and the Soviet Union (Andersson and Rindzeviciute 2015: 4).

Historians of the future[5] point to the postwar era as a crucial moment in the rise of both scientific and political interest in the future. Fearing that it had fallen behind the Soviet practice of forecasting, "prognostik," the U.S. government invested tremendous resources in various techniques and technologies of "pre-vision" as a way of assessing and countering the alleged Soviet threat (Andersson 2012: 1420; Connelly et al. 2012: 1433). This investment began during World War II as the nation's leaders sought to discern how quickly the Soviet Union would recover from the global conflict and be in a position to challenge the United States militarily (Connelly et al. 2012: 1433). This early work was followed by a concerted effort to assess Soviet intentions and capabilities for developing nuclear weapons and waging war against the United States (Connelly et al. 2012: 1433). Such "modern forms of divination," Connelly et al. (2012) explain, were embraced by politicians and policymakers during the Cold War and, consequently, served to "cloak" geopolitical power in the "mystique of clairvoyance" (1459).

The postwar period, then, was a time that saw the return of the "future on a grand and global scale" (Andersson and Rindzeviciute 2015: 3). It was a period during which the future became a clearly articulated temporal domain within scientific and political practice (Andersson and Rindzeviciute 2015: 1). In the immediate aftermath of World War II the future was seen as posing unique challenges to both East and West and, thus, to be a vital sphere of influence and intervention (Andersson 2012: 1429, 1414). That is, the end of World War II capped a process of decolonization initiated after World War I that brought to an end an imperial system that had structured the global order for hundreds of years. In its place, the United States emerged as a global power ready to assert itself in the international arena. Escobar (1995) points specifically to 1945 as the moment when the nation's economic and military power was unrivaled and, concomitantly, when the entire Western political-economic system became its charge (32).

In this context change itself was viewed as a threat, as it raised questions about the validity of a Western-defined status quo (Andersson 2012: 1415). The early years of the Cold War were marked by concerted efforts to tame and control the future as both the United States and the Soviet Union sought to turn the openness of the future to their advantage (Andersson 2012: 1414). "Futurology" thus became a practice of "world making" through which dominant social institutions and actors sought to manage a rapidly changing world by creating a stable global order that would protect and sustain the status quo (Andersson 2012: 1429; also see Andersson 2019). The future emerged in the postwar era as a political and temporal space dominated by bipolar interests and, thus, as a key temporal and conceptual space within which geopolitical battles would be fought (Andersson and Rindzeviciute 2015: 4; Andersson 2019, Andersson 2012: 1430). Indeed, as Engerman (2012) explains, the Cold War conflict was "a battle as much over future time as over present-day space" (1407; also see J. Andersson 2012: 1411). The aftermath of World War II also saw the rise of the national security state and with it the emergence of the future as a central concern of United States security policy discourse and practice. As Yergin (1977) argues, the key tenet of national security at this moment was to prepare for "war just over the horizon," that is, for hostile potentialities that could materialize in both the proximal and distal future (193).

The future orientation of security discourse and practice and the conception of the Cold War as a battle over the postwar future frame my analysis of how the nation's policymakers and politicians leveraged the nation's identity as the "great nation of futurity" in its ideological contest with the Soviet Union.

Foreign Policy, National Identity, and Discourse:
Construing Self and Other

I understand national identity, foreign policy, and discourse to be inextricably, dialectically, and functionally intertwined. Hansen (2006) explains that articulations of foreign policy draw upon discursive representations of identity and, in so doing, constitute, reproduce, and sustain them (1). Those representations, in turn, serve to legitimate the attendant foreign policy proposals (Hansen 2006: 21). Foreign policy, then, is a dialectical discursive practice, as the discursive construction of identity both constitutes foreign policy and is produced by it (Hansen 2006: 23; Dalby 1990: x). Moreover, foreign policy is not a neutral practice that engages the world "as it is" but a political and semiotic practice that actively constructs that world by ascribing

[8]   *The Great Nation of Futurity*

meaning to the people, places, and relations comprising it (Hansen 2006: 6). It is through foreign policy discourse that "boundaries are constructed, spaces demarcated, standards of legitimacy incorporated, interpretations of history privileged and alternatives marginalized" (Campbell 1998: 68). As a political performance that creates and sustains figural and material boundaries, foreign policy discourse serves to render as foreign particular events, actors, and ways of being (Ashley 1987: 51; Shapiro 1988: 100).

Like all meaning-making practices, foreign policy discourse creates meaning by asserting relations of identity and difference. That is, the production of national identity within and through foreign policy involves assertions of difference and exclusionary practices whereby the identity of Self is constructed in relation to some Other (Wodak et al. 1999: 4; Hall 1996: 4; Nayak 2006). Indeed, the assertion of difference is an essential means by which the identity of Self is secured and sustained (Connolly 1991: xiv). As Campbell (1998) argues, "the logic of identity" that operates within foreign policy discourse mandates difference and, consequently, falls prey to "the politics of negation and the temptation of otherness" (70–71). Through this process, the array of discursively constituted others is rendered, at one and the same time, as "essential to the truth of the powerful identity and a threat to it" (Connolly 1991: 66).

Because it embodies the "most fundamental divisions of inside and outside, us and them, domestic and foreign," the state is key to the creation of national identity (Connolly 1991: 201). It ensures the integrity and reality of Self by imposing a scheme of "vision and division" onto geopolitical relations (Campbell 1998: 70; Bourdieu et al. 1994: 7–8; Connolly 1991: ix). Indeed, the very existence of the state, Campbell (1998) insists, depends upon the discursive construal of some Other as challenging or threatening its legitimacy and viability (12). All too often these practices involve disseminating "electrifying" images designed to construe any suffering of Self as caused by outside perpetrators (Silver 2008: 94).

Given that the national Self is typically represented in laudatory terms, the foreign Other is typically construed as an inferior subject as positive declarations about Self implicate an implicit, typically negative, evaluation of those deemed Other (Shapiro 1988: 100; Campbell 1998: 70). The positive meaning of the national Self is constituted relationally vis-à-vis "the other . . . what it is not . . . what it lacks . . . what has been called its constitutive outside" (Hall 1996: 4, 1992: 188). Othering, then, is a highly consequential act of differentiation; it is at once an act of discursive and political power by means of which "we" impose "'our' concept of 'them' as being 'them' and act accordingly" (Shapiro 1988: 101, 90; Dalby 1990: 18). In this way, the assignment of difference and the ability to impose meaning on spaces and those who occupy them confers power and privilege to Self (Connolly 1991: xiv; Dalby 1990: 28). Accordingly, American foreign policy discourse can be understood as a "geopolitical code" that strategically positions the Other in the nation's "imaginative enactments of its own survival and hegemonic struggles" (Shapiro 1988: 111–112).

This conception of national identity as a sociopolitical construct is rooted in Benedict Anderson's (1983) theory of nations as "imagined political communities" that have no ontological status apart from the cultural practices that imbue them with textuality (6; Campbell 1998: 11). And while multiple sociopolitical practices play a role in constructing national identity, discursive practice is central to both the formulation and expression of national identity (Wodak et al. 1999: 29). As Connolly (1991) puts it, assertions of national identity rely on an "indispensable discursive field" of differences, dangers, and demonizations that delineate Self from Other (39).

This discursive differentiating of the national Self from some Other is particularly salient in national security policy discourse,[6] which conceptualizes security as the "spatial exclusion of Otherness" and relies on "discourses of danger" to legitimate practices ostensibly aimed at protecting the nation from these dangers (Campbell 1998: 70; Dalby 1988: 416). In fact, the ceaseless projection of dangers and threats through foreign policy discourse is a necessary condition of existence for the state (Campbell 1998: 13). In order to secure their identity, states proselytize an "evangelism of fear," which highlights the contingent and perilous condition of the world (Campbell 1998: 61). In other words, securing a state's affluence and privilege requires, in part, rendering the state as imperiled by what it deems to be perpetual global threats (Connolly 1991: 23, 202).

My analysis of how American national identity is articulated and rhetorically deployed in Cold War foreign policy discourse assumes that foreign policy, itself, is a discursive practice dialectically related to the identification of a national Self and a foreign Other. This framework conceptualizes foreign policy as grounded in and, simultaneously, constitutive of relations of identity and difference that are deemed to hold between Self and Other. My analysis is concerned specifically with the ways particular temporal schemes are used to identify the American national Self, differentiate that Self from various Others, and, importantly, render those Others as national security threats. In the following section, I map out the theoretical precepts underlying my analysis of the temporal nature and function of American national identity within foreign policy discourse.

Identity Construction as Spatiotemporal Practice

Distinguishing Self from Other involves, Dalby (1990) explains, "spatial and temporal deferment of the Other" (18). Foreign policy practice plays a particularly potent role in this process and, thereby, in the constitution of national identity, by situating peoples and societies in a spatiotemporal scheme of "inside and outside, self and other" (Campbell 1998: 62). Such inscription creates moral distinctions through a delineation of space and time that constitutes a "geography of evil" according to which dangers are construed as emerging from remote foreign lands (Campbell 1998: 88). These delineations are central to security practice that renders the Other as a threat by situating it in a spatiotemporal domain different from and foreign to that occupied by Self (Dalby 1990: 13).

Said (1978) attributes these spatiotemporal delineations to the "universal" and "arbitrary" practices of "imaginative" geography and history (54–55). That is, the "objects or places or times" that constitute the political and historical world are constituted through a "poetic process, whereby the vacant or anonymous reaches of distance are converted into meanings for us here" (Said 1978: 55). By accentuating what is spatially and temporally near and distant, these practices serve to shore up and intensify a nation's or a people's sense of Self (Said 1978: 55). The "imaginative geography of the 'our land–barbarian land' variety," Said (1978) explains, involves demarcating our familiar space and their unfamiliar space (54). Such spatial differentiations identify the territory and mentality of the Other and assign meanings, roles, and values to them (Said 1978: 54). O'Tuathail (1996) similarly explains that spatial delineations stem from not only from routine conflicts over naming and ownership rights of particular spaces; they are also the product of conflicts between incongruous "images and imaginings," conflicts over how the world ought to be envisioned (14–15).

According to Said (1978), such "imaginative, quasi-fictional" designations also have a vital temporal dimension, as our knowledge of " 'long ago' or 'the beginning' or 'at the end of time' " are largely poetic creations that do more than merely situate people and events along a timeline of past, present, and future (55). Fabian (1983) emphasizes this temporal dimension, noting the central role "naturalized-spatial time" serves in ascribing "meaning to the distribution of humanity in space" (25). Time, in his words, has semiotic power in that it creates meaning for Self and Other and mediates the relations between them (ix). Focusing on anthropology, he emphasizes the imperialistic implications of the discipline's conception of temporality and the Other that situates human societies on a "temporal slope, a stream of Time—some upstream, others downstream" (Fabian 1983: 17). Such politically consequential temporal schemes are an important dimension of foreign policy inscription, as time, along with space and responsibility, is one of the key concepts through which political constituencies are conceptualized and talked about (Hansen 2006: 46).

Such temporal imaginings are grounded in "solidarities" important to constituting national identity and maintaining the modern nation state (Tavory and Eliasoph 2013: 918). Drawing on Anderson (1983), Tavory and Eliasoph

(2013) argue that the citizens of a given nation share an understanding of the nation's trajectory and orient to "the same landscape-like temporal horizon" (917–918). This trajectory and horizon are the product of a nation's people seeing themselves as situated within a common temporality and subject to similar experiences (Tavory and Eliasoph 2013: 917–918). Such solidarities are reinforced and sustained by juxtaposing the temporality of Self with the temporality of Other. In Andersson and Rindzeviciute's (2015) words, it is through such differentiation between Our time and Their time that we see time operating as a "powered affair involving the legitimacy of the state" (2).

The function of such temporal schemes is twofold. First, placing the Other in a temporal space removed from that occupied by Self renders that Other as temporally distant, and, thus, different, from Self (Fabian 1983: 26). In addition, such schemes embed a politics and ideology of time that construe Self and Other differently in terms of progress and modernity (Fabian 1983: x, xii). Self is identified with temporal concepts of modernity, progress, and development while Other is typically located "earlier on the time path of 'progress'" and, thus, as non-modern, backward, and underdeveloped (Dalby 1990: 21). In this way, Fabian (1983) argues, time plays a crucial role in constituting power and relations of inequality (ix).

The analysis at the heart of this book examines how the temporal differentiation of the American Self from the nation's various Others manifests linguistically and functions rhetorically within Cold War foreign policy discourse. Key to this discursive process is the particular claim on the global future made through articulations of American national identity. In what follows, I argue that this claim is a fundamental dimension of the rhetoric and ideology of American exceptionalism.

Exceptionalism in U.S. Foreign Policy: America as Future

National identity, exceptionalism, and temporality came together in interesting and dynamic ways in post–World War II foreign policy discourse, a discourse that has deployed a particular conception of American national identity to legitimate a foreign policy of absolute security (Bacevich 2002, 2021; Hunt 1987; Layne 2006; McCartney 2004; Pfaff 2010). This policy has entailed shaping, through economic, political, and military means, the international environment in ways that accord with American geopolitical interests and goals. As Fousek (2000) explains, the nation emerged from World War II "prepared to usher in a new golden age in its own image," an image grounded in the conviction that the American political-economic system represents the future of the postwar era (2). Consequently, national security would be concerned with creating a geopolitical environment based on and amenable to American political, economic, and military interests.

[12]   *The Great Nation of Futurity*

While this postwar program was unique to its historical moment, it was, nevertheless, but one moment in the conceptual and discursive working out of the nation's identity and geopolitical purpose. Borrowing from Campbell (1998), we can understand American national identity as being continuously constituted through "*a stylized repetition of acts*" and a "*regulated process of repetition*" (10; emphasis in the original). Postwar foreign policy discourse participates in this performative process by reaffirming a conception of the United States that has long characterized its foreign policy discourse: an exceptional nation "designed by Providence to live as a more perfect community" led by a form of government "accommodating to the perfectibility of man" (Schlatter 1962: 42; Lapham 2011: 14). Symbolically, America has claimed the special geopolitical role of exemplifying how other nations ought to organize their political and economic institutions, treat their citizens, and engage with the wider world (Schlatter 1962: 42; also see Bacevich 2002; Herring 2008a, 2008b; Layne 2006).

The conviction that America is an exceptional nation—that it is not only distinctive but "exemplary"—has undergirded that nation's sense of Self throughout its history (Bell 1989: 41). McCrisken (2003) points out that scholarship of the last several decades concerning the history and practice of foreign policy has pointed to the enduring impact that exceptionalist claims have had on foreign policy discourse and practice (2). He further argues that, although there is little empirical evidence that American foreign policy has, in fact, *been* exceptional, the *belief* that the nation is exceptional has consistently anchored and legitimated its foreign policy precepts and practices (McCrisken 2003: 2; also see Restad 2015).[7] Exceptionalist appeals within foreign policy discourse have proven to be a "cultural reality and potent force" as well as a convenient shorthand for explaining America's place and purpose in the larger world (McElvoy-Levy 2001: 23; Kammen 1993: 11). Campbell (1998) notes that foreign policy texts redound with statements identifying the United States as an exceptional nation that bears global responsibilities that have been forced upon it (31). In sum, the presumption that America occupies a unique and superior place among the nations of the world has grounded its approach to foreign relations "from the days of Manifest Destiny to the era of the American Century" (Whitcomb 1998: 23, 21).

Claims of exceptionalism within foreign policy discourse are not, however, ideologically innocuous (Hall 1992: 203). They participate in the discursive process of othering whereby in deeming Self to be exceptional some Other is deemed less than exceptional, as the excluded that is outside the spatial, temporal, and moral domains occupied by Self. Rodgers (2004) contends that because the construction of a national Self entails "conjuring up its antitypes," exceptionalist discourse simultaneously creates a "we" and a "them" (23). In fact, the exceptionalist narrative is distinguished from other discourses of difference for its "hyperconcentration" on the external Other

(Rodgers 2004: 23). This discursive process is both a symbolic and material act: it designates an Other against which the behavior of Self is judged and defined and against which the identity of Self is enacted (Dalby 1990: 7, 4). As McEvoy-Levy (2001) argues, the rhetoric of exceptionalism has served as the "'nationalistic' expression of a distinctly American sense of identity," an identity grounded in the juxtaposition of the American Self with a nefarious Other (27). Indeed, what Silver (2008) has termed the "sense of indignant vulnerability" felt by Americans since the early years of the republic has been one of the nation's most unique and persistent cultural artifact (94).

The temporal scheme embedded within the rhetoric and ideology of American exceptionalism participates in the broader discursive and political process of Othering that, as noted earlier, is endemic to foreign policy discourse. In fact, the imaginative practices whereby the Other is temporally and spatially deferred lie at the heart of exceptionalist arguments. Rodgers (2004) explains that "exceptional" should not be understood merely as designating uniqueness or difference vis-à-vis others but as signifying a "deviation from a rule," namely, the rule of history (23). As such, claiming oneself to be exceptional situates that Self in a rarified time and place, as exceptionalist arguments simultaneously posit and create an "imagined . . . 'here' and 'elsewhere' in which, in an important sense, history itself runs by different dynamics" (Rodgers 2004: 23). This spatiotemporal scheme situates the exceptional American Self outside the historical tendencies that hold sway over other places and peoples (Rodgers 2004: 23).

Of particular interest here is that American claims of exceptionalism are qualitatively different from claims put forth by other nations. This distinctiveness, Whitcomb (1998) argues, arises from the temporal nature of American exceptionalist ideology (23, 21; also see McEvoy-Levy 2001: 23). According to Stephanson (1995), all nation-states lay claim to being unique in some way or, in the case of empires, to being the "anointed focal point of world or universal history" (xii). What sets American exceptionalism apart is that it has "envisaged a transcending 'end' of history" engendered by the creation of a global community modeled on America's self-image (Stephanson 1995: xii). Indeed, Dalby (2008) argues that the nation's relations with the global community have been grounded in the conviction that "America is the telos of history" (427). As Westad (2007) puts it, the nation's political symbols and images serve the teleological function of rendering "What is America today" as what "will be the world tomorrow" (9).

Bacevich (2021) likewise argues that American geopolitical practice has been grounded in the exceptionalist assumption that the nation is uniquely qualified to designate history's terminus and to ensure mankind's safe passage to that destination (5). Once arrived at, this "end of history" would signify the culmination of the ideological development of human society and the global triumph of Western liberal democracy as the ultimate form of human

[14] *The Great Nation of Futurity*

government (Fukuyama 1989: 1). Consequently, the temporal domain of the future would give way to a perpetual, unchanging present defined by American geopolitical interests, values, and goals.

The conviction that America comprises a "special people with a special destiny" is, in short, the preeminent idea that historically has bolstered America's relations with the rest of the world (Wood 2002: xxiii; Fousek 2000: 4). This exceptionalist rhetoric construes America as the quintessential exceptional nation and, as such, as standing "singularly and fortuitously" separate from history's trends and tendencies (Rodgers 2004: 25). As the nation in which the laws and reason of history manifest, America is not subject to the rules and norms that govern other peoples and places (Rodgers 2004: 25). America, in this view, is the "locus" for the future; it is, in the words of Hanson Baldwin, military editor of *The New York Times*, "the key to the destiny of tomorrow" (Sardar 1999: 13; Hanson, as quoted in Whitcomb 1998: 23).

The current study examines how the United States drew on the rhetoric of American exceptionalism in order to stake a claim on the global future and, thereby, attempted to force the "stream of history" in a direction that served its interests. Specifically, I provide a fine-grained linguistic and rhetorical analysis of how this claim was enacted in Cold War foreign policy discourse. As I outline in the following section, I adopt a critical discourse analysis framework and deploy the critical concepts of space-time and legitimation to conduct my analysis. Moreover, I focus my analysis on documents drawn from key moments of the Cold War—its *formulation* in the aftermath of World War II, its *enactment* in 1950s and 1960s, its *reassertion* in the late 1970s and early 1980s, and its *reformulation* in the late 1980s.

ANALYTIC FRAMEWORK AND DATA

This study adopts a critical discourse analysis (CDA) approach to examine the temporal aspects of American national identity and how that identity was deployed in foreign policy discourse at particular moments during the Cold War. CDA is concerned with the role of language in society and the role of society in language, the dialectical relationship that holds between discourse and context, and the cultural and historical aspects of meaning (Young and Harrison 2004: 1). Moreover, this analytic framework understands discourse to be an important social practice through which relations of power are created, legitimated, reproduced, and challenged (Fairclough 1989, 2003; van Dijk 2008, 2009; Wodak and Meyer 2001). It posits language to be "an irreducible part of social life, dialectically connected to other elements of social life," and, as such, that analysis of social relations, phenomena, and problems must attend to language (Fairclough 2003: 2). CDA sees discourse analysis as an important means for examining how the relations of power are maintained, reproduced, and resisted.

Power concerns both the asymmetrical relationships that exist between discourse participants, as well as the unequal roles social actors play in the production, dissemination, and consumption of discourse (Fairclough 1995: 1). Ideology, which is embedded in and enacted through discourse, is a central means of enacting power and is understood as "representations of aspects of the world which contribute to establishing, maintaining, and changing social relations of power, domination, and exploitation" (Fairclough 2003: 9). As Lemke (1995) explains, the political is "profoundly textual," with ideology serving as the link between the textual—the recordings of meanings we make—and the political—the "chronicle of our uses of power in shaping social relations large and small" (1). Although representations, ideologies manifest in social action and social identities by being "'enacted' in ways of acting socially, and 'inculcated' in the identities of social agents" (Fairclough 2003: 9).

As noted earlier, the means through which the future is imagined, made meaningful, and projected is an important site for critical social analysis. Discourse, in particular political and policy discourse, plays a significant role in creating and disseminating projections of the future (Dunmire 2011; Edelman 1971, 1988; Fairclough 2003, 2004; Graham 2001, 2002; Jaworski et al. 2003; Jaworski and Fitzgerald 2008). As Fairclough (2003) explains, discourses serve not only to represent people, places, and events as they are now or as they were at some prior moment (124). They are also projective in that, through their efforts to create or stifle change, social actors employ discourses that embed images of possible worlds that may differ from or align with the status quo (Fairclough 2003: 124). Futurology, Fairclough (2003) insists, has come to serve an important role in the projective function of discourse by legitimating "injunctions" about what can or must be done (167). That is, while anyone can make claims about the future, certain people and institutions within a given social order claim and/or have been granted the "socially ratified power of prediction," which enables them to exert a degree of power over how the future is imagined, shaped, and controlled (Fairclough 2003: 167).

My analysis examines the linguistic construal of space-times embedded in Cold War foreign policy discourse and the ways they function rhetorically as legitimation devices within that discourse. While I explicate the concepts of space-time and legitimation separately in what follows, it's important to note that they are "dialectically intertwined" (Fairclough 2003: 224): particular space-times function as legitimation devices, and, concomitantly, acts of legitimation draw on space-time contrasts and construals. I focus my analysis of space-times on identifying the temporalities assigned to different geopolitical actors and constituents; my analysis of legitimation concerns the justificatory

[16] *The Great Nation of Futurity*

claims that build upon the various spatiotemporal positionings and identities embedded in Cold War discourse.

Space-Time

Fairclough (2003) identifies "space-time" as a social phenomenon germane to critical discourse studies that can be operationalized and studied at the textual and linguistic level (151). He grounds his explication in Bakhtin's (1981: 84) conception of the "literary artistic chronotope" and Harvey's (1996) conception of space and time as socially constructed phenomena.[8] Far from being naturally occurring phenomena, space and time are constituted through the various social practices, including discourse, that comprise a given social order (Fairclough 2003: 224). His conception holds that the "construction of space and the construction of time are closely interconnected" (151). He further explains that the consequential nature of different space-times derives, in part, from aligning "particular spatio-temporalities . . . with particular social relations and social identities" (152). Analysis, then, should consider the "intersection" of space and time in the construction of "different space-times" that coexist in any social order (Fairclough 2003: 151). Moreover, analysis should attend to the connections between different space-times and, relatedly, how they are discursively connected to and construe social identities and relations (Fairclough 2003: 152). As such, an important focus of critical analysis is to examine the discursive means by which relations between past, present, and future are constructed; particular spaces are connected with particular temporalities; and different space-times are built up and connected within texts (Fairclough 2004: 151).

Such an analytic approach understands that a key means of ordering the social world, and making a claim to power within that world, involves situating and differentiating peoples and places in temporal terms (Bussey 2007: 56). As Hansen (2006) puts it, "political spaces and subjects are constituted in time," and, thus, time is an important means through which social relations and identities are created and contested (46). She further explains that the future is a particularly important marker of identity within foreign policy discourse (46). That is, such discourses rely on contrastive space-times that situate peoples and societies at different moments along the temporal trajectory of past, present, future, with Self typically identified as future relative to Other and, concomitantly, Other identified in terms of its proximity to Self as future (Hansen 2006: 48).

I understand space-time to involve the association of physical spaces (nations, geographical regions) and the people who occupy them with a moralized temporal domain of past, present, future. Take, for example, the following three excerpts from my data:

- "ancient ways of making a living" within non-Western societies
- America as "the last island of freedom"
- the Soviet Union "runs against the tide of history"

In each of these phrases particular geopolitical spaces—non-Western societies, America, the Soviet Union—are situated in or aligned with different temporal domains. In the first excerpt, we see "non-Western" peoples being designated as past through the use of the adjective "ancient" to characterize how they support themselves economically. Moreover, this use of "ancient" implies a contrast with "modern," which situates non-Western peoples temporally as past relative to the "modern" West. The use of the island metaphor and the adjective "last" in the second example creates a temporal relationship between America and freedom in which America is rendered as not only the locus of and refuge for freedom but as its *last* refuge. Consequently, the future prospect of freedom—whether "freedom" is sustained into the future— is construed as depending on America, on its survival as a free nation, and on its geopolitical status and role. Finally, in the third excerpt the Soviet system is characterized as regressive through the metaphorical construal of human history as a "tide." This metaphor assumes a telos according to which human history is oriented toward a goal and progresses naturally toward it. Representing the Soviet Union as "running against" this tide renders it as opposed to progress and, thus, as regressive and oriented to the past.

I identify the space-times comprising Cold War foreign policy discourse by focusing on a range of linguistic features and conceptual signifiers that index temporality, generally, and futurity, specifically (see Table 1.1). Moreover, in keeping with the scholarship on identity construction, my analysis assumes that the discursive construal of America as the "great nation of futurity" is grounded in relations of identity and difference and that the discursive construal of these relations draws on temporal themes that are essential to constituting them (Hansen 2006: 48).

In terms of process,[9] I examined my data for signifiers of futurity and considered how they served to identify and position different global actors and constituents temporally. For example, in my analysis of Henry Luce's "American Century" rhetoric (Chapter 3), I noted the use of nominal and modal contrasts (e.g., "progress" vs. "survive"; "ought" vs. "must") in his representation of the issues facing the United States and Britain and the actions each were oriented to in 1941. I then considered the different space-times indexed by these contrasts and how they positioned the two nations vis-à-vis the postwar future. In analyzing of the discourse of modernization theory (Chapter 4), I noticed the prevalence of nouns and verbs indexing future-oriented mental states and process (e.g., "aspire," "hope," "want") in statements about the "underdeveloped countries" and considered the space-time indexed by this lexis relative to that assigned to nations at the center[10] of the geopolitical environment. In

[18] *The Great Nation of Futurity*

Table 1.1. LINGUISTIC AND CONCEPTUAL MARKERS OF FUTURITY

Tense: will,[a] going to, shall

Aspect:
- Prospective meaning: I am going to leave.
- Present progressive: is pursuing, is developing
- Future perfect: She will have arrived by 2:00 tomorrow.
- Inchoativity: He continues to work on the plan.

Modality: would, will, should, could, must, can, ought

Verbs, nouns designating future-oriented mental Processes, states: anticipate, anxious, desire, seek, fear, intention, aspiration, hope, see, envision

Time adverbials: now, then, soon, by 2025, eventually, next

Hypothetical, conditional, irrealis statements: Should we fail, the effect will be far reaching.

Forward-looking verbs: continue, aim, plan, become, survive

Movement/motion: toward, forward/backward, lunge, drive, momentum, tempo

Metaphors:
- Build, create, invest, grow
- Horizon, frontier
- Space: we will go in three weeks
- Movement: the deadline is fast approaching
- Resource: time is running out
- Journey, path
- Turning point
- Wave, tide

Nominals: survival, progress, the year 2025, potential, tomorrow, purpose, aspiration, effect

Adjectives: next, new, last

Speech acts: warn, propose, promise, threaten, predict

Genre: instructions, procedures, blueprints, proposals, policy

Concepts: change, repetition, development, movement, stability, imminence, volition, agency

Conjunctions, prepositions: before, after, in front of, behind

Sources: Aiezza (2015), Bergs (2010), Bondi (2016), Comrie (1976), de Saint-Georges (2013), Evered (1983), Fairclough (2003), Fleischman (1982), Glasbey et al. (2002), Lakoff et al. (1991), Schneider (2006), Ultan (1978), and Wekker (1976).
[a]For discussions of whether "will" is a tense or a modal, see Fleischman (1982), Palmer (2001), and Salkie (2010).

my analysis of documents produced by the Committee on the Present Danger (Chapter 5), I found that the present progressive aspect was used in statements about the Soviet Union's military plans and actions (e.g., "The Soviet military budget is growing") and examined these statements in terms of the geopolitical future projected through their aspectual profile.

I then considered how these space-times created relations of identity and difference between different actors and constituents. In Luce's rhetoric, the contrast between American and British space-times created a Self/Other contrast that rendered America as the nation best situated to design the postwar global future. In modernization theory discourse, the space-time occupied by the periphery was construed as past relative to that occupied by both the United States and Soviet Union. As such, I determined that modernization theory embedded a Self/Other contrast between the United States and the people of the periphery that rendered Their future as both a potential threat to Our future and as a crucial site of the Cold War conflict. In terms of the CPD documents, I compared the types of present progressive actions attributed to the United States and Soviet Union and identified a Self/Other contrast rooted in the nature of the future each superpower's actions were oriented to.

The Self/Other contrasts I identified in my data set are presented in Table 1.2, along with some additional samples of the temporal language through which the contrasts were realized. These contrasts and the temporal markers they embed occur to different degrees and in different forms throughout my data set.

My analysis of Self/Other contrasts is grounded in Hansen's understanding that the national Self is not always or necessarily constituted against a "radical" Other. That is, she argues that the relationship between Self and Other isn't necessarily a binary, dichotomized relationship because not all Others are radical Others (Hansen 2006: 37). Rather, analyses of foreign policy discourse reveal "degrees of difference and Otherness" and a more complex set of identities for Self than the dichotomized binary conception allows (Hansen 2006: 37). "Identity construction involves," Hansen (2006) explains, "not a single Self-Other dichotomy but a series of related yet slightly different

Table 1.2. TEMPORALITY OF SELF/OTHER CONTRASTS

Ch.	Self/Other dyad	Linguistic and conceptual realization of temporal contrasts
3	• U.S./Britain	• Progress, purpose *versus* survive, endure
	• U.S./periphery	• Technology, progress *versus* primitive, stagnant
	• U.S./Soviet	• True promise of freedom *versus* false promise of Bolshevik revolution
4	• U.S./periphery	• Aspirations realized through peaceful means *versus* aspirations
	• U.S./Soviet	realized through violent change
		• Upward spiral of development *versus* downward spiral of stagnation, decay
5	• Cold War Soviet other/detente Soviet other	• Immutable existential threat *versus* cooperative partner
		• Aimless, drifting, degenerative *versus* purposeful, driven, regenerative
	• U.S./Soviet	• Universal, democratic, peace and unity *versus* hegemonic,
	• U.S. future/Soviet future	imperialistic, conflict and discord
6	• Active/passive U.S.	• U.S. will shape the new era *versus* U.S. will be shaped by the
	• U.S./periphery	new era
		• Zones of peace, stability, hope *versus* zones of war, instability, despair

[20]   *The Great Nation of Futurity*

juxtapositions," including contrasts between Self and a "variety of non-Selves" and a host of "less-than-radical" Others (Hansen 2006: 37, 39–40). These non-radical Others can include different temporal versions of Self (Wæver 1996) as well as Others that are differentiated from Self in terms of temporal distance. While this form of differentiation juxtaposes Self and Other, it doesn't necessarily place them in a hostile relationship (Hansen 2006: 40). As I demonstrate in the analytic chapters, while the American Self is juxtaposed to a radical Other, it is also contrasted with less-than-radical Others (i.e., Britain, the periphery) as well as with alternative versions of the American Self.

In sum, I examine how America's temporal identity is constituted in Cold War foreign policy discourse through space-time contrasts embedded within and realized through the Self/Other dyad. My analysis focuses on the linguistic and conceptual temporalization of different political actors and spaces and the relationships created between them. I also examine the ways in which these spatiotemporal identities and relationships serve to legitimate the nation's approach to foreign policy at particular moments in the Cold War era.

Legitimation

The rhetorical act of providing "good reasons, grounds, or acceptable motivations"—that is, acts of legitimation[11]—maintains social orders and institutions by providing "explanations and justifications for how things are and how things are done" (van Dijk 1998: 255; Fairclough 2003: 219). As Berger and Luckmann (1966) point out, all acts of language can be understood as serving a legitimating function (12). Legitimation becomes particularly salient, however, at moments of crisis and change that raise questions about identity and an individual or group's identification with the shared concepts and beliefs underlying social institutions and orders (van Dijk 1998: 257; Martin-Rojo and van Dijk 1997: 529).

A central concern of this study is how America's claim on the geopolitical future is discursively legitimated. Specifically, I examine how America's conception of the future and its proclaimed geopolitical role as agent of the future are rendered as valid and necessary at different moments of the Cold War. I consider how the nation is discursively authorized to project the future, prescribe that future for others, and serve as a guide to it. Three legitimation techniques are relevant to this examination: authorization, moral evaluation, and mythopoesis (van Leeuwen 2008).

In his outline of the four major categories of legitimation, van Leeuwen (2008) explains authorization legitimation as involving appeals to some form of authority, including the authority of tradition (108). To the query "Why do X?" this legitimation move responds, "Because that is what we have always done" (108). In this way, authorization legitimation has a temporal character, as a given activity or policy is legitimated by an invocation of traditions or customs grounded in past practice.

To this temporal conception of authorization, the present study adds appeals to the future, specifically: authorization grounded in projections of the future ("future projection authorization") and authorization grounded in temporal location ("temporal location authorization"). Future projections authorization is a type of "futurological prediction" (Fairclough 2003: 167) whereby some person or institution claims the authority to project the future both in terms of future "realities" and future consequences: If we do X, then Y will/could happen; Because Y is going to happen, we must/should/will do X; To prevent Y from occurring, we must/should/will do X. Temporal location authorization sanctions a recommendation or prescription because it comes from actors who situate themselves as further along "the proper rate of evolution" than some Other: This is the way *we* did it, so it is the way *you* should/must/will do it. In this rhetorical move, Self claims the role as model or guide for how things ought to be done. In terms of foreign policy discourse, both of these forms of futurological authorization rely on invocations of national identity, either by declaring the national Self as authorized to project the future or by claiming the authority to prescribe the future for some Other.

Legitimation by moral evaluation, that is, the legitimation of actors and actions by evoking some system of values, is also relevant to the current study (van Leeuwen 2008: 109). As Oddo (2014) explains, this legitimation device serves to evaluate Self morally by positing a binary relationship according to which We are heroic, freedom loving, and rational and They are savage, freedom-hating, and irrational (525). This formulation operates according to what van Dijk (1998) has termed the "ideological square": the discursive polarization of Us and Them, which emphasizes Our positives and Their negatives and suppresses Our negatives and Their positives (267). My analysis focuses on the temporal means by which Self and Other are morally evaluated.

Hansen (2006), as noted earlier, argues that evaluations of Self and Other can be constructed along spatial and temporal axes whereby Other is constituted as less than Self by being situated outside the geographical and temporal spaces occupied by Self. I follow Hansen by focusing on the discursive means by which Self and Other are temporally situated and how these temporal locations serve to legitimate, or delegitimate, different global actors in moral terms. I also examine the moral lexis used in relation to competing conceptions of the future and how this lexis renders Our claim on and plan for the future as legitimate and Their claim as illegitimate.

The legitimation strategy of mythopoesis involves the use of stories and narratives to legitimate actions and the actors proposing and engaging in them. Such narratives can take shape as moral tales about a protagonist who undertakes what is deemed to be a legitimate course of action and who subsequently reaps the rewards entailed in or brought about by that action (van

[22]   *The Great Nation of Futurity*

Leeuwen 2008: 117). Cautionary tales, in contrast, involve stories about the negative consequences suffered by an actor who fails to abide social norms, conventions, or practices (van Leeuwen 2008: 118). Whether it is realized as a moral or cautionary tale, the strategy of mythopoetic legitimation involves narratives about identity, action, and consequence.

While such stories can be set in the past as stories about past actions and outcomes, they can also be oriented to the future as stories in which a proposed course of action is legitimated or delegitimated through projections of its future consequences: If we take action A, then B will be our reward; If we pursue action C, then D will be our fate. As Mische (2009) explains, projections of the future often take shape in various narrative forms that serve as "templates for future action" (701). In terms of my analysis, I consider how such narratives of the future serve to legitimate or delegitimate possible courses of action through projections of benefits and harms. I also consider how they can render Other as illegitimate by projecting the harms entailed in actions being undertaken by Other.

Legitimation via mythopoesis manifests in two ways in my data. As I demonstrate in Chapter 5, the re-securitization of the Soviet Union in the mid-1970s and early 1980s is legitimated by Ronald Reagan's rhetorical performance of the "grand story of America" (Oddo 2011: 298). His telling of this story serves to legitimate American claims on the global future and, at the same time, warn the nation about the dangers that inhere in Soviet claims. Through this story Reagan reminds the nation of its fundamentally exceptional character and its unique responsibility for the global future. The strategy of mythopoesis underlying American claims on the post–Cold War future, the focus of Chapter 6, takes shape as the American jeremiad. I demonstrate how the George H. W. Bush and Clinton administrations drew upon the themes embedded within the jeremiad to make the case that the nation must take an active role in shaping the post–Cold War geopolitical future. Taken together, the administrations tell the story of a nation of high moral purpose that faces obstacles and challenges as it works toward completing its providential mission.

Data Set

My data set[12] comprises documents drawn from four "critical discourse moments" (Chilton 1988) of the Cold War during which the nation's postwar identity and geopolitical purpose took center stage in the face of various global changes, challenges, and uncertainties. Each moment was marked by explicit concerns about both the future of America's geopolitical status and role and the nature of the global future. Specifically, my analysis focuses on documents produced in the 1940s at the inception of the Cold War,[13] which focus on America's role in the post–World War II world; in 1950s and 1960s, which focus on how the nation's Cold War foreign policy strategy would be enacted; in the 1970s and early 1980s, which call for the revival of the Cold War; and at the conclusion of the Cold War in the late 1980s and early 1990s, which outline the geopolitical mission of the United States for the post–Cold War era.

Formulation. The Cold War came into being at a moment marked by substantial geopolitical changes brought about by World War II, the rise of the United States as the dominant global power, the waning of European imperialism, and the liberation of previously colonized people. As noted earlier, it was a moment that brought to the fore questions about what the postwar world would look like and the role the United States would play in shaping that world. As Fabian (1983) argues, decolonization and "temporal pluralism" threatened the political and economic status and security of the West and, thus, posed particular problems for the international order (144). I analyze three texts that played an important role in addressing these issues: Henry Luce's 1941 essay "The American Century," President Truman's 1947 "Special Message to the Congress on Greece and Turkey," and the 1950 policy document National Security Council Resolution 68, "United States Objectives and Programs for National Security" (NSC 68).

Although published in early 1941, several months before the nation entered World War II, Luce's essay was very much focused on the aftermath of the war, specifically on the role the United States should play once hostilities ended. His essay laid the groundwork for an activist geopolitical identity and role as he urged the nation's leaders to project American values, principles, and interests throughout the world. President Truman further articulated this geopolitical mission in his speech on aid to Greece and Turkey, which marked "America's 'declaration of Cold War'" and outlined the Truman Doctrine (Judge and Langdon 1999: 24). The speech declared communism to be a global threat and mapped out America's responsibility in addressing that threat: it would be the policy of the United States to provide economic and military aid to any nation or people deemed vulnerable to a communist insurgency (Judge and Langdon 1999: 24). This speech is also significant for identifying particular parts of the world as the "underdeveloped areas," a spatiotemporal designation that would reverberate throughout American foreign policy for years to come. NSC 68 was a top secret document that declared the Soviet Union to be an "immediate" military threat to the "free world" and outlined the military and economic means by which the United States would address that threat (Judge and Langdon 1999: 66). The policies presented in NSC 68 were concerned not only with the containment of the Soviet Union but also with enabling the United States to create actively a geopolitical environment conducive to its political, economic, and ideological interests.

[24]   *The Great Nation of Futurity*

Enactment. The second phase of my analysis concerns the period of the 1950s and 1960s during which the United States engaged in a "hot" cold war with the Soviet Union in the newly decolonized areas. This was a time when the idea of the future became the focus of scientific, political, and ideological attention and served as a key weapon in and a site of the battle between East and West (Andersson and Rindzeviciute 2015: 3; Andersson 2019; Connelly et al. 2012). Furthermore, the fact that the Soviet Union was viewed by many in the world as offering a compelling alternative vision of the future gave added urgency to American claims that it was the nation best suited to shape the postwar global future. Consequently, articulations of American national identity—its values, capabilities, responsibilities, and mission—were projected onto the conceptual space of the future as the nation's leaders proclaimed the possibilities and potentialities of global society that they insisted were intrinsic to the American political-economic system.

My analysis examines documents that outline a particular articulation of the nation's Cold War policy, "modernization theory" (MT), which came to prominence in the Cold War and served as the basis for the nation's foreign policy and military strategy in Vietnam. As Restad (2012) notes, MT was a key concept, along with "manifest destiny," "imperialism," "leader of the free world," and "new world order," through which the American identity and sense of mission was articulated (60). An influential social scientific theory, it held sway among United States policymakers because it offered an explanation of the nation's place and purpose in the postwar world and a program for managing the vagaries of that world in ways that supported its Cold War strategy (Gilman 2003: 13, 3; Latham 2000: 13). The present study focuses on three key MT texts—Staley's *The Future of Underdeveloped Countries*, Millikan and Rostow's *A Proposal: Key to an Effective Foreign Policy*, and Lerner's *The Passing of Traditional Society*.

Reassertion. During the 1970s the mainstream of the foreign policy establishment deemed the United States to be nearing a relaxation of tensions with the Soviet Union and, thus, the diminishing of difference between the two superpowers. This period of "detente" ran from 1969 to 1979 and was embraced by the Nixon, Ford, and Carter administrations (Gaddis 2005: 286; Dalby 1990: 46). According to the Committee on the Present Danger (CPD), however, detente posed a "clear and present danger" not only to the nation's security, geopolitical status, and mission, but also to the global future. By asserting that the Soviet Union continued to pose an existential threat to Western liberal democracy, the CPD ushered in the "second Cold War" (Dalby 1990; Halliday 1983).

This declaration of a second Cold War involved reestablishing a fundamental relationship of difference between the United States and the Soviet Union. By resituating the Soviet Union as America's radical Other, the CPD also reclaimed America's purported unique geopolitical identity and status.

Moreover, the CPD's "present danger" discourse also involved specific characterizations of the present and projections of the future through an "anticipatory regime." This discursive regime created a symbiotic relationship between a dangerous present and catastrophic future and embedded a "moral economy in which the future sets the conditions for possible action in the present" (Adams et al. 2009: 249). My analysis focuses on the linguistic details of the CPD's public position papers as well the iterative and intertextual nature of the CPD project. That is, I connect the CPD threat discourse to prior articulations of the Soviet threat presented in NSC 68 and to the public performance of the CPD argument provided by contemporaneous speeches of President Reagan.

Reformulation. The final phase of my analysis focuses on the ending of the Cold War in the late 1980s and early 1990s. This moment was initially touted as representing the "end of history" and, with it, the end of the Soviet Union as the radical Other against which the nation had defined itself for over 40 years. Given that assertions of national identity are often generated in relation to some danger or threat deemed to be facing the nation (Campbell 1998; Connolly 1991), the demise of the Soviet Union raised new questions about the nation's identity and the role it would play in the post–Cold War era.

This portion of my analysis focuses on foreign policy statements and national security policy documents from the George H. W. Bush and Bill Clinton administrations, both of which oversaw the ending of the Cold War and the inception of the post–Cold War era. Although generally deemed an American victory and a vindication of its values and way of life, the ending of the Cold War was, nevertheless, characterized in foreign policy discourse as a moment of geopolitical uncertainty and challenge. This context gave rise to questions from politicians and policymakers concerning the nation's geopolitical identity, role, and purpose that asked whether the nation would reap the benefits of its "victory" over the Soviet Union by extending its political-economic system globally to those societies that "remain stuck in history" (Fukuyama 1989: 17) or turn inward, thereby ceding reign of the future to others.

The design of this data set is not meant to account for the entirety of the Cold War period or provide an exhaustive analysis of foreign policy discourse produced during the Cold War. Rather, my goal is to demonstrate the temporal dimension of America's exceptionalist identity, namely, its proclaimed unique role vis-à-vis the future and how that identity and role were discursively created and used in foreign policy discourse. I ground this demonstration in different texts and genres drawn from different moments of the Cold War, moments that are distinct yet interconnected. They are distinguished by the fact that they are separated in time and that each is characterized by its own geopolitical issues and dynamics. They are connected by the fact that they are moments during which questions about the nation's identity and geopolitical role were of central concern to American policymakers, politicians, and pundits, as were questions about the political-economic character of the geopolitical future.

Broadly speaking, the questions concerned the role the United States would play with respect to the evolution of the postwar geopolitical future and whether that future would be amenable to the nation's proclaimed interests and values. As such, my data set enables me to examine the relationship between construals of American national identity and futurity and the linguist and rhetorical means by which that relationship is realized and sanctioned. Additionally, it enables me to demonstrate the consistency of the temporal dimension of American national identity across different geopolitical contexts, as well as to identify some of the patterns and differences in how this identity is discursively created. More broadly, my analysis of this data provides additional insight into the potent role futurity plays in political discourse and into the linguistic, discursive, and rhetorical means by which the future is construed and claimed for ideological and political purposes.

CHAPTER OVERVIEW

This introductory chapter is followed by a review chapter, four discourse analytic chapters, and a conclusion. Chapter 2, "America's Most Precious Resource," outlines the temporal dimensions of the discourse and ideology of American exceptionalism, focusing on how futurity has figured historically in articulations of the nation's geopolitical place and purpose. I begin with a brief review of early conceptions of exceptionalism and then consider how exceptionalist appeals have functioned rhetorically within foreign policy discourse. The chapter concludes with a discussion of the temporality of the core components of the exceptionalist ideology. Chapter 2 lays the groundwork for the argument I develop in the four subsequent discourse-analytic chapters concerning how the identity of the United States as the "great nation of futurity" has figured in the nation's Cold War foreign policy rhetoric.

In Chapter 3, "Vistas to the Future," I examine conceptions of the nation's geopolitical status and purpose in the immediate aftermath of World War II and at the onset of the Cold War. I focus primarily on Henry Luce's 1941 essay "The American Century," President Truman's 1949 speech "A Special Message to Congress on Greece and Turkey," and National Security Resolution 68 promulgated in 1950. I examine the space-times and Self/Other contrasts embedded within these documents and consider how they identified and positioned different global actors and constituents in temporal terms.

I begin by analyzing the temporal implications of the change in the nation's security posture from "national defense" to "national security" and how that change positioned the United States with respect to the future. I then examine how discursive representations of postwar space-time positioned the United

States in relation to two Others: the Soviet Union and what President Truman termed the "underdeveloped areas." I demonstrate how the future was invoked to create an antagonistic relationship between the two superpowers and how the relative temporal positioning of the United States and "underdeveloped areas" was used to legitimate an interventionist foreign policy in the newly decolonized areas. Finally, I examine the contrastive construals of two American Selves and how each positioned the nation in relation to the future. Taken together, my analysis of the Luce, Truman, and NSC 68 statements demonstrates how the geopolitical future was rendered as the central concern of postwar foreign policy and how that policy instrumentalized the geopolitical future and claimed it as the special province of the United States.

Chapter 4, "New Vistas of Opportunity," examines how conceptions of the nation's identity, geopolitical purpose, and temporal positioning were articulated and deployed at a time when both the United States and the Soviet Union were making claims on the postwar future. I focus on the discourse of modernization theory as laid out in Eugene Staley's *The Future of Underdeveloped Countries*, Max Millikan and Walter Rostow's *A Proposal: Key to an Effective Foreign Policy*, and Daniel Lerner's *The Passing of Traditional Society*. My analysis identifies the space-time contrasts embedded in these texts and how these contrasts legitimated a projection of the future grounded in American interests, history, and identity. I demonstrate how both the Soviet Union and the "underdeveloped areas" were situated temporally relative to the United States and how that positioning rendered each as a particular type of threat to America's vision of the global future. I also demonstrate the discursive means through which the future of the newly decolonized societies was aligned with U.S. foreign policy interests and goals and how a historically specific vision of the future was transformed into a universal, inevitable future. In sum, this chapter demonstrates that America's efforts to secure and wield power drew upon contrasting projections of the global future that pitted an American future against a Soviet future and appropriated the future of the newly decolonized societies as part of its Cold War strategy.

In Chapter 5, "Alerting America," I focus on the moment when some in the foreign policy community insisted that the policy of détente was undermining the nation's geopolitical position and ceding the global stage to the Soviet Union. Their response was to reclaim the nation's special geopolitical status and role by reigniting the American–Soviet tensions that had animated the Cold War in the 1950s and 1960s. My analysis centers of the position papers issued by the CPD in the 1970s and 1980s that sought to re-identify the Soviet Union as an existential threat to the United States and the future of the liberal capitalist order. I draw on the concept of "securitization" (Buzan and Wæver 2003) from critical security studies to examine the temporal resources used to resituate the Soviet Union as America's radical Other. I demonstrate that the purported "present danger" posed by the Soviet Union was created through projections of alternative futures that reconstituted relations of identity and difference between the two superpowers and through the management of the temporal distance between the present moment and a purported catastrophic future.

I then examine the iterative nature of this securitization process (Stritzel 2007) by linking the CPD's threat discourse to prior articulations made in the 1950s and to the public performance provided by Ronald Reagan. I show that the CPD's construal of the imminent threat posed by the Soviet Union of the 1970s and 1980s drew on rhetorical strategies used to construe an imminent Soviet threat in the 1950s. The final portion of my analysis demonstrates how, as both a candidate and president, Reagan both reaffirmed the nation's claim on the global future and legitimated the re-securitization of the Soviet Union.

This chapter, in sum, examines the discursive response to the policy of détente, which had posited an easing of tensions between the two superpowers and the possibility of a cooperative rather than adversarial relationship. What we see in this response is the potency and resilience of a particular temporal conception of the nation's identity and purpose, that it occupies a unique place and plays a special, preordained role in the history of mankind.

The final analytic chapter, "From 'the American Century' to 'the End of History,'" examines the foreign policy discourse of the two presidents who oversaw the ending of the Cold War and helped usher in the post–Cold War era, George H. W. Bush and Bill Clinton. It analyzes how American national identity was construed in the absence of a radical Other and at a moment of ostensible geopolitical triumph. I identify the linguistic and rhetorical means by which the nation's exceptionalist identity was asserted and reaffirmed and how that identity was used to sanction an activist foreign policy aimed at creating a post–Cold War future amenable to the nation's interests and goals. I situate this discourse within the American jeremiad, a genre that has served historically to articulate the nation's identity and geopolitical purpose. My analysis is organized around three central themes of the jeremiad—chosenness, declension, and prophecy—and identifies the spatiotemporal contrasts that draw upon and reaffirm the nation's unique status vis-à-vis the global future.

The concluding chapter, "The Future of the American Future," summarizes and consolidates the analyses presented in the four preceding analytic chapters and considers the ideological implications of the American claim on the global future. I argue that this claim represents a "chronological imperialism" whereby politicians and pundits sought to colonize the future in the service of the nation's Cold War interests by universalizing a particular vision of the future that denied alternative conceptions of local and global futures (Galtung, as quoted in Andersson 2006: 281). I then shift my focus from the Cold War to the present moment and consider how the concept of American exceptionalism has figured in the discourse generated within the context of Donald

Trump's presidency, his contest of the 2020 election results, and the January 6 Capitol insurrection. I argue that the rise of Trumpism has been viewed by many as a moment of crisis and reflection regarding America's identity and geopolitical purpose and that these concerns focus on the status of America as the "great nation of futurity."

CHAPTER 2

"America's Most Precious Natural Resource"

The Temporality of American Exceptionalism

AMERICAN EXCEPTIONALISM AND FUTURITY

The aim of this chapter is to draw out the temporal elements of America's self-proclaimed identity as an exceptional nation, particularly the claim to the future this identity entails.[1] My interest here lies not in establishing the importance of exceptionalism to American national identity and foreign policy. Those arguments, as I've indicated in the preceding chapter, have already been made. In short, the belief in exceptionalism traces back to the initial arrival of Europeans in North America and is expressed through and sustained by such iconic appellations as "the empire of liberty" and "the last, best hope of earth" (Hodgson 2009: 10). Nor am I concerned here with the debate regarding whether America has been an exceptional nation, a debate that, as I also noted in Chapter 1, has received considerable scholarly attention. Rather, I examine the temporal logic embedded in the central components of the nation's exceptionalist ideology and rhetoric. Specifically, I consider the ways the American brand of exceptionalism positions the United States temporally and the relations of identity and difference implicated in that positioning. I argue that at its core, the claim of exceptionalism locates America in a privileged position with respect to the future and, concomitantly, with respect to its relations with other nations and peoples.

In what follows, I draw out the sense of futurity embedded in early articulations of the nation's identity. This discussion is organized around the three components of the American exceptionalist ideology that McCrisken (2003) has identified as proving "relatively consistent throughout American history"

The Great Nation of Futurity. Patricia L. Dunmire, Oxford University Press. © Oxford University Press 2023.
DOI: 10.1093/oso/9780197658222.003.0002

(8): America as "the elect" nation endowed with a special destiny, as "separate and different from the rest of the world," and as exempt from the laws of history that impact the ascendancy and decline of all preeminent nations (McCrisken 2003: 8; also see McCartney 2004: 403).

In brief, conceptualizing America as comprising a special people—the "elect"—with a special destiny—a world-historical "mission"—renders the nation as a "beacon" for the perpetual improvement of human society and as the exemplar of what other nations and peoples ought to be and should aspire to (McCrisken 2003: 9). Realizing this destiny requires that the nation undertake the "divine errand" assigned to it by Providence, an errand guided by a "predetermined historical design," the "apex" of which is understood to rest in the New World (Bercovitch 2012: 39, 99). America as a land and a people "separate and different" from the rest of the world further entails the idea that the American experiment represents something unprecedented in human history: the "opening of a grand scene and design," a "marked epoch in the course of time," and an opportunity to "begin the world over again."[2] Finally, the contention that the nation is not subject to the typical forces and tendencies of history that have governed the fate of other republics situates America outside of history, as the nation that will "escape the 'laws of history'" (Rodgers 2018: 230; McCrisken 2003: 10). As the exceptional nation, America is rendered as the leader of global progress tasked with advancing human achievement and relentlessly pursuing its ultimate goal of forming "a more perfect union" (Preamble of the U.S. Constitution, as quoted in McCrisken 2003: 10). In short, America is conceived of as the nation that "would inherit the future" (Bell 1975: 195).

Special Nation, Special Destiny

Although de Toqueville was the first to use the term "exceptional" to characterize the United States, the concept has been linked to the arrival of the Puritans in New England and the belief that it was the new "promised land," and the Puritans, the new "chosen people" (McCrisken 2003: 1, 9). This original act of colonization was understood as providentially blessed and as intended to fulfill the divine purpose of creating a society that would ultimately lead to the improvement of the world's people (McCrisken 2003: 9). In his address "A Model of Christian Charity," John Winthrop (1630) explained to his fellow migrants aboard the Arbella that in setting out for the New World "We are entered into a covenant with [God]. We have taken out a commission" and that safe passage would be evidence that God had "ratified this covenant and sealed our commission." He was careful to warn, however, that the success of their venture was not assured. Explaining that "with the eyes of all people" upon New England, the "city on a hill," Winthrop cautioned that "we shall be

[32] *The Great Nation of Futurity*

made a story and a by-word throughout the world" should "we . . . deal falsely with our God in this work we have undertaken."

This belief that they were undertaking a divine errand, Bercovitch (2012) contends, was rooted in the Puritans' conviction that they were "elect" and an expectation that they would achieve great things on behalf of humankind (38). As the "redeemer nation," they understood themselves as having been commissioned by God to rehabilitate themselves and the world (McCrisken 2003: 9). As such, the early migrants viewed their emigration from England as an attempt to reform rather than disengage from the world (Bercovitch 2012: 38). In sum, the Puritans viewed themselves as divinely charged—as "called" and "chosen"—with the task of completing a "predetermined historical design" that would reach its "apex in the New World" (Bercovitch 2012: 7–8, 39, 99).

Rodgers (2018) demonstrates that throughout the nation's history the phrase "as a city on a hill" has been transformed from being an expression of the modest aspirations of the early Puritans to a declaration of America's global mission and responsibility (32). That is, he explains that Winthrop declared that the Puritan settlement would represent a model only for "succeeding *plantations*"; he did not view it as setting the "pattern for *the world*" (Rodgers 2018: 69, emphasis added; also see Hodgson 2009).[3] Despite the modesty of Winthrop's ambitions, the iconic phrase has been taken "prophetically," as "contain[ing] all that was to come afterward" (Rodgers 2018: 32). By the latter half of the 17th century exuberant references to Winthrop's metaphor proliferated as religious leaders deployed "tropes of self-importance" to assure their congregants that they were the new chosen people (Rodgers 2018: 73, 81). For example, in a 1674 sermon Increase Mather linked New England to the ancient Israelites in order to identify the Puritans and their geographical environment as recipients of a divine promise, proclaiming that "God hath covenanted his people . . . without a doubt the Lord Jesus hath a peculiar respect unto this place, and for this people" (as quoted in Murphy 2009: 18).

Rodgers (2018) further explains that although "A Model of Christian Charity" was not a significant text in the nation's early history, its appropriation for nationalistic ends dramatically changed how the text was understood and used (124). The status of "A Model" as a foundational text was "invented" by being "rediscovered and remade" by national leaders and pundits searching for texts on which to ground the meaning, significance, and identity of the new nation, as well as by those offering reassurances concerning the nation's continued promise and status as a formidable global power (Rodgers 2018: 124–125, 247–248).

For their part, the Founding Fathers drew upon late 17th-century Puritan rhetoric in their declarations that the new nation was destined to be the vanguard of progressive development in the world and, thus, was a nation assigned an "extraordinary obligation" to the world's people (McCrisken 2003: 10; Hunt 1987: 191). In this view, America would serve as the "theatre for displaying the illustrious design of Providence" with the success of the Revolution representing the "fulfillment of God's plan" (Colonel David Humphries, as quoted in Bercovitch 2012: 122, 123). This plan, however, extended beyond colonial territory, as the patriots saw themselves to be "acting for the benefit of the whole world and of future ages" (Benjamin Rush speaking in 1783, as quoted in Bercovitch 2012: 127). John Adams (1765) characterized the nation's inception as the "Opening of a grand scene and Design in Providence for the Illumination of the Ignorant and the Emancipation of the slavish Part of Mankind all over the Earth." Echoing the redemptive mission proclaimed in the late 1600s, Thomas Paine (1776) explained that by seeking independence from Great Britain, the colonies "have every opportunity . . . to form the noblest purist constitution on the face of the earth. We have it in our power to begin the world over again. . . . The birthday of a new world is at hand" (113–114).

In his 1789 inaugural address George Washington declared that Providence had "entrusted" to its people "the preservation of the sacred fire of liberty, and the destiny of the Republican model of Government." In his first inaugural address Thomas Jefferson (1801a) characterized America as a "rising nation" that was "advancing rapidly to destinies beyond the reach of the mortal eye." As the nation blessed by an "overruling Providence," Jefferson identified the young nation as "the world's best hope" and, consequently, as the nation destined to serve all of mankind by "ameliorat[ing] the condition of man over a great portion of the globe" (Jefferson 1801a, 1801b). In his final State of the Union address, James Monroe (1824) averred that the nation's newly formed institutions were spawning "an important epoch in the history of the civilized world. On their preservation and in their utmost purity everything will depend."

At its inception, the United States was understood to comprise a chosen people entrusted with the divine errand of revolutionizing the way governments would function and people would be governed. It was through its revolutionary character that the young republic would "'give law to the rest of the world' . . . as 'an empire of liberty,' . . . 'an empire of virtue'; . . . 'a great and mighty Empire; the largest the World ever saw'" (Bercovitch 2012: 114). As Hunt (1987) tells it, for the Founding Fathers the America Revolution represented evidence of America's progress and exemplified the type of political progress other nations "were destined to receive" (95). Moreover, Paine's "vision of a glorious future" rendered America as the nation that would breathe new life into "a gray, spent world" by "restarting the clock of time" (Hunt 1987: 19; Rodgers 1998: 22). Rodgers (2018) similarly explains that with the American Revolution came a temporal reconfiguration away from the "older logic of typological history," according

[34] *The Great Nation of Futurity*

to which historical development was prescribed by the Bible (129). This conception of time and history was eventually replaced by the temporal logic of "nationalist time," which involved a leap "forward to the promise of the future" and a celebration of the nation's severing its ties to the past (Rodgers 2018: 129–130).

The conviction that the nation figured as a preeminent actor and force in the Almighty's plan for humankind served as a "civil religion" during and immediately after the American Revolution (McCartney 2004: 404). Bolstered by an expansive vision and an unwavering belief in their "future greatness," Revolutionary leaders saw themselves as "harbingers of a New World Order" that was universal in its appeal and would alter history's course (Herring 2008b: 11–12). Rodgers (2018) notes that in reading their writing one cannot help but be "struck by the force of the future tense" (129). "Raptures" about the nation's "future glory," Silver (2008) similarly notes, pervade Revolutionary discourse (253). This nationalist rhetoric uprooted the nation's divine mission from its scriptural grounding by transforming "providence" into a "belief in human progress" and the possibility of unending "secular improvement" (Bercovitch 2012: 93–94). Their revolutionary project, the patriots were sure, presaged the inception of a new age in global politics and, as such, would serve as a "beacon" to the world's people (Herring 2008b: 16). Fourth of July orators similarly insisted that the fledgling nation "was bent on future glory" (Rodgers 2018: 129). "To what height of national greatness may we not aspire?," David Ramsey asked Independence Day celebrants in 1794 (as quoted in Rodgers 2018: 130).

This conviction was further sustained in the post-Revolutionary period through claims about the universal meaning and impact of American independence. With the emergence of a profound confidence in the American project in the 1820s, influential orators regularly characterized the United States as the exemplary nation that was "'admired by the kings of the world,' the 'bright example' toward which 'the longing eyes of millions are turned,' and the 'beacon . . . to which the nations look for light and guidance'" (Rodgers 2018: 139). In 1833 Robert Rantoul, a member of the 32nd Congress, declared that the American Revolution

> is not only a marked epoch in the course of time, but it is indeed the end from which the new order of things is to be reckoned. It is the dividing point in the history of mankind; it is the moment of political regeneration of the world. (as quoted in Bercovitch 2012: 143)

During a Fourth of July celebration in 1834, radical orator Orestes Brownson urged his audience to understand that the "Birth-day of Freedom" was the outcome of not just the warring British and colonial armies; "the past and the future" had also done battle as "the spirit of immobility and the spirit of progress" met "in terrible conflict" (as quoted in Rodgers 2018: 152). As the original colonies expanded across the continental United States, Americans came to conceive of their nation as charged with a "world historical covenant and mission" (Rodgers 2004: 24). In 19th-century nationalist discourse the conditional nature of Winthrop's admonition concerning the fate of the American experiment was washed away by the "inflowing tides of patriotism" (Rodgers 2018: 146).

The belief that America was providentially endowed with an exceptional character and destiny found expression in and through the jeremiad. As a literary genre, the American jeremiad forged a framework of national identity based on the idea of America as an "unfolding prophecy," as a "child of prophecy and promise" (Bercovitch 2012: xiii, 69). Since the nation's founding the jeremiad has served as a political and rhetorical vehicle for sanctioning America as a nation destined to fulfill a divine mission on earth (Bercovitch 2012: xv, xii). In Bercovitch's (2012) view, the idea of a predetermined mission manifests, in part, through the "insistent temporality" of the jeremiad's rhetoric, which conceptualized the Pilgrim's New England venture as representing "the climax of history" and the "pattern" of what lay ahead (143–144). Through this "heroic errand" the nation would serve as a "model" to others and, ultimately, would bring "history itself to an end" (Bercovitch 2012: 20, 12). The turn of the 17th century saw the "sacred" Puritan jeremiad transformed into the "profane" American jeremiad (Bercovitch 2012: 93). This latter version ultimately came to articulate a "vision so broad and so specifically American in its application" that it would be sanctioned as a flexible guide to a secular future (Bercovitch 2012: 92).

Entailed in the concept of destiny, the "sure ground" of exceptionalism and the premise of American national life (Bell 1975: 205; Schlesinger 1977: 515), is the view that America embodies the future. As the "anointed nation," America is understood to be exceptional because it has been granted a special destiny—"a prefixed trajectory of spatial and temporal aims"—by divine Providence (Stephanson 1995: xiv). Indeed, Mohlo and Wood (1998) note that although all nations articulate their own distinct geopolitical role, the claim of a special geopolitical destiny is uniquely American (1998: 4). Key to this claim, what further distinguishes America from other republics, is the insistence that the nation's destiny is necessarily progressive. In fact, a commitment to progress was deemed to be so important to the nation's destiny that in 1840 the editors of the *Democratic Review* declared "progress—indefinite, unpausing progress" as the nation's preeminent creed (227). Heeding this law would ensure a destiny whereby the nation would become the "perfect specimen" of the republican form of government (Tarnas 1993: 58).

As Edwards and Weiss (2011) explain, to its adherents, American exceptionalism proclaims a telos of continual progress whereby the nation moves through time in a relentless pattern of ascension as it strives to become "a more perfect union" (1). This conception of American progress is undergirded by what Appadurai (2013) terms "trajectorism": a conceptualization of temporality according to which "time's arrow" points in a singular direction toward a known destination (225). Trajectorism is a fundamental epistemological and ontological disposition that assumes that human affairs proceed along "a cumulative journey from here to there, or more exactly from now to then" (Appadurai 2013: 225). Accordingly, the American trajectory, in the words of 18th-century Protestant theologian Jonathan Edwards, construes the nation's development as preparing "the way for the future, glorious times" (as quoted in Bercovitch 2012: 99).

The nation's exceptionalism, then, lay in what it, the "great experiment for the demonstration of higher purposes," was to become and what it presaged for the future of humankind (Stephanson 1995: 21). The new nation was seen as embodying potentiality: its exceptionalism lay not in what the nation was but in what it could become, in its relentless advancing and broadening expectations of what is possible and its unceasing quest for progress (McCrisken 2003: 10). Although "a nation of but yesterday," America would "aspire" to an unprecedented "height of national greatness" (David Ramsey speaking in 1794, as quoted in Rodgers 2018: 129–130). As an idea, America was conceived of as a "unique mission . . . in time and space, a continuous *process*" that would be the site of the final realization of God's grace (Stephanson 1995: 6, emphasis in the original; Schlesinger 1977: 515). In the words of Walt Whitman (1871), "America . . . counts . . . for her justification and success . . . almost entirely on the future. . . . For our New World I consider it far less important for what it has done, or what it is, than for the results to come." The nation, Lapham (1992) notes, has always been about "becoming, not being; about the prospects of the future, not about the inheritance of the past" (2).

By manifesting God's grace, so the thinking went, America, as the ultimate realization of the Western tradition, would provide the blueprint for the future development of Western civilization, a conviction captured in the inscription on the national seal: "novus ordo seclorum," (New Order of the Ages) (Mohlo and Wood 1998: 6). In short, the creation of the United States was understood as ushering in an unprecedented age of social and political relations (Rodgers 1998: 21). The nation's political and cultural leaders insisted that most important to the young nation were not the cultural traditions of the past but its inhabitants' ability to adjust to their new environment, an adjustment that would engage them with the demands of the present and the possibilities of the future (Nash Smith 1950: 41). Declaring that "the past is dead," Herman Melville insisted that the American experiment had "endowed" the future "with such a life that it lives to us even in anticipation" (as quoted in Schlesinger 1977: 518). This patriotic rhetoric espoused a nationalist sentiment that proclaimed the future of the new nation to be "unbounded";

"the future, and the future alone, was what mattered" (Rodgers 2018: 149; Stephanson 1995: 41).

Separate and Different

America was deemed uniquely positioned to claim the future because it was seen as not just geographically but also temporally separate and different from Europe: it was characterized as a country that began "with no history" and, thus, had "liberate[d] its descendants from history" (Bell 1975: 198; Schlesinger 1977: 518). In this thinking, Europe was temporally identified as past and, thus, as the new nation's temporal Other against which it would juxtapose its own identity as the nation of the future. The United States was the nation that had made a "heroic break with the past" and, thereby, had obliterated "history's chains and encagements" (Rodgers 2018: 130). "Anticipations of escape from ordinary history," Rodgers (2004) explains, are endemic to conceptions of the nation's past (24).

In the words of 19th-century poet James Russell Lowell, America was "something without precedent" (as quoted in Kammen 1993: 8). Irving Howe similarly argued that the nation was exempt from "the historical burdens that have overwhelmed Europe" (as quoted in Kammen 1993: 10–11). According to Madsen (1998), Benjamin Franklin believed that because it was not burdened with Europe's complicated history the new nation was uniquely suited to create a rationally based democratic society (36). For Thomas Jefferson, Stephanson (1995) explains, the past was nothing more than "a sedimentation of obstacles" that stood in the way of individual freedom and happiness (22). Having fled the "crushing nightmare of history," Jefferson saw Americans as uniquely situated and capable of developing a form of society unknown in the history of mankind (Stephanson 1995: 22).

According to John O'Sullivan (1839), editor of *The United States Magazine and Democratic Review*, the United States occupies a "disconnected position as regards any other nation" and, as such, has "but little connection with the past history of any of them." In 1842 the editors of the *Democratic Review* similarly noted that "probably no other civilized nation . . . has . . . so completely thrown off its allegiance to the past as the American" (225). Indeed, the "whole essay of our national life and legislation," they insisted, "has been a prolonged protest against the dominion of antiquity" (*Democratic Review* 1842: 225). To be American, John Quincy Adams declared, was to "cast off the European skin" and "look forward to . . . posterity rather than backward" toward ancestry (as quoted in Lapham 1992: 2). What distinguished Americans, then, was that "our thoughts and energies . . . are engrossed . . . of the future toward which this unparalleled movement is bearing us on" (*Democratic Review* 1840: 227).

The editors of the *Democratic Review* further declared the temporal separateness of the United States by contrasting its conception of the future to that of the Europeans. Europe's ruling class, they insisted, offered only a stunted conception of the future, which held that "the future should continue, as closely as possible, the perpetual reproduction of the past" (*Democratic Review* 1840: 227). The European future, Ralph Waldo Emerson (1844) noted, was "closing in ... to a narrow slit of sky"; this "fast contracting future" was, in fact, "no future." Europe was governed by the past, which served, Melville averred, as a "textbook of tyrants" (as quoted in Stephanson 1995: 41). America would upend this tyranny of history by fixing its gaze wholly on the future: its "eyes" would be "forever bent forward, and rarely cast behind" it (*Democratic Review* 1840: 227). The nation would be governed, Melville declared, by the future, "the Bible of the Free" (as quoted in Stephanson 1995: 41).

Given this break from the past, the new nation was claimed to be uniquely positioned to take hold of its potential and "begin the world over again" (Rodgers 2018: 130; Paine 1776). Its "birth," O'Sullivan (1839) insisted, represented the "beginning of a new history ... which ... connects [the nation] with the future only." In North America lay the "empire of the future" and, thus, the site where the "world's great age would begin anew" (Nash Smith 1950: 11). As "pioneers of the world," Americans were, Melville proclaimed, "the advance-guard sent to break a new path in the New World that is ours," a position that created a distinctive temporal space for the United States and, thereby, relegated all other nations to "our rear" (as quoted in Ceasar 2012: 18). The nation's unique temporality sanctioned its role as "the vanguard" of humanity's future (Kagan 2006: 12). As a "new, different, and superior society," America would exemplify how other nations should develop their societies (McKeever 1989: 45). By focusing its energy on realizing the "grand though shadowy anticipations [that] are forever vaguely present before our minds," the nation would create a sense of hope for the future for the world's people (*Democratic Review* 1840: 227; Bell 1989: 46). As an emerging force on the world scene, North America was the place "toward which the old nations of Europe 'turn with hope in their eyes'" (Nash Smith 1950: 41). Eighteenth-century European philosophers likewise viewed Americans as "the hope of the human race" and the new nation as "the model" of social and political development (Turgot, as quoted in Commager 1974: 35).

Because it was charged by "the movement of history" to bring to fruition the democratic age, the new nation was sure to "inherit the future" (Restad 2012: 17; Bell 1975: 195). "The far reaching boundless future," O'Sullivan (1839) insisted, would be "the era of American greatness," with the nation's destiny being realized in the "expansive arena of the future." America was, O'Sullivan (1839) declared, "the great nation of futurity." Echoing O'Sullivan, Ralph Waldo Emerson (1844) designated America as the "country of the future," a "country of beginnings, of projects, of designs, and expectations." The

American future, he pointed out, was "open" and "expanding" and, as such, held unlimited promise and potential. Forty years later, Andrew Carnegie attributed America's claim on the future to the accelerated tempo of its material progress, noting that "The Old nations . . . creep on at a snail's pace; the Republic thunders past with the rush of the express" (as quoted in Commager 1974: 34). America, in short, was deemed the "locomotive of human progress" (McCartney 2004: 401).

That Providence had destined America to be the nation of the future was made manifest in its unique physical and spatial character. In addition to its commitment to liberty, virtuousness, and commercial acumen, the nation's geographical expansiveness "destined" it to achieve global prominence (Rodgers 2018: 129). That is, within the discourse of American exceptionalism, both the nation's location and geography render it as the place of the future: as both the site of potentiality and promise and the space within which that promise could and would be realized. Thus, this siting of the future in America stems not just from the new nation's temporal separation from Europe but also from its geographical separation and territorial uniqueness.

In a very literal sense, the Puritans saw their future as located in *New England* and conceived of their flight to the New World as the only means for accessing that future. By migrating, they left the status quo that reigned in the Old World and a hereditary system that greatly limited an individual's prospects and sought on the American continent a place where they could create new social forms, practices, and norms (McCrisken 2003: 9). Fleeing the European past had liberated the New England immigrants from Europe's trials and tribulations, thereby enabling them to find "their own exceptional future" as an "exemplar or model for the future progress of liberty and democracy" (Rodgers 1998: 29; Mohlo and Wood 1998: 4). The land of New England was the place that, in the words of John Cotton, "God spied out for thee" and "made room for thee" (as quoted in Sanford 1974: 17). Providence, the Puritans believed, had sent them to this new Eden because it was "the place where the Lord will create a new Heaven, and new Earth" (Edward Johnson, as quoted in Schlesinger 1977: 514). This Puritan millennialism prophesized a spiritual renewal across the globe and the exceptional role the "chosen people living under providential blessing" would play in that renewal (Hunt 1987: 20). By siting the millennium in New England, mankind's redemption was linked to a particular people and a particular place, in a "new land" that was . . . "the climax of redemptive history"; it was deemed a land and a place that represented the fulfillment of "divine prophecy" (Schlesinger 1977: 515; also see Bell 1975: 198; Kammen 1993: 8).

The American continent, because it was physically separate from the Old World of Europe, was also seen as removed from and untouched by its traditions and presumptions (McCrisken 2003: 10). Rather than being a mere extension of European culture and history, the New World was understood

[40] *The Great Nation of Futurity*

to be "different in nature and in man," and, thus, as different in history and destiny (Commager 1974: 21). As the "last order" in history, America was unprecedented and unsullied, free from "ancient arrangement" (Stephanson 1995: 41). Within this view, the "'scenes of antiquity' were of interest only as 'lessons of avoidance'" (Stephanson 1995: 41). Deemed by exceptionalist rhetoric as a "virgin land," America was designated as a place of opportunity, invention, and creation where people could engage with principles, values, and ideas that had no currency anywhere else (McCrisken 2003: 10).[4]

Indeed, the progressive future imagined by American Enlightenment thinkers required a "break from the past" embodied in European institutions that were held to be infertile ground for a "forward-looking world view" (McCartney 2004: 405). Accordingly, they championed North America as a "continental tabula rasa" and "redemptive land" that would serve as the site of a new era in the history of mankind and upon which the progressive vision of the Enlightenment could be realized and sustained (McCartney 2004: 406; 2006: 37). American geography, they insisted, represented a "literal break from the past" and, as such, presented the ideal location for enacting the principles and convictions of a new era (McCartney 2004: 406).

Exempt from Laws of History

The physical separateness and isolation of the New World was understood not only as dislodging America from Old World traditions but also as placing it outside the laws of history that had led to the ruin of other republics. That is, underlying America's claim of exceptionalism has been the assumption that it is not destined to rise and fall like its predecessors; rather, it would develop along a trajectory of perpetual ascension. Being exceptional meant being an "exception from a rule, from the common tide of change, from time itself" (Mohlo and Wood 1998: 15). This was the view of the Founding Fathers, who held fast to the conviction that the new republic would not fall victim to the corruption and decadence that had led to the ruin of the Old World (Commager 1974: 21). In his inaugural address, President Washington (1789) insisted that the new nation was uniquely suited to the task of preserving "the sacred fire of liberty and the destiny of the republican model of government," an "experiment entrusted to the hands of the American people." He reaffirmed this view in his farewell address, noting that the nation's "detached and distant situation" would shield it from the "insidious wiles of foreign influence" that have proven to be among "the most baneful foes" of republicanism (Washington 1796). Consequently, America would be able to "pursue a different course" (Washington 1796).

Thomas Jefferson (1801a) likewise insisted that as a nation "kindly separated by nature and a wide ocean from the exterminating havoc of one quarter of the globe" and "with room enough for our descendants to the thousandth and thousandth generation," America was unlikely to "endure the degradation of others." Geographical distance, in sum, would inoculate the "innocence" of the New World against the "corruption" of the Old (McKeever 1989: 45). Positioned to pursue a path of perpetual ascension rather than eventual decline, the new nation was naturally predisposed, so the thinking went, to lead the world to a progressive future. The nation's "progressive exceptionalism" made it particularly well suited to replace Europe as the vanguard nation (Adas 2009: 1698). Its future prospects, and thus those of the world, were endless.

The prospects and survival of America and the ideals it represented were further assured by a seemingly boundless continent that provided ample space in which the progressive future could come to fruition. The western portion of the continent, which appeared to offer seemingly limitless resources, was held to be "a land of endless promise" and as evidence that Americans had settled in a special place that would provide all that was needed to sustain the American democratic experiment (McCartney 2006: 29–30; Madsen 1998: 89). Virginians seeking to invest and grow their wealth, Anderson (2005) explains, trained their eyes on the future, which they saw as residing in the West (28). Jefferson designated the western territory as "the chosen country" and argued that the nation had been territorially blessed with sufficient space for sustaining countless generations of future citizens (Onuf 2000: 15). Such geographical expansiveness would enable the "swelling masses of the future" to realize the American ideal of a self-sufficient and independent existence and to claim their own futures (Stephanson 1995: 41, 22).

This expansiveness of the land was believed, moreover, to presage future greatness for the new nation, as it was the site upon which divinity's design would be made manifest (Bell 1975: 198). As Weinberg (1958) explains, early Americans interpreted the natural grandeur of the continent as symbolizing the nation's exceptionalism and its unrivaled potential; it signified the future trajectory along which the nation would develop into "a still greater nation" (48). A look into the future was a look to the West, to the spaces in which new states would arise and new beginnings would ensue (Silver 2008: 253–254). This perspective was grounded in the belief that a nation's destiny could be discerned by carefully examining, in the words of geographer Andrew Guyot, "the theatre, seemingly arranged by Him for the realization of a new social order, towards which humanity is tending with hope" (as quoted in Nash Smith 1950: 42). "The order of nature," Guyot insisted, "is a foreshadowing of that which is to be" (as quoted in Nash Smith 1950: 42).

In the 19th-century American imagination, the western frontier represented the outer limits of the "exceptionalist world" and the place where the nation's exceptional character and purpose would be made and perpetuated (Rodgers 2004: 37). It represented a "*figural* outpost, the outskirts of the advancing kingdom of God" and signified "prophecy and unlimited prospects" (Bercovitch 2012: 163, emphasis in the original). The Louisiana Purchase of 1803 made apparent "vaster horizons of national greatness" and bolstered the view that "nature has destined the far-flung boundaries for the sake of America's glory" (Weinberg 1958: 48). This foreign policy coup was viewed as the beginning of the nation's "anticipatory hopes" of a day when its "boundaries shall be those which nature has formed for a great, powerful, and free state" (Joseph Chandler, as quoted in Weinberg 1958: 48). Likewise, the Lewis and Clark expedition in the early years of the 19th century was seen not merely as an exploration of the western territory; its importance lay "on the level of the imagination" in which the expedition represented "the enactment of a myth that embodied the future" (Nash Smith 1950: 17).

The conviction that nature, rather than politics, determined a country's boundaries, as well as its destiny, derived from the "metaphysical dogma" of "geographical predestination," which held that nature had destined natural boundaries for all nations (Weinberg 1958: 43). This was held to be especially true for America, "the nation of special destiny" (Weinberg 1958: 43). Although other nations subscribed to this principle, the American variant was distinctive in that it served as a call for "indefinite future expansion" across the continent as a means of ensuring the republic's continued success (Weinberg 1958: 44–45, 129). That is, the destiny of the nation was believed to be immanent in a geography that would ensure the United States a place of prominence over other nations (Nash Smith 1950: 43).

Because the West was viewed as the site of the "truly American society of the future" (Nash Smith 1950: 45) the nation's destiny would be realized, O'Sullivan (1839) warned, only by expanding into this "untrodden space of the future." As Weinberg (1958) put it, "the hand of nature seemed to beckon to a terminus just beyond the horizon, to a boundary which demanded all effort" (71). Moreover, many of the proponents of Manifest Destiny subscribed to "sun symbolism," which held that the future has a "sense of direction" and "lay westward, following the sun" (Sanford 1974: 3–4). With each push westward the nation achieved a higher level of progressive development (Nash Smith 1950: 37). America's destiny was a "directional destiny—from east to west" (Hostetler 2011: 129). Expansion was imperative, then, if the nation was to realize its true potential as "the great nation of futurity."

The impetus toward continental dominion assumed that Americans, a people not bound by the laws of history, had an obligation to the future of republican ideals to expand into the West. Proponents of expansion held the view that Providence had "entrusted the fullest achievement of the moral glory of man to the best of human material, the mighty American democracy" (Weinberg 1958: 128). As Congressional Representative Duncan put it, the "indefinite future expansion" of the nation's territory would enable "the area of freedom" to be extended "as far and as wide as the American continent,"

"AMERICA'S MOST PRECIOUS RESOURCE" [43]

thereby ensuring the "fulfillment of a moral mission delegated . . . by Providence itself" (as quoted in Weinberg 1958: 129; Weinberg 1958: 1).

As the civil religion of the mid-1880s, Manifest Destiny comprised both the idea that the nation had the right to control its future and the insistence that its people were endowed with a unique virtue. Taken together, these convictions distinguished the American project "from anything known . . . in the history of the world" (Bell 1975: 199). Belief in the nation's Manifest Destiny further assumed, as noted earlier, that history followed a linear path of progressive development directed by divine Providence and natural law (Sanford 1974: 11). Its disciples subscribed to the concept of *translatio imperii*: the dual idea that a singular preeminent force or people served as the vanguard of civilization and that westward movement was the geographical tendency of historical progress (Stephanson 1995: 18). Manifest Destiny, then, was much more than "a mere land grab"; it was a particular articulation of the progressive ideal of which America was the ultimate manifestation (Ceasar 2012: 16).

Understanding western expansion to have global implications, advocates stressed the "moral urgency" of their project by warning that "nothing less than the future of the world" was at stake (Hunt 1987: 30; Stephanson 1995: 7). As "God's emissary," the nation had a moral duty advance the cause of freedom and democracy wherever and whenever it could (McCrisken 2003: 13). O'Sullivan (1839) insisted that by granting the nation a "magnificent domain of time and space," Providence had destined it "to manifest to mankind the excellence of divine principles; to establish on earth the noblest temple ever dedicated to the worship of the Most High—the Sacred and the True" (427). Increasingly, the call to expand was grounded in the conviction that liberty and national greatness were inextricably linked and that the future viability of both depended upon territorial expansion (Weinberg 1958). Whereas the prospects of other republics had been limited and, thus, ultimately unsustainable, the whole of the American continent was believed to provide the space needed to ensure the unceasing perpetuation of republican ideals. Speaking in 1848 in support the Mexican War, Senator Sydney Breese urged his fellow senators to allow the nation to "expand to our true and proper dimension, and our liberty will be eternal; for, in the process, it will increase in strength, and the flame grow brighter, whilst it lights a more extensive field" (as quoted in Hunt 1987: 31).

Not only did the nation's future reside in the West; its very existence as a republic depended on access to the western frontier, as acquisition of new lands was further declared essential to both the nation's salvation and defense. By turning toward the ever-expanding and shifting western frontier the Americans were eschewing "the backward pull of Europe" and its degraded past and turning toward a future of unlimited possibility (Bell 1989: 57; Hostetler 2011: 128). The acquisition of western territory, so the thinking went, would inoculate the new nation against European corruption and degradation and,

[44]   *The Great Nation of Futurity*

thereby, ensure its salvation and survival. Expansionists argued that a republic with a growing population but limited territory would eventually meet its demise; as such, they insisted western expansion was necessary for ensuring the nation's "salvation" (Hunt 1987: 30). According to Fredrick Jackson Turner's (1920) "frontier thesis," expansion was necessary to the nation's future economic and social welfare because the frontier offered a "gate of escape" from domestic pressures and "the bondage of the past" (38). The frontier of the New World was the place where Old World traditions and institutions would end and human society would start anew (Rodgers 2004: 26). The trope of expansion as salvation ultimately gave way to a trope of expansion as defense, as "extending the area of freedom" was touted as a defensive act essential to protecting the young republic from foreign dangers, namely, the European Other that threatened to encroach upon the nation's territory and principles (Weinberg 1958: 109).

Taken together, the central components of American exceptionalism can be understood as embedding a host of concepts that index futurity. "Special nation, special destiny" comprises the ideas of a telos of progress, becoming rather than being, potentiality and promise, aspiration and anticipation, hopes and desires, and a nationalist rhetoric cast in the future tense. "Separate and different" aligns with the characterization of history and tradition as fetters on the future and of the American future as a boundless, expansive space of possibility, opportunity, and new beginnings. Finally, "exempt from laws of history" entails a development scheme that assumes perpetual ascension rather than eventual degradation and, concomitantly, a commitment to vanguardism. In the following section, I examine the role exceptionalist appeals have played in foreign policy discourse and how these appeals embed and reproduce the conception of America as exemplar of the global future.

EXCEPTIONALISM AS LEGITIMATION

Since the early days of the American republic, the ideology of exceptionalism has functioned rhetorically not just to give meaning and coherence to the nation but to guide and legitimate its geopolitical relations and actions. That is, what Madsen (1998) terms the "prescriptive force" of exceptionalism has both motivated the nation to play an active role on the global stage and rationalized that role and the actions it entails (9). The conviction that America is a special nation with a special destiny has played a consistent and prominent role in shaping the nation's foreign policy (McCrisken 2003: 5; Hunt 1987; McEvoy-Levy 2001; Restad 2012). In fact, exceptionalism has been the one clear conceptualization of the nation's foreign policy (Lepgold and McKeown 1995: 369). For McCartney (2006), the concept of mission helps explain the motivations and goals of the nation's foreign policy and its particular brand of exceptionalism (10, 26).

The legitimating function of the exceptionalist ideology can be seen in the early years of the nation's approach to foreign relations, namely, in arguments surrounding its "Manifest Destiny" and the conviction that, as the agent of a divinely inspired errand, the young republic had a right and duty to expand westward (Bercovitch 2012: 160). According to 18th-century Congregationalist pastor Joseph Bellamy, westward migration and annexation of adjacent land were sanctioned by the nation's responsibility to "manifest to mankind the excellence of the divine principles of our Revolution" (as quoted in Bercovitch 2012: 142). In an address to Congress in 1845, William Gilpin (1974/1873) declared that the nation's "*untransacted destiny*" was to "establish a new order in human affairs . . . to teach old nations a new civilization—to confirm the destiny of the human race—to carry the career of mankind to its culminating point" (124, emphasis in original). This "right . . . to spread over [the] whole continent," Representative Charles C. Winthrop declared in 1846, is a right that "will not be admitted to exist in any nation except the universal Yankee nation!" (as quoted in Pratt 1927: 795).

It was this uniquely American destiny, proponents of expansion insisted, that entitled those moving west to lands occupied by people deemed not part of the "progressive narrative," that is, those deemed not to be contributing to or participating in the advance of civilization (Deneen 2012: 42). Concerned about a rapidly growing "restless population," President Washington urged movement to contested lands as a means of ensuring the future of the republic (Herring 2008b). This "covetousness" for land occupied by others was warranted by Americans' conviction that the preeminence of their institutions and ideology endowed them with privileged access to western lands (Herring 2008b: 58–59).

By 1846 use of the phrase "Manifest Destiny" had become commonplace after Massachusetts Representative Robert Winthrop invoked it in his argument to Congress that it was "the right of our manifest destiny" to secure title to Oregon from the British (as quoted in Pratt 1927: 795). Both the phrase and concept, however, are attributed to the writing of John O'Sullivan, who first articulated the concept of Manifest Destiny, though not the phase, in his 1839 essay "The Great Nation of Futurity" (Pratt 1927). Noting that "America is destined for better deeds" than European monarchies and aristocracies, O'Sullivan (1839) explained that the nation's people were moving west "with the truths of God in our minds" and "beneficent objects in our hearts." As for "the nation of human progress," which had Providence on its side, he was adamant that "no earthly power can . . . set limits to our onward march" (O'Sullivan 1839). The nation's "high destiny" was the "entire development of the principle of our organization" and, thereby, the establishment on earth of

[46]   *The Great Nation of Futurity*

"the moral dignity and salvation of man" (O'Sullivan 1839). America alone, O'Sullivan insisted, had been "chosen" to undertake this "blessed mission to the nations of the world, which are shut out from the life-giving light of truth" (O'Sullivan 1839).

In his essay in the summer of 1845 advocating the annexation of Texas from the Republic of Texas, O'Sullivan distilled the nation's right to expand westward into the phrase "manifest destiny," which he defined as America's divinely sanctioned mission to "overspread the continent allotted by Providence for the free development of our yearly multiplying millions." O'Sullivan's conceptualization of Manifest Destiny subsequently appeared in a December editorial in the New York *Morning News* concerning the nation's claim to Oregon, which insisted that it was

> *the right of manifest destiny to overspread and possess the whole of the continent* which Providence has given us for the development of the great experiment of liberty and federated self-government entrusted to us . . . and with His blessing we will firmly maintain the incontestable rights He has given, and fearlessly perform the high duties He has imposed. (as quoted in Pratt 1927: 796, emphasis in original)

In sum, the doctrine of expansion whereby the nation would achieve "continental dominion" was justified because "God wills it"; America was "the continent of the future" (Weinberg 1958: 112, 129; Andersson 2006: 285). The policy of Manifest Destiny, according to its adherents, would extend America's revolutionary promise to the "untrodden space of the future" and to peoples deemed to have been left out of its progressive project. Nascent within the American Revolution, so the thinking went, lay the culmination of humanity's evolution.

The legitimating function of exceptionalist appeals, of course, has not been limited to actions taken in the early years of the republic; rather, it "runs from seventeenth-century Puritan thought, to the Revolution, to the mid-century doctrine of Manifest Destiny, to late nineteenth-century American imperialism, to Wilsonian idealism, to cold war anti-communism, and George W. Bush's unilateralism" (Ceasar 2012: 10). In concert with Manifest Destiny, American exceptionalism has proven to be an enduring and infectious ideology that has resounded across the globe through a host of foreign policy decisions motivated by the nation's commitment to carrying out its self-proclaimed divinely sanctioned mission to "remake the world" in the American image (Herring 2008b: 180).

McCrisken (2003) argues that within foreign policy discourse American exceptionalism has taken shape as "exemplary exceptionalism" and "missionary exceptionalism" (11). In the exemplary approach, the United States assumes a relatively passive posture toward other nations by presenting itself as a "model" for others to emulate and a "beacon" for the improvement of humankind (McCrisken 2003: 11; also see Brands 1998). The missionary approach, in contrast, advocates for interventionist and expansionist policies aimed at proactively shaping other societies in ways that serve the interests of the United States (McCrisken 2003: 11; also see Bacevich 2021). An important assumption embedded in both forms of exceptionalism is that "inside every foreigner there is the potential, even desire, to be an American" (McCrisken 2003: 11). Restad (2012) argues that its claim of exceptionalism has compelled the nation to "expand, model, lead the way, and meddle," a foreign policy approach based on the fact that America historically has been claimed to be God's choice for leading the world's people to "the end of history" (71).

Within foreign policy discourse, the legitimating function of exceptionalist appeals evinces an important and consequential temporal dimension. As McKeever (1989) explains, the unifying function of national myths does not reside solely in an account of the past; it also resides in "a utopian vision of the future" (44). The American utopia, however, isn't reserved just for the United States; it is held out as a vision of the world's future. That is, embedded within the exceptionalist claim is a temporal scheme that situates America as further along a trajectory of past–present–future than the rest of the world and, thus, as representing "the wave of the future" (Commager 1974: 45). America's claimed insight into the future, Bacevich (2021) insists, is the "lingua franca of American statecraft" (6). It undergirds the enduring belief that the American experience represents "a template for the future of less fortunate peoples and less developed cultures" and, thus, as embodying the aspirations of all the world's people (Adas 2001: 1696). As Secretary of State Madeline Albright (1998) put it, "we are the indispensable nation . . . we see further than other countries into the future." America's mission, accordingly, is to ensure a safe and prosperous future for all the world's people and, thereby, lead them "toward a new and better age" (McCrisken 2003: 24; McCartney 2006: 12).

Burrow (2009) similarly points out that the history of the nation's foreign policy has been grounded in the idea that America embodies the future (439–440). McCartney (2006) identifies as a "staple" of the nation's identity the belief that America is more advanced than other nations and has a unique understanding of how societies ought to be developed and organized (24). It is these attributes that ostensibly qualify the United States to change the world accordingly (McCartney 2006: 24). At significant moments in America's geopolitical history, the nation's leaders have insisted that foreign policy serve to "illuminate a boundless future" in order to promote American interests and, thereby, the interests of humankind (McCrisken 2003: 14).

The discourse and ideology of American exceptionalism, in sum, embeds a teleology of progress that identifies America as the nation of the future, an identity that, throughout its history, has been used consistently to guide and legitimate its foreign policy. The conviction that America, as both an idea and a geographical place, manifests not only what civilization *could* be but also what it *ought* to be has been key to the nation's identity and geopolitical purpose. In the words of Hannah Arendt, the nation's leaders have designated America as the nation that has deciphered "the mysteries of the whole historical process—the secrets of the past, the intricacies of the present, the uncertainties of the future" (as quoted in Smith 2012: 206–207).

CONCLUSION

The characterization of America as an exceptional nation not just different from but superior to other nations is grounded in efforts in the early years of the republic to answer the question "What was the nation to become, and how was this identity to be reflected in its international behavior?" (Hunt 1987: 17). The result was a conception of the nation's place and purpose imbued with "prescriptive force," which oriented the nation's leaders to an expansionist, missionary agenda focused on securing the nation's institutions and values and extending its conception of governance throughout the world. As I aimed to show in the preceding discussion, this global errand was sanctioned by a temporal logic that situates America in a temporally privileged position. That is, at its founding, the rhetoric of exceptionalism rendered America as an unprecedented experiment in republicanism unburdened by the history and corruption of "Old Europe." It was the nation that would focus its attention and energy on the future, serving as the vanguard of republican ideals and practices and, thereby, as "history's vanguard" (Bacevich 2021: 6). Furthermore, this rhetoric placed the nation outside the ordinary laws of history and, thus, as able to realize its inherently progressive destiny of ensuring the betterment of all the world's people.

These early conceptions of American exceptionalism have survived to the present day as the ideology Americans have repeatedly returned to in order to understand what the nation and its people represent and where they are headed; it is the aspect of national identity that "permeates" the nation's history (Madsen 1998: 14, 1). Although a malleable idea open to interpretation, American exceptionalism has been "the single most powerful agent" in conceptions of and arguments about the nation's identity (McCrisken 2003: 8; Madsen 1998: 1). Moreover, the nation's claim of exceptionalism was "nourished" by the nation's 20th-century triumphs in World War II and the postwar era, animated by the Cold War struggle with the Soviet Union, and used to explain the subsequent collapse of the Soviet Union (Hodgson 2009: 10). In the chapters that follow, I examine how the temporal dimension of the nation's exceptionalist identity, its claim of being the "great nation of futurity," manifested and functioned within texts and genres from consequential moments in the America's Cold War conflict with the Soviet Union.

CHAPTER 3

"Vistas to the Future"

Shaping the Postwar Future

INTRODUCTION

In this chapter, I analyze the different space-times embedded in foreign policy statements made in the early years of the post–World War II era and examine how they positioned different global actors and constituencies vis-à-vis the future. Following Wæver (1996) and Hansen (2006), my analysis of the Self/Other trope considers both the radical and "less-than-radical" Others through which American national identity and geopolitical purpose are construed and legitimated. Specifically, I identify and examine four Self/Other pairings: the United States/Britain (European) dyad, the United States/Soviet Union dyad, the United States/periphery dyad, and the active/passive American Self dyad.

Regarding the United States/Britain (European) dyad, I identify the different space-times assigned to each global actor and analyze the implications these assignments have for their respective agentive capacity. In terms of the United States/Soviet Union dyad, I demonstrate how the temporal domain of the future was invoked to create an antagonistic relationship between the two nations at the center of the postwar global system. My analysis of the United States/periphery dyad considers how construals of space-time positioned each along the temporal trajectory of past–present–future and how that positioning legitimated American intervention in the periphery. Finally, my analysis of the active/passive American Self dyad considers how the nation's geopolitical role and purpose were construed and legitimated through contrasts between two American Selves, each of which is identified in terms of its

---

The Great Nation of Futurity. Patricia L. Dunmire, Oxford University Press. © Oxford University Press 2023.
DOI: 10.1093/oso/9780197658222.003.0003

posture with respect to the global future and projections of the future ostensibly entailed in those postures.

My data set centers on three documents key to the working out of United States national security policy in the postwar era: Henry Luce's 1941 essay "The American Century"; President Truman's 1947 speech "A Special Message to Congress on Greece and Turkey" (Truman 1947, March 12); and the 1950 policy document for National Security Council Resolution 68, "United States Objectives and Programs for National Security" ("NSC 68"; May 1993).[1] Each played a significant role in the development and evolution of postwar national security discourse. In brief, Luce's essay introduced a temporal conception of national security by arguing that the nation must reorient its security policy away from defense of territory to creation of the global future. Luce's concepts were operationalized through President Truman's speech to Congress that called for aid to Greece and Turkey. This speech outlined the "Truman Doctrine," which advocated a globalized conception of national security that situated the superpower conflict in the periphery and, thereby, designated geographically distant spaces as within the purview of the U.S. security policy. Finally, NSC 68 formalized the core ideas from Luce and the Truman Doctrine into a security policy whereby the United States would work actively to shape the global environment in its own image as a means of countering the supposed Soviet threat.

The Cold War conflict between the United States and the Soviet Union can be understood, I contend, in temporal terms as a battle over the postwar future. Through the policy of containment, the United States sought to prevent the Soviet Union from expanding its political-economic system into spaces beyond its immediate security perimeter. However, given that movement through space also involves movement through time (Charteris-Black 2011: 211), the containment policy can also be understood as focused on preventing Soviet communism from expanding temporally into the future as the ideological system that would define postwar geopolitics. As Buzan (1997) puts it, the Cold War conflict bore the mark of temporality as it was a conflict over which of "two mutually exclusive systems" would shape "the future of industrial society" (6).

In the following analysis, I demonstrate how this temporal interpretation manifests in foreign policy discourse generated at the inception of the Cold War and, moreover, how this discourse granted the United States a privileged role in shaping the postwar geopolitical future. My aim is to explore how the United States was discursively positioned vis-à-vis the postwar future and how the nation's claim of exceptionalism figured in that positioning. I argue that through various space-time and Self/Other contrasts, the foreign policy documents examined herein aligned different geopolitical actors with different space-times in such a way as to render the postwar global future the special province of the United States.

[52]   *The Great Nation of Futurity*

SHAPING THE POSTWAR FUTURE

Henry Luce and "The American Century": Staking a Claim on the Future

In his highly influential 1941 editorial in *Life* magazine Henry Luce (1999 [1941]) claimed the twentieth century as "The American Century" and, in so doing, articulated the nation's geopolitical purpose primarily in temporal terms. That is, he advocated for a foreign policy conceived not in terms of defending particular geographical spaces but in terms of creating "the world of the 20th Century" (170). He insisted that if "the world of the 20th century . . . is to come to life in any nobility of health and vigor," it "must be to a significant degree an American century" (168). Such a future would be one in which "a system of free economic enterprise—an economic model compatible with freedom and progress" would occupy the center of the international system (169). As the world's "most powerful and vital nation," it would be up to America, the 20th century's exceptional nation, to determine whether this future "shall prevail or not" (170, 169).

By conceiving of the nation's purpose in this way, Luce staked a claim on the future of the post–World War II era. The nation's right to this future derived from its status as a dominant global power, as Luce explained that the 20th century is "ours not only in the sense that we happen to live in it but it is ours also because it is America's first century as a dominant world power" (167). For Luce, this power meant power over time, the power of the United States to influence, if not control, the way the present moment would evolve into the future. In what follows, I argue that Luce staked this claim by advocating for a particular conception of space-time for the postwar era: a reorientation of the nation's security policy away from a space-time grounded in local geographical spaces toward a space-time grounded in an American conception of the global future.

Luce's essay inaugurates a relationship between different space-times that would come to characterize subsequent articulations of the postwar geopolitical context. Although writing as war raged in Europe, he focused his essay not on the co-present events in Europe but on the meaning those events hold for the future, or, more specifically, for America's vision of the future. In so doing, Luce reorients the temporal context of the war away from the present fighting in Europe to the future of the American Century. He initiates this transformation by beginning his essay with a lament about the future that, at present, seems to be defined by events in Europe:

1. As we look toward the future—our own future and the future of other nations—we are filled with foreboding. The future doesn't seem to hold anything for us except conflict, disruption, and war. (159)

Luce's lament is echoed in a subsequent articulation of the problem the war in Europe poses to the United States, a problem involving a temporal shift from the known present to an unknown future:

2. The trouble is not with the facts. The trouble is that clear and honest inferences have not been drawn from the facts. The *day-to-day present* is clear. The issues of *tomorrow* are befogged. (160)

In this excerpt Luce divides geopolitical space-time between the "day-to-day present" and "tomorrow." The former signifies the present and near-term future and is the domain of facts and certainty; the latter signifies the more distant future and is the domain of obscurity and inference. As will be seen below, this temporal demarcation aligns with geographical distinctions and, ultimately, with differentiations in the agentive capacity of particular global actors.

As excerpt 2 suggests, Luce characterizes the problem currently facing the United States not as a material one of co-present threats and dangers but as a futurological one of discerning the meaning of the present moment for the global future and, relatedly, of bringing clarity and purpose to that future. Importantly, it is a problem that only Americans, as the "inheritors of all the great principles of Western civilization," can address (170). As can be seen in the following excerpts, Luce draws on temporal distinctions between an American Self and a British Other to position the United States as uniquely suited to shape the postwar future. That is, he grounds America's special capacity in the "striking contrast between our state of mind and that of the British people," a contrast owing to the temporal orientation of each nation's physical and mental energies:

3. [T]hey are fighting for their lives . . . they have no further choice . . . they are faced with a supreme task . . . defending, yard by yard . . . their island home. (159)
4. With us it is different. We do not have to face any attack tomorrow or the next day. Yet we are faced with something almost as difficult. We are faced with great decisions. (160)

As can be seen in excerpt 3, the British present is rendered as a dynamic situation in which its citizens are engaged with co-present material events unfolding around them. Theirs is a local space-time coded within an imperative deontic modality of *must*, a modality of "necessity and survival" (162, 159). Indeed, They have "no further choice" but to focus on physical survival (159). As can be seen in excerpt 4, Our present isn't defined by such physical threats, as Luce assures the nation that "We do not have to face any attack tomorrow or

[54]   *The Great Nation of Futurity*

the next day" (160).[2] Rather, American space-time is coded within a modality of *ought* and is oriented toward "great decisions" concerning the postwar future. This deontic coding of American and British space-times orients both to the future (Palmer 2001: 97). The space-times are distinguished, however, by the nature of those futures and the actions each entails. While the British future is a proximal one of fighting for survival, the American future is a distal one of "choice and calculation," of determining what the postwar global future should be (167, 162). America's unique geography and location separates it from the troubles roiling Europe, thereby enabling it to focus on the future and "the future only" (O'Sullivan 1839).

Luce imbues the choices and calculations facing the nation with significance by invoking what I term the *alternative-futures trope*, which projects alternative future scenarios and aligns them with different geopolitical actors. In so doing, he draws on the legitimation strategy of future projection authorization through which, as explained in Chapter 1, an actor claims the authority to project future reality in order to sanction an action or proposal. The trope is typically realized through conditional statements along the lines of "If the future develops in a direction determined by Us, good things will accrue to global society; if the future develops in a direction determined by Them, bad things will accrue to global society." The alternative futures projected through such statements contrast "good futures" with futures that are deemed "profoundly undesirable" (Andersson 2019: 2). Although conditional, such statements, nevertheless, embed authoritative projections of the future. Such projections mediate relations between Self and Other and serve to legitimate policies and actions pursued by Us and de-legitimate policies and actions pursued by Them. The alternative-futures trope can be seen in the following excerpt:

5. There is one fundamental issue which faces America as it faces no other nation. . . . *If* America meets it correctly, *then*, despite a host of dangers and difficulties, we can look forward and move forward to a future worthy of men. . . . *If* we dodge the issue, we *shall* flounder for ten or 20 or 30 bitter years in a chartless and meaningless series of disasters. (160)

Through this conditional statement Luce projects two alternative futures: a "future worthy of men" versus a future of "a chartless and meaningless series of disasters." If the nation makes the correct choices and calculations, the former will come to fruition; if not, the world will suffer the latter.

In addition to these alternative futures, this statement juxtaposes alternative identities and geopolitical roles for the United States. That is, the Self/Other dyad in play here is two versions of the American Self: an active American Self versus a passive American Self. "If" America embraces an active role regarding the global future, "then . . . we can look forward and move forward to a future worthy of men"; "If we" assume a passive posture and "dodge the issue" then the world "shall flounder . . . in a chartless and meaningless series of disasters" for several "bitter years" to come. As such, along with the alternative-futures trope, Luce draws on what I term the *shape-the-future trope*, which juxtaposes two American Selves in terms of the posture the nation assumes with respect to the future: an active American Self takes a "purposeful stance oriented toward" the future while a passive Self does not (Mische 2009: 701). The shape-the-future trope engages the issue of whether the nation will, in the words of H. G. Wells (1987), "let . . . [the future] happen to us" or whether it will work to shape the future in ways that accord with the nation's interests. Luce, not surprisingly, urges the nation to take charge of the future by working to shape the trajectory of 20th-century geopolitics. In so doing, he invokes and perpetuates America's exceptionalist identity and its capacity for the future, a responsibility that "faces no other nation" (160).

The nation's unique responsibility and capacity vis-à-vis the future is reinforced through Luce's use of a spatiotemporal lexis to contrast America to "other nations":

6. Other nations can *survive* simply because they have *endured for so long*. But this nation, conceived in adventure and dedicated to the *progress* of man—this nation cannot truly *endure* unless there courses through its veins . . . the blood of *purpose* and enterprise and high resolve. (171)

While They are identified with the concepts "survive" and "endure," We are identified with "progress" and "purpose." In Luce's words we hear echoes of colonial rhetoric in the characterization of Europeans as a static people who survive by enduring, by merely continuing to exist and sustain the status quo. Americans, however, are perpetually on the move, advancing through time and space toward continual improvement. What's important to other nations is their past, their capacity to have existed in a particular state across time; what distinguishes the United States is its need to move purposefully through time in pursuit of "manifold projects and magnificent purposes" (171). The United States, in short, must embrace its role as the agent of the future.

With Luce's temporal reorientation from present to future comes a spatial reorientation away from a territorially bound understanding of defense to an extraterritorial conception of creating a "world environment." Noting that "the plain meaning of the word defense is defense of American territory," Luce asks whether "our national policy today is limited to defense of American territory?" (161). "It is not," he responds, insisting that "no man can honestly say that as a pure matter of defense . . . of our homeland . . . it is necessary to get into this war" (162). Moreover, he contends that the aims of the war,

[56]   *The Great Nation of Futurity*

which "America and America alone" can determine, cannot be stated in terms of "vastly distant geography," such as deciding the "boundaries of Uritania" (164–165).

Rather, "some big words like Democracy and Freedom and Justice," words that capture ideals that are "especially American" and "do mean something about the future as well as the past," best articulate the aims of America's geopolitical mission (165). According to Luce, however, America has failed in this mission and, thus, must reclaim and commit to its global purpose:

7. [Americans] have failed in their part as a world power—a failure which has had disastrous consequences for themselves and all of mankind . . . the cure is this: to accept wholeheartedly our duty and opportunity as the most powerful and vital nation in the world . . . to exert upon the world the full impact of our influence, for such purposes as we see fit and by such means as we see fit. (165)

America must embrace its geopolitical mission because it is "responsible, to herself as well as to history, for the world-environment in which she lives" (166). In sum, Luce configures postwar space-time as follows:

"America's vision of our world," Luce explains, "has within it the possibilities of such enormous progress as to stagger the imagination" (170). Transforming this vision into reality, however, will require a change in the metaphorical conception of the nation's global purpose. Luce argues that Herbert Hoover's earlier characterization of America as "the sanctuary of the ideals of civilization" does not befit the actual and potential role the United States does and should occupy within global society (171). As such, he urges politicians and citizens to see the nation as "the powerhouse from which the ideals" of Western civilization, namely, "Freedom and Justice," would "spread throughout the world" (171).

Table 3.1. CONFIGURATION OF POSTWAR SPACE-TIME

Actor	Spatiotemporal orientation	Behavior	Objective
Britain; other modern nations	Local, present	Physical action (defend, fight)	Defend territory, endure
America	Global, future	Mental, persuasive action (decide, exert influence, promote, incite)	Create world environment

"VISTAS TO THE FUTURE" [57]

This transition from "sanctuary" to "powerhouse" reconfigures the space-time of the nation's geopolitical purpose and, therein, its relationship to the global community: whereas sanctuary is oriented to the "is" of America as a place and way of life, powerhouse is oriented to the "could be" of global society. That is, as sanctuary, America is construed as a rarefied, even sacred place set apart from the rest of the world that serves as a preserve for civilization's ideals and principles and offers a refuge for people desiring to live by those ideals. America represents a place to which people come when, in the words of Thomas Paine, "home should afford neither friendship nor safety" (Paine 1997 [1776]: 22). As powerhouse, however, America is conceived of as the source of that life, rather than its mere location. Consequently, the powerhouse metaphor transforms America from being a place *to which* people retreat to being the site *from which* something is generated and disseminated to places beyond itself. The civilized life, in turn, is not a state of being that resides in and characterizes a particular place; it is a potential—a future—that awaits all of global society and will be provided by the United States.

By construing and juxtaposing alternative space-times, Luce rendered America as uniquely capable of shaping the postwar geopolitical future and, thereby, claimed the 20th century as "The American Century." Indeed, he invoked the shape-the-future trope by declaring that the key reason for the United States to enter the war was its responsibility for "shaping the future of America and the world" (166). Luce insisted, however, that realizing the nation's destiny to "reorder a world destroyed" (Herring 2008b: 594) would require a different spatiotemporal conception of its security and geopolitical purpose. American security and prosperity should be understood in temporally and geographically expansive terms, as requiring the creation of a world environment hospitable to its values and interests. As such, America's contemporary Manifest Destiny was to be the "powerhouse" of a global future in which an economic system of free enterprise and a sociopolitical system of freedom and progress could survive and flourish. In what follows, I examine how politicians and policymakers subsequently elaborated and operationalized Luce's vision by translating it into calls for action and policy prescriptions.

The Truman Doctrine: Transforming Postwar Space-Time

On March 6, 1947, six days before delivering the speech that outlined what became known as the Truman Doctrine, President Truman gave an address at Baylor University on foreign economic policy (Truman 1947, March 6). In it he situates the global community at a pivotal moment, as occupying a temporal space in which the future, in Luce's terms, is "befogged":

[58] *The Great Nation of Futurity*

8. The global community has reached *a turning point in history*. National economies have been disrupted by war. *The future is uncertain everywhere.* Economic policies are in *a state of flux*. (Truman 1947, March 6)

President Truman draws on the metaphor of a turning point to construe the present moment as one of decisive change for the global community: the world has reached a point when the geopolitical future will be markedly different from the past. However, he deems the specific direction of this change, that is, the future to which this change will lead, to be "uncertain everywhere." As such, the President insists on the certainty of geopolitical change yet hedges on the character of the future resulting from that change. In so doing, he creates a temporal space for the United States to assume the role as agent of the postwar future, as uniquely capable of providing clarity and resolve in an "atmosphere of doubt and hesitation":

9. [T]he *future* pattern of economic relations *depends upon us*. The world is waiting and watching to see *what we will do*. The choice is ours. *We can lead* the nations to *economic peace* or we *can plunge* them into *economic war*. (Truman 1947, March 6)

In excerpts 8 and 9 we see Truman drawing on both the alternative-futures and shape-the-future tropes to underscore and legitimate his call for American global leadership. That is, he authorizes his call to action by projecting two alternative futures—a future of "economic peace" and a future of "economic war"—that he insists could define the global future. Through the deontic modal "can" President Truman renders the United States as the nation capable of determining which future will come to fruition. Whether the geopolitical future is one of peace or one of war depends on which American Self takes hold in the postwar era. That is, to bolster his case for American global leadership, the president creates a moral contrast between an active American Self and a passive American Other. While the former "can lead the nations to economic peace," the latter "can plunge them into economic war." He further insists that "unless we act, and act decisively," global trade will revert to the past, to the "pattern" that held sway in the "seventeenth and eighteenth centuries." As was the case in Luce's argument for the American Century, the nature of the global future depends on which temporal American Self emerges.

President Truman's call for the nation to assume a leadership role in shaping the global future was given added urgency in his address to Congress requesting economic aid for Greece and Turkey. Decisive action is imperative, he insists, to counter the claim being made on the global future by a "militant minority . . . led by Communists." In making this request for aid he renders Greece and Turkey as sites of a struggle between two competing conceptions of political-economic organization. Not surprisingly, the American conception was legitimated by a moral lexis that contrasts Our positive actions, behaviors, and values, with Their negative actions, behaviors, and values. While We help other free nations "survive," "restore internal order" and "stability," and enable others to become "self-supporting," They "exploit human want and misery," "create political chaos," and "impose their will, their way of life" on others.

My focus here, however, is the spatiotemporal dimensions of President Truman's security discourse. In this section I examine how he construed the postwar environment in spatiotemporal terms and how that construal both reinforced America's identity as the nation of the future and authorized calls for the United States to assume a leadership role in shaping the postwar global future. As we'll see, these construals involved transforming local space-times into global space-times and juxtaposing and evaluating alternative projections of the global future. I begin with the Truman Doctrine speech delivered on March 12, 1947, and then consider how the linguistic and rhetorical features comprising it redounded in subsequent speeches and statements on foreign and national security policy.

As explained in Chapter 1, the president's address to Congress on March 12, 1947, marked "America's 'declaration of Cold War'" and outlined the Truman Doctrine (Judge and Langdon 1999: 24). The speech declared communism to be a geopolitical threat and outlined a policy response according to which the United States would provide economic and military aid to any nation deemed vulnerable to a communist insurgency (Judge and Langdon 1999: 24). In his address to Congress, the president identified Greece and Turkey as two nations in urgent need of such aid. This urgency, the president insisted, derived from the fact that two alternative futures were currently in play in the Mediterranean region: a future of freedom, stability, and independence, and a future of chaos, extremism, and oppression.

To convince the nation's citizens and legislators that the situation in Greece was one that could "endanger the welfare of this nation," the president had to resolve a spatiotemporal problem, namely, that of rendering a geographically distant situation in the periphery as a "crisis" that demands "immediate and resolute action" by the United States. In other words, he sought to render the postwar era as an era in which local space-times are directly connected to the global space-time of the nation's struggle against international communism. President Truman, in short, sought to transform "vacant or anonymous reaches of distance . . . into meanings for us here" (Said 1978: 55). As I will demonstrate, the president connects these space-times by chaining together local events in Greece and Turkey and the global consequences those events entail, thereby linking "different scales of social life, the local, national, regional, and global" (Fairclough 2003: 151).

[60]   *The Great Nation of Futurity*

As can be seen in the following excerpts, the president deploys a lexis of survival and a modality of necessity and urgency to define the present situation in Greece as a crisis over its future:

10. Assistance is *imperative* if Greece is *to survive* as a free nation.
11. Greece *must* have help to import the goods *necessary* to restore internal order and security *so essential* for economic and political recovery.
12. The *very existence* of the Greek state *is today threatened*.
13. Greece *must* have assistance *if it is to become* a self-supporting and self-respecting democracy.

In these statements President Truman construes the Greek crisis in terms of its future, not only its ability to survive as a free nation and to become an independent, orderly democracy, but also its capacity to continue to exist. He offers a similar assessment of Turkey:

14. The *future of Turkey* as an independent and economically sound state *is clearly no less important* to the freedom-loving peoples of the world than the future of Greece.
15. Turkey has sought assistance from . . . the United States for *the purpose of effecting that modernization necessary* for the maintenance of national integrity.

According to the president, the United States is the sole agent able to ensure a future of peace, prosperity, and independence for Greece and Turkey as he declares that: "The United States must supply this assistance. . . . There is no other country to which democratic Greece can turn. No other nation is willing and able to provide the necessary support for a democratic Greek government."

President Truman subsequently transforms the space-time of the crises in Greece and Turkey by construing local events affecting the Greek and Turkish people as portents of a broader crisis that would have a global impact, warning that "If we falter in our leadership, we may endanger the peace of the world." That is, President Truman legitimizes his call for economic assistance by projecting the catastrophic future that awaits the global community should the United States not assume its leadership position. The President foreshadows this legitimation strategy by connecting local space-time to global space-time in the opening sentences of his speech:

16. The gravity of the situation which *confronts the world today necessitates* my appearance before a joint session of the Congress. The *foreign policy and the national security of this country are involved*. One aspect of the present situation . . . concerns Greece and Turkey.

"VISTAS TO THE FUTURE" [61]

In the span of three sentences, the president resituates the present economic situation in Greece and Turkey within a global context as a situation that "confronts the world today" and frames it within an obligational modality as a problem that "necessitates" the nation's attention and implicates its national security policy. This rhetorical move effaces the spatiotemporal divide that confines the present crisis to the periphery and, as such, as ostensibly outside the purview of *national* security policy. Consequently, the president situates the periphery within the jurisdiction of American national security policy.

President Truman elaborates his opening claim by detailing the spatiotemporal trajectory by which the crisis in Greece would become a global crisis, thereby further blurring the temporal boundary between now and future and the spatial boundary between here and there. While referencing a map, the president presents an early articulation of the domino theory[3] by mapping out a hypothetical future that projects the consequences of a failed Greek state onto the space-time of the global community:

17. *It is necessary only to glance at a map* to realize that *the survival and integrity of the Greek nation are of grave importance in a much wider situation.*
18. *If Greece should fall* under the control of an armed minority, *the effect* upon its neighbor, Turkey, *would be* immediate and serious.
19. Confusion and disorder *might well spread* throughout the entire Middle East.
20. Moreover, the disappearance of Greece as an independent state *would have a profound effect* upon those countries in Europe . . .
21. Collapse of free institutions and loss of independence *would be disastrous* not only for [European countries] but for the world.
22. Discouragement and possibly failure *would quickly be* the lot of neighboring people striving to maintain their freedom and independence.
23. *Should we fail* to aid Greece and Turkey in this fateful hour, the effect *will be far reaching* to the West as well as to the East.

These statements extend a geographically specific situation temporally and spatially to its final culmination as a future "effect" that "will be far reaching to the West as well as the East." The president projects this future through material (e.g., "might well spread," "would have a profound effect") and relational ("would be disastrous," "would be immediate and dangerous," "are of grave importance") process clauses. These clauses, in turn, set up relations of probability and identity between the hypothetical failure of Greece and the future regional and global consequences entailed in that failure. And despite the irrealis nature of these statements—their epistemic status as projections of consequences stemming from a hypothetical situation (i.e., the failure of Greece, failure to aid Greece)—the president's construal is rendered as an objective assessment that is apparent from a mere "glance at a map." Moreover, the prevalence of the modal auxiliary "would" (as opposed to "could") for coding the likelihood of these future consequences further bolsters the certitude of the president's account. In sum, the president presents a spatiotemporal trajectory whereby the present crises of Greece and Turkey are extrapolated to the global future:

| present/local | $\rightarrow\rightarrow\rightarrow$ | future/global |
| economic crisis in Greece, Turkey | | collapse of free institutions, loss of independence |

In Truman's proposal concerning Greece and Turkey, we see the alternative-future and shape-the-future tropes working in concert to project the alternative futures that lie ahead for the global community and to declare the urgency of America assuming a leadership role in shaping the global future. That is, in mapping out the consequences of a failed Greek state, President Truman projects an alternative future that would come to be if the United States assumes a passive posture and evaluates that future through a negative moral lexis: a future "controlled by an armed minority" that would spread "confusion and disorder." By implication, the preferred future created by the United States taking an active role will be a positive future of independence and freedom, order and stability (see Table 3.2).

The alternative-futures trope is deployed again through two metaphors—investing and gardening—used to characterize the implications of the United States providing, or refusing to provide, aid:

24. The United States contributed $341,000,000,000 toward winning World War II. This is *an investment in world peace and freedom*. The assistance that I'm recommending for Greece and Turkey amounts to $\frac{1}{10}$ of 1% of this investment. . . . *The seeds of totalitarian regimes are nurtured by misery and want. They spread and grow in the evil soil of poverty and strife.*

Table 3.2. CONTRASTING FUTURES OF U.S. ACTION, INACTION

U.S. inaction → negative future	U.S. action → positive future
• Controlled by armed militants	• Rule by a peaceful majority
• Confusion and disorder	• Stability and order
• Disappearance of independent states; collapse of free institutions	• Survival and integrity of independent nations and free institutions
• Discouragement, failure, disaster	• Encouragement, achievement, success

Both metaphors embed a temporal scheme that projects the future outcome of present action: investing yields future financial benefits; gardening yields future horticultural benefits. Moreover, each entails the concept of growth: growing one's wealth and growing one's garden. As Chilton (1996) explains, the concept of growth typically bears a positive connotation (184). Accordingly, the investment metaphor characterizes American aid to Greece and Turkey as positive, as enabling the growth and accumulation of something of value, in this case, "world peace and freedom." Chilton (1996) further argues, however, that growth takes on a wholly negative connotation when used to characterize Soviet actions because it signifies "germination and proliferation," "spread and infiltration," concepts that cohere with the portrayal of the Soviet Union as expansionist (184). Comparatively, then, the two metaphors positively evaluate U.S. action and, thereby, render it as legitimate while implicitly rendering Soviet action as illegitimate.

The president's construal of the Greece/Turkey situation as a portent of two possible global futures is rearticulated in his argument that the issue of financial assistance entails a broader decision concerning how members of the global community ought to live. Specifically, he invokes the alternative-future trope by reframing the crises in Greece and Turkey as a contest over which of two "alternative ways of life" should characterize the global future, insisting that "At the present moment in world history nearly every nation must choose between two mutually exclusive ways of life." "Our way of life" is characterized through a moral lexis of freedom, liberty, and democracy:

25. *Our way of life* is based upon the will of the majority and is distinguished by free institutions, representative government, free elections, guarantees of individual liberty, freedom of speech and religion, and freedom from political oppression.

"The second way of life" is characterized through a moral lexis of force, terror, and oppression:

26. *The second way of life* is based upon the will of a minority forcibly imposed upon the majority. It relies on terror and oppression, a controlled press and radio, fixed elections, and the suppression of personal freedom. . . . The seeds of totalitarian regimes are nurtured by misery and want. They spread and grow in the evil soil of poverty and strife. They reach their full growth when the hope for a better life has died.

Further contrasts are created through a future-oriented lexis of hope and destiny. Invoking the gardening metaphor (excerpt 26), the president construes Their way of life as grounded in and nurtured by "misery and want"; it is a way

[64] *The Great Nation of Futurity*

of life based in a system that reaches its full potential only after "the hope for a better life has died." Our way of life, however, "keep[s] that hope alive" and enables "free peoples to work out their destinies in their own way." In short, an authentic future for Greece and Turkey resides in "The American way."

This juxtaposing of alternative ways of life gets us to the heart of the Truman Doctrine, an approach to national security intended to ensure that Our way of life prevails over Theirs. The president explains that a "primary objective" of the nation's security policy is "the *creation of conditions* in which we and other free nations will be able to *work out a way of life free from coercion.*" This objective requires that the United States be "willing to help free peoples to maintain their free institutions and their national integrity *against aggressive movements that seek to impose* upon them totalitarian regimes." U.S. foreign policy "must . . . support free people who are resisting attempted *subjugation by armed minorities or outside pressures.*" Taking on this global responsibility is incumbent on the United States, then, because of its unique status as the agent of the global future: "The peoples of the world look to us for support in maintaining their freedom. If we falter in our leadership, we may endanger the peace of the world—and we shall surely endanger the welfare of this Nation."

The conceptions and arguments comprising the Truman Doctrine were repeated and elaborated in subsequent speeches by the Truman administration. Before considering how the Doctrine was formalized as Cold War policy in NSC 68, I will briefly review how its construal of the global security environment and the U.S. role vis-à-vis that environment was presented in subsequent policy statements.

As explained earlier, a central concern at the beginning of the postwar era was the future political and economic development of newly decolonized nations in the periphery. For the Truman administration this concern was essentially a concern about the future prospects of global society:

27. The people of the earth *face the future with grave uncertainty*, composed almost equally of *great hope and great fear*. (Truman 1949, January 20)
28. we can see that . . . this *new day* . . . which *is dawning*, may go on to a *glorious noon* or it may *darken and drizzle out*. (Acheson 1950, January 12)[4]

Taken together, these statements project two diametrically opposed futures that could define the postwar world: a future of great hope and glorious noon or a future of great fear and darkness. Through policy statements about the nation's plans and goals for the periphery, the administration aligns these alternative futures with the ideological systems jockeying for position at the center of the geopolitical stage. It does so, as can be seen in Table 3.3, through a future-oriented lexis of hope, desire, and determination to connect the future of the periphery with the United States and distance it from the Soviet Union.

The American future is rendered as an authentic future rooted in mankind's genuine wishes, desires, wants, and longings, a future that will be created by Americans "determined to work" on behalf of "all nations and all peoples." The Truman administration stakes a claim on the Asian future by invoking its unique ability to "know" the type of future the people of Asia "desire," "want," and "hope" for, knowledge stemming from the temporal location of America relative to that of Asia. That is, American knowledge of the Asian future is rooted in a configuration of postwar space-time that situates Asia on a social, political, and economic developmental path forged by the West and, concomitantly, endows America with special insight into the future that lies ahead for the peoples of Asia. This space-time is distilled in the president's temporal juxtaposing of Asia as "old" and America as "new":

29. We believe that we have much in common with the peoples of the Far East. Their *older* civilization has much to teach us. We hope our *new developments* may be of help to them. (Truman 1950, October 17)

As excerpts 30–33 show, Truman draws on the legitimation strategy of temporal location authorization, which, as explained in Chapter 1, anchors a claim of legitimacy in the relative temporal positioning of different actors, societies, etc. Here we see that America's legitimacy as the agent of the global future derives from its temporal location as future relative to Asia, a position from which it claims the authority to know what the Asian people want: a future rooted in American principles and historical experience. In a nationwide radio address on October 17, 1950, President Truman employs a rhetorical strategy through which he proclaims a particular want the Asian people have and then immediately identifies the American principles, historical experiences, and actions that will ostensibly fulfill that want:

30. *We know* that the peoples of Asia *cherish* their freedom and independence. We *sympathize with this desire* and we *will help to attain and defend* their independence. *Our entire history* proclaims our policy on this point. Our men *are fighting now* in Asia to help secure . . . freedom and independence. (Truman, October 17, 1950)
31. *We know* that the peoples of Asia . . . *want* their farmers to own their land and to enjoy the fruits of their toil. That *is* one of our great national *principles*. That *is* the basis of our agriculture and *has strongly influenced* our form of government. (Truman 1950, October 17)
32. *We know* that they *want* their industrial workers to have their full measure of freedom and rising standards of living. That *is* the basis of our industrial society in this country. (Truman 1950, October 17)

Table 3.3. AGENTS OF THE FUTURE

United States	Soviet Union
• "The American people *desire, and are determined to work for,* a world in which all nations and all peoples are free to govern themselves as they see fit, and to achieve a decent and satisfying life." (Truman 1949) • "[O]ur people *desire, and are determined to work for,* peace on earth—a just and lasting peace—based upon genuine agreement freely arrived at by equals." (Truman 1949) • "aided by all who *wish* to live in freedom from fear . . . *want* relief from lies and propaganda . . . *desire* truth and sincerity . . . *desire* self-government and a voice . . . long for economic security . . . *desire* freedom of speech, freedom of religion, and freedom to live their own lives" (Truman 1949) • "Our allies are the millions who *hunger and thirst* for righteousness." (Truman 1949) • "Our real interest is . . . to do just exactly what *the peoples of Asia want.*" (Acheson 1950, January 12) • "in a manner consistent with *mankind's deep longing* for a respite from fear and uncertainty" (Acheson 1950, March 16) • "*the real promise of freedom*" (Acheson 1950, November 30) • "[T]he affirmative values of our society have been *deeply inspiring.*" (Acheson 1950, November 30) • "striving to make our society worthy of the *hopes* that free men everywhere have placed in it" (Acheson 1950, November 30) • "will give many people *a real stake in the future.*" (Truman 1951, January 8) • "*hopes for the future*" (Truman 1951, January 8)	• "A conception of life based in a *false philosophy* which *purports* to offer freedom, security, and greater opportunity to mankind." (Truman 1949) • "*Misled* by that philosophy, many peoples have sacrificed their liberties only to learn to their sorrow that *deceit and mockery, poverty and tyranny,* are their reward." (Truman 1949) • "Penetration either through ignorance, or because they believe these *false promises.*" (Acheson 1950, January 12) • "They have always . . . maintained the *pretense* that they are the *interpreters of the aspirations* of peoples far beyond their borders." (Acheson 1950, March 16) • "They have conducted . . . a foreign policy . . . designed to keep the peoples of the world in a state of deepest *apprehension and doubt.*" (Acheson 1950, March 16) • "the *false revolution* of communism" (Truman 1950, October 17) • "makes the *false claim* that it stands for progress and human achievement" (Truman 1950, October 17) • "*the false promise* of Bolshevik imperialism" (Acheson 1950, November 30) • "the *illusion* that . . . they are helping along the *inevitable course of history*" (Acheson 1950, November 30) • "*tried* to identify themselves with *the cause of progress* . . . surely one of the most *cynical* efforts of which history offers record" (Truman 1953, January 7) • "the *distorted* Marxist interpretation of history" (Truman 1953, January 7)

(continued)

Table 3.3. CONTINUED

United States	Soviet Union
• "help these people *develop . . . and re-shape their societies*" (Truman 1953, January 7) • "answer the *desires* of the people for advancement" (Truman 1953, January 7) • "help these countries *grow and flourish* in freedom" (Truman 1953, January 7)	• "[T]hey seem to believe that *history is on their side.*" (Truman 1953, January 7) • "[T]hey are trying to *boost 'history' along*, at every opportunity, in every way they can." (Truman 1953, January 7) • "*would lead* the world back *into slavery and darkness*" (Truman 1953, January 15)

33. *We know* that they *need* to produce more food and clothing and shelter. We *can make* a special contribution by sharing . . . the productive techniques *which we have discovered in our own experience.* (Truman 1950, October 17)

Although the American future is a wholly positive future of freedom, economic security, abundance, and righteousness, it is by no means assured, as it is, President Truman warns, "directly opposed by a regime with contrary aims and a totally different conception of life" (Truman 1949, January 20). As can be seen in the right-hand column of Table 3.3, the Soviet future is rendered as a false future rooted in a flawed philosophy that promises freedom and opportunity but delivers tyranny and poverty, rewards sacrifice with misery, and answers uncertainty with even greater apprehension and doubt. Moreover, the Soviets are represented as false prophets who make "false promises" and offer flawed interpretations of other peoples' "aspirations" and the course of history. President Truman warns that if Soviet efforts to "boost history along," efforts guided by the mistaken belief that "history is on their side," succeed, the world will be led "back into slavery and darkness." In sum, the Soviet system represents a direct threat to "our dream of the future—our picture of the world we would hope to have when the communist threat is over" (Truman 1953, January 15).

Consequently, in addition to defending against "Soviet expansion," the nation's "purpose" must be, Secretary of State Acheson insists, "building the kind of world in which our way of life can flourish. We must continue to press ahead with the building of a free world which is strong in its faith and in its material progress" (Acheson 1950, March 16). As President Truman explains in his 1949 inaugural address, the United States can build this world by sharing its technical knowledge and expertise with nations in the periphery. According to the president, in this expertise and knowledge lay the future of progress, advancement, and prosperity the "underdeveloped areas" aspire to:

[68] *The Great Nation of Futurity*

34. [W]e must embark on a bold new program for making the benefits of *our scientific advances and industrial progress available for the improvement and growth of underdeveloped areas.* ... Their economic life *is primitive and stagnant.* Their poverty is *a handicap and a threat* to them and to more prosperous areas. ... I believe that we should *make available to peace-loving peoples the benefits of our store of technical knowledge in order to help them realize their aspirations for a better life.* (Truman 1949, January 20)

Through this statement, President Truman designates newly decolonized societies as the "underdeveloped areas" and, in so doing, ushers in a global space-time that would undergird the nation's foreign policy in the postwar era. Specifically, he presents a conception of postwar space-time according to which the American present—its scientific advances, industrial progress, and store of technical knowledge—is the locus of and means to the future for the "underdeveloped areas." Assuring this future is essential to protecting the nation from the "threat" posed by impoverished nations. In sum, by setting its foreign policy sights on the "underdeveloped areas," the president identifies the nation's "last frontier—the non-Western future itself" (Sardar 1993: 187). As we'll see in Chapter 4, this spatiotemporal designation ramifies through subsequent articulations of American foreign policy, as well as conceptions of geopolitical space-time. In the final section of this chapter, I examine how the Truman administration's earlier articulations of postwar policy and the space-times embedded within it were articulated in official national security policy.

National Security Council Resolution 68: "Fostering a World Environment"

Created in the spring of 1950, National Security Council Resolution 68 (NSC 68)[5], "[O]ne of the most significant studies of the entire Cold War period," outlined the rationale for the containment policy and the political and military means by which that policy would be pursued (Leffler 1992: 313).[6] Its policy goals aligned with those presented in earlier speeches and statements from the Truman administration and "reaffirmed the geopolitical and ideological basis of the nation's foreign policy" (Leffler 1992: 359).[7]

In its assessment of the postwar security environment, NSC 68 creates a "discourse stage" (Cap 2010) upon which the security environment facing the United States is presented as comprising nascent yet very real threats to the nation's future as a geopolitical power, explaining that global power has "increasingly gravitated" to two "centers," the Soviet Union and the United States (May 1993: 25). NSC 68 construes the post–World War II world as comprising two clearly demarcated and antithetical worlds: the "Free World" of the "West" and the "Communist World" of the "East." Moreover, it declares that

35. The gravest threat to the security of the United States within the *foreseeable future* stems from the *hostile designs* and formidable power of the USSR, and from the nature of the Soviet system. The political, economic, and psychological warfare which the USSR *is now waging* has *dangerous potentialities for weakening the relative world position of the United States.* (77)

NSC 68 projects a negative Soviet future through the phrases "foreseeable future," "hostile designs," and "dangerous potentialities." This near-term future is evident in the present moment, which is characterized through the actions and orientations of each geopolitical center with regard to each other and the world community. As can be seen in the following excerpt, the Soviet Union is represented as undertaking expansionist actions through which it "seeks to impose" its political-economic system "over the rest of the world." The United States, in contrast, is represented as a rising nation whose future is threatened by the Soviet Union:

36. The Soviet Union . . . *is animated* by a new fanatical faith, antithetical to our own, and *seeks to impose* its absolute authority over *the rest of the world.* Conflict . . . *is waged* . . . by *violent or non-violent methods* in accordance with the dictates of expediency. . . . It is in this context that this Republic and its citizens *in the ascendancy* of their strength stand in their *deepest peril.* The issues that face us are momentous, involving the *fulfillment or destruction not only of this Republic but of civilization itself.* (25)

Through the statements in excerpts 35 and 36 NSC 68 configures the present moment as comprising oppositional centers and maps out the divergent trajectories along which that present could develop in the future. That is, latent within these construals of the "present crisis" are "dangerous potentialities" that presage the "weakening [of] the relative world position of the United States" and the "fulfillment or destruction" of America and "civilization itself." Indeed, NSC 68 raises the question of whether the global community will "long tolerate this tension [of equilibrium-without-order] without moving toward some kind of order, on somebody's terms" (52). At issue is which superpower will extend the current scope of its political-economic system across time and space by shaping the future of those living in the periphery, and which will be contained within its present geopolitical domain of influence. As Chilton (2004) explains, locating the center in another's space typically positions that other as a principal causal agent and renders its movement beyond that center as threatening (146). As can be seen in excerpt 36,

[70]   *The Great Nation of Futurity*

such threatening movement is apparent in NSC 68's construal of the Soviet Union as an aggressive global actor that "is animated," "seeks to impose," and "wage[s]" conflict by "violent and non-violent methods." The American "Republic," along with civilization, is placed in a relatively passive position as the target of those aggressive actions.

Of interest here is the document's contrastive representation of Soviet and American space-times and how this representation delegitimizes the geopolitical goals and ambitions of the Soviet Union and legitimates those of the United States. The Soviet Union's expansionist movement is characterized through a space-time anchored in and oriented to the geopolitical plane of the here-and-now and as proceeding horizontally across that plane outward, into territory beyond its deictic center. In NSC 68's construal of a Soviet-defined future, the "ascendancy" of the "Republic and its citizens," which at present stand in "their deepest peril," will have been thwarted, its potential unrealized, and its very existence, and that of "civilization," destroyed. United States space-time, however, is oriented toward a higher, transcendent geopolitical plane and purpose. The prepositional phrase "in the ascendancy" positions the nation as moving upward from its deictic center, movement that is non-threatening, as it is oriented toward a "higher" place above the current geopolitical plane. As such, the American future is not just better than the Soviet future; it is exceptional, as it resides on a geopolitical plane that transcends the vagaries of the current world environment.

This rendering of the "present crisis" and the alternative futures it projects are crystallized in the document's construal of the raison d'être that defines each global actor (see Table 3.4).

Noteworthy here are the referential expressions—"purpose" and "design"[8]—used to represent each superpower's intentions and aims and, relatedly, the alternative futures each entails. NSC 68's juxtaposing of purpose and design locates each global actor's goals in different space-times: the United States in the deterritorialized and atemporal abstract plane of "purpose" and the Soviet Union in the temporally and spatially anchored material plane of "design." United States "purpose," in turn, collocates with a series of abstract concepts: "integrity," "vitality," "free," "dignity," "worth," and "the individual." Consequently, the United States is rendered as a nation that acts in accord with a spatially and temporally transcendent purpose and is guided by equally transcendent ideals and values.

The "Soviet Union," in contrast, is metonymically rendered as "The Kremlin" and is anchored in the present moment through pronominal references to political actors who exist and act in time and space, namely, "those who control the Soviet Union and the international communist movement" and "their absolute power." The "fundamental design of the Kremlin" is also tethered to the here and now through prepositional phrases that index geographical territories ("in the Soviet Union" and "in areas"), the temporal adverb "now," and

Table 3.4. UNITED STATES "PURPOSE," KREMLIN "DESIGN"

Fundamental Purpose of the United States:

"In essence the fundamental purpose [of the United States] is to assure the integrity and vitality of our free society." (26)

Consequences:

- Our determination to create conditions under which our free and democratic society can live and prosper
- Our determination to fight if necessary to defend our way of life

Fundamental Design of the Kremlin:

"The fundamental design of those who control the Soviet Union and the international communist movement is to retain and solidify their absolute power, first in the Soviet Union and second in the areas now under their control." (26)

Requirements:

- The dynamic extension of their authority and the ultimate elimination of any effective opposition to their authority
- The complete subversion or forcible destruction of the machinery of government and structure of society in the countries of the non-Soviet world and their replacement by an apparatus and structure subservient to and controlled from the Kremlin

its representation as a staged process ("first," "second"). Moreover, the Soviet design collocates with wholly negative concepts: "control," "absolute power," "complete subversion," and "forcible destruction."

These statements are also significant for their contrastive use of lexico-grammatical forms for construing future actions. The "fundamental purpose of the United States" will be realized through the productive processes of creating conditions that support a democratic way of life and of fighting and defending that life. However, the use of the nonfinite verb forms "to + verb" ("to create," "to fight," "to defend") eliminates the deictic function tense and aspect and serve to specify the temporality of processes (e.g., "we are working to maintain"; "we will fight to defend"). And although the nebulous constructs "our society" and "our way of life" orient the nation's purpose to the domestic domain, they leave unspecified the geopolitical spaces implicated in the actions that will "assure" the nation's well-being. The means by which the Kremlin design will be implemented, however, are presented not as processes but as wholly negative outcomes: "dynamic extension of . . . authority," "ultimate elimination of . . . opposition," and "complete subversion or forcible destruction" of non-Soviet societies. And although nominalized forms obscure temporality, they do reify processes by imbuing them with a sense of materiality lacking in verbal forms.

Through its polemical portrayal of the world's two superpowers, NSC 68 construes the global environment as one in which the United States cannot

[72] *The Great Nation of Futurity*

realize its fundamental purpose in a world that includes a Soviet Union, and the Soviet Union cannot implement its design in a world that includes a United States. At its heart, the U.S.–Soviet conflict is not a physical/material one, but an ideological one; it is a conflict between two diametrically opposed conceptions of how societies ought to be politically and economically organized. That is, despite claims that the Soviet system is "crowding in" on the territory of the free world, the problem actually derives from the supposed inability of the global environment to sustain the perpetuation of two antithetical ideological systems. As NSC 68 explains, the "breadth of freedom" and its "long continued existence ... in the world" can't be tolerated by a system that has a "formidable capacity to act with the widest possible tactical latitude" (28, 35).

Several statements do construe the threat environment in material terms by indexing geopolitical spaces and specific moments in which the Soviet Union is taking aggressive actions. NSC 68 argues, however, that these actions are not the nation's primary concern because its "marked atomic superiority over the Soviet Union which inhibits aggressive Soviet action" (May 1993: 76).[9] When the Soviets do act aggressively, NSC 68 construes that action as merely symptomatic of the actual threat posed by the Soviet Union. Regarding Czechoslovakia, for example, it explains that

37. The assault on free institutions is world-wide now ... *a defeat of free institutions anywhere is a defeat everywhere*. The shock we sustained in the destruction of Czechoslovakia was not in the means of Czechoslovakia's material import to us. ... But when the *integrity* of Czechoslovak institutions was destroyed, it was in *the intangible scale of value that we registered a loss more damaging than the material loss we had already suffered*. (29)

As did President Truman's plea for aid to Greece and Turkey, NSC68 obliterates the spatiotemporal divide separating the core from the periphery by declaring that "a defeat of free institutions anywhere is a defeat everywhere." Consequently, the "destruction of Czechoslovakia" foretells a future in which the Kremlin's "idea of slavery" has subjugated the American "idea of freedom" (27). This distal future, in turn, mandates that the "immediate objectives" of the nation's security policy focus on "developing the moral and material strength of the free world" (30).

And herein lies the expansionist nature of the "fundamental purpose of the United States." Through the metaphors "integrity" and "vitality" NSC 68 conceptualizes national security in terms of the present internal state of American society and its capacity to endure into the future. That is, the integrity of a thing or entity has to do with it existing with its material wholeness intact. Consequently, "integrity" indexes the present state of "our free society" by conceptualizing the United States within the traditional status quo model

(Chilton 1996: 61). "Vitality," however, extends the scope of national security to include the task of ensuring the nation's capacity to endure into the future. Metaphorically, vitality renders "our free society" as a living, dynamic being that must be able to regenerate itself. Assuring this vitality requires an offensive posture that will enable the United States to reproduce itself across time and space.

Like any living thing, "our free society" requires a particular environment if it is to secure its future well-being. Thus, a key goal of U.S. national security must be to create a global environment favorable to American values and interests, as NSC 68 declares that "Our overall policy at the present moment may be described as one designed to *foster a world environment in which the American system can survive and flourish*" (40; emphasis added). NSC 68 further explains that this plan to "change the world situation" is "a policy which we would probably pursue *even if there were no Soviet threat*" (32, 41, emphasis added). Indeed, unless the United States is willing to "risk the future on the hazard that the Soviet Empire . . . will spontaneously destroy itself from within," an offensive, expansionist posture is essential to ensure the viability of the Free World and, thereby, that of the United States (69).

Such an offensive program requires security policy to be territorially and temporally expansive. Thus, the battle to "assure the integrity and vitality of our free society" must be waged beyond the nation's deictic center, "abroad" throughout "the Free World" and "the Soviet world." And it must also be waged according to a timeframe that extends beyond the contingencies of the present and proximal future. NSC 68 does temporally anchor security strategy to a specific moment and event: "an initial surprise atomic attack of weight which it is estimated the USSR will be capable of developing by 1954" (56). The nation's "overall policy," however, extends beyond this moment to the "non-definite future space" of "as long as necessary" (Chilton 2004: 160; May 1993: 79).

American efforts to "create conditions" within global society, although expansive, are portrayed in NSC 68 as being of a different order than the imperialistic machinations of the Soviet Union: while Soviet design is oriented to expansion as subjugation, U.S. purpose is oriented toward expansion as elevation. Important here is the use of verb forms to conceptualize the nation's plans and actions that either invoke or cohere with the building metaphor (e.g., "building a successfully functioning political and economic system," "create a world society"). In addition to evaluating American efforts positively by invoking the conceptual metaphor GOOD GOVERNING IS CREATING, the building metaphor and its cognates orient those efforts in an upward, progressive direction (Charteris-Black 2011: 205). In topographical terms, building metaphors orient movement along a vertical trajectory (Charteris-Black 2004: 94; Koteyko and Ryazanova-Clarke 2009: 120). NSC 68's conceptualization of the nation's efforts to build a free and democratic world society,

[74]   *The Great Nation of Futurity*

then, collocates with the ascendancy metaphor to construe the nation's expansionist tendency as oriented vertically toward a future geopolitical space in which freedom, democracy, and prosperity reign supreme.

Although expansive, NSC 68 renders the nation's plans and objectives as not self-interested by insisting that they are taken on behalf of the future of global society. In making its case that the United States is best suited to unleash the potential of the periphery, NSC 68 invokes the nation's identity as the exemplary agent of the future. It, not the Soviet Union, is the nation that manifests the world's hopes and aspirations and, as such, is best able to futurize the periphery. This claim is grounded in a construction of geopolitical space-time according to which, as Adam (1995) puts it, "other" time is constructed against the "backcloth of 'own' time" (7):

38. Translated into terms relevant to the lives of *other people*—our system of values *can become* perhaps a powerful appeal to millions who *now seek* or find in authoritarianism a refuge from anxiety, bafflement, and insecurity. (42)

39. The *potential* within us of bearing witness to the values by which we live *holds promise* for a dynamic manifestation to the rest of the world of the *vitality* of our system. (42)

40. As we ourselves demonstrate power, confidence, and a sense of moral and political direction, so the same qualities *will be evoked* in Western Europe . . . Latin America, Asia, and Africa and the real *beginnings of an awakening* among the Soviet totalitariat. (44)

41. An affirmative decision to summon up the *potential* within ourselves *would evoke the potential* strength within others. (44)

42. The psychological impact [of United States action]—the *revival of confidence and hope in the future*. (73)

43. *awaken and arouse the latent* spiritual energies of free men everywhere and obtain their enthusiastic support for a positive program *going far beyond* the frustration of the Soviet design and *opening vistas to the future*. (75–76)

As can be seen in these excerpts, the as-of-yet untapped potential inherent in the American people and the nation's system of values holds the promise for those seeking a better life. By acting with confidence and power, America can evoke and awaken the power and confidence currently dormant in others, thereby enabling them to realize their potential, expand their vision of what's possible, and renew their faith in the future. In short, America has the power and capability—indeed, the responsibility—to open "vistas to the future" for all the world's people.

If Our future is one that "affirm[s] the constructive and hopeful instincts of men" and is "capable of fulfilling their fundamental aspirations," Their future must do the opposite. Accordingly, NSC 68 attributes the Kremlin's strength to its "ideological pretensions" to which "vulnerable segments" of the "free world," Asia in particular, have fallen prey:

44. The Asiatics have been impressed by what has been plausibly portrayed to them as the rapid advancement of the USSR from a backward society to a position of great power. Thus, in its *pretensions* to being . . . a *model "scientific" society*, the Kremlin cynically identifies itself with *the genuine aspirations* of large numbers of people. (35)

The Soviet Union cynically exploits people's desire for a better future in order to reap the "benefits" that derive from its "international crusade" (35). Its claim of being a model of a modern society is a mere "pretension," as "Soviet ideas and practices run counter to the best . . . and strongest instincts of men, and deny their most fundamental aspirations" (36). It is, in the end, a false prophet of the future, a charlatan that promises progress and liberation but delivers regression and oppression.

CONCLUSION

The focus of this chapter was on the linguistic and rhetorical means by which foreign policy discourse in the near aftermath of World War II and the inception of the Cold War staked an American claim on the global future and how that claim drew upon and affirmed the nation's identity as the "great nation of futurity." I demonstrated how different global actors were aligned with particular space-times, the means by which these space-times were differentiated and evaluated, and how America was rendered as uniquely capable of shaping the postwar future. In his essay, Luce proposed that the nation's foreign policy shift from focusing on defending local spaces to pursing a mission of shaping the global future. This reorientation away from local space-time to global space-time was grounded in the author's call for the nation to make the 20th century the American Century by assuming role as the "powerhouse" of the global future. Through his speech outlining the Truman Doctrine, as well as subsequent speeches, President Truman construed the postwar geopolitical environment in temporal terms in such a way that authorized a leadership role for the United States in determining the future of that environment. He offered a globalized conception of security rooted in a change in timescales that construed geographically distant and remote spaces and happenings as immediate and urgent threats to American security. He also contrasted the American and Soviet systems in such a way as to identify the future of the periphery with the American system. NSC 68 formalized this temporal conception of the global environment through a security policy grounded in a contrast between the geopolitical futures entailed in the American and Soviet political economic systems. This contrast served to render the American future as the authentic future for global society and the Soviet future as ensuring its eventual ruin.

My analysis further demonstrated that this foreign policy discourse created and deployed relations of difference between the American Self and three Others (Britain, Soviet Union, and the periphery), as well as between two conceptions of the American Self, to position the United States in a unique role vis-à-vis the global future. These relations were created through modal contrasts, moral and future-oriented lexis, and several future-oriented conceptual metaphors. It also drew on two rhetorical tropes—alternative futures and shape the future—to project the different futures that could develop out of the postwar environment and, at the same time, underscore and authorize the necessity of America assuming a global leadership role in shaping the new era. That is, postwar security discourse presented the specter of an alternative future as its own sort of threat that allowed for the possibility that global society would evolve along lines hostile to American interests. This threat to the future, in turn, served to legitimate an expansionist and interventionist geopolitical role for the United States.

In the following chapter, I consider how the contest over the shape and character of the global future manifested in a particular articulation of Cold War policy and, moreover, how that discourse positioned the future of the periphery as the terrain upon which the Cold War would be waged.

CHAPTER 4

"New Vistas of Opportunity"

Modernizing the Other

INTRODUCTION

The focus of this chapter concerns how the temporal identity of America manifested and functioned within the social scientific theory underlying the nation's approach to foreign policy in the 1950s and 1960s, "modernization theory" (MT).[1] I examine the space-time contrasts embedded within the development scheme promoted by modernization theory, how those space-times created Self/Other contrasts, and how those contrasts, in turn, positioned America in a privileged position vis-à-vis the global future. My analysis focuses on two Self/Other dyads: United States/Soviet Union and United States/periphery. I identify the space-times assigned to each constituent and consider how those space-times position them relative to the global future.

I argue that MT rendered the Cold War as a conflict over the future development of what President Truman termed the "underdeveloped areas" and identified the United States as uniquely qualified to guide that development. I further argue that MT legitimated this role by construing both the "underdeveloped areas" and the Soviet Union as threats to the postwar geopolitical future. This argument is grounded in a linguistic and rhetorical analysis that demonstrates how: (1) modernization theorists staked an American claim on the global future by using contrastive space-times to construct relations of identity/difference, and (2) this American future was legitimated through these relations and through the naturalization and universalization of the sociopolitical temporal order underlying MT. In sum, this chapter considers how discursive projections of what the future would and ought to be were deployed

The Great Nation of Futurity. Patricia L. Dunmire, Oxford University Press. © Oxford University Press 2023.
DOI: 10.1093/oso/9780197658222.003.0004

in foreign policy discourse as part of American postwar efforts to secure and wield geopolitical power.

The post–World War II era, as noted in Chapter 1 and demonstrated in Chapter 3, is particularly ripe for such an analysis because it brought to the fore questions about what the geopolitical environment would look like and the role the United States could and should play in shaping it. These questions were given added urgency by the fact that the Soviet Union, considered by some policymakers and social scientists to provide a "better example of development than anything the West had to offer," was making tangible gains in the decolonizing world (Gilman 2003: 43). The Soviets, Gilman (2003) argues, "appeared to many to occupy the rhetorical high ground in the early post-war period" (42). The United States, consequently, faced a crisis of legitimacy as the nation's leaders had to decide, according to Walter Rostow, a prominent modernization theorist, whether it was going to "observe or participate in this struggle over which so much of our destiny hinges" (as quoted in Gilman 2003: 45). The nation's leaders opted to participate and did so, as I demonstrate below, by deploying a temporal scheme that identified America as the true nation of the future and, thus, as the "kind of society 'development' should strive to create" and the decolonized peoples should seek to emulate (Gilman 2003: 2).

MODERNIZATION AS COLD WAR POLICY

Emerging in the late 1950s and developed during the 1960s, MT outlined a development program that supported the nation's Cold War policy by delineating a "singular path of progressive change" that provided policymakers with a plan for restructuring postcolonial societies (Gilman 2003: 3; Latham 2000; Pearce 2001). The central premise of MT held that the political and nationalistic movements of the "Third World" could be managed through political and economic development programs (Alqvist and Rhisiart 2015: 93; Sardar 1993: 180).[2] It was a prescriptive "theory of the future . . . based in foresight and prediction about the course of human welfare" that its champions claimed provided a blueprint for restructuring newly decolonized societies (Appadurai 2003: 218). A primary goal of modernizing efforts was to identify "potential threats" and eradicate "future trouble spots" within nationalistic movements in the "underdeveloped areas" (Alqvist and Rhisiart 2015: 93).

As Tipps (1973) points out, MT arose as the response of political elites and intellectuals to the inception of the Cold War and the new and increasing role of "Third World" societies in geopolitics (200). The theory held great promise in the eyes of policymakers, as it offered a means for directing the development of the newly decolonized areas and responding to the Soviet Union's "surging geopolitical and ideological power" and its efforts to "chip away at the 'underdeveloped periphery'" (Gilman 2003: 13; Latham 2000: 2). MT constituted a "metalanguage" that "supplied . . . a sense of the 'meaning' of postwar geopolitical uncertainties" and an "implicit set of directions for how to effect change in that dissilient world" (Gilman 2003: 5). This metalanguage was imbued with "exceptionalist assumptions" concerning the nation's geopolitical place and purpose and its temporal status relative to newly decolonized societies (McCrisken 2003: 23). As Gilman (2003) explains, modernization theorists insisted that the shape of the future toward which the "third world" ought to orient itself was "discernible in the contemporary United States" (5).

The following analysis focuses on three key MT texts—Eugene Staley's *The Future of Underdeveloped Countries*, Max Millikan and Walter Rostow's *A Proposal: Key to an Effective Foreign Policy*, and Daniel Lerner's *The Passing of Traditional Society*—and examines the linguistic and rhetorical means through which what policymakers deemed the "official future" was constructed, deployed, and reified (Connelly et al. 2012: 1422). The importance of these texts derives from their influence on the nation's approach to decolonizing societies during the 1950s through the 1960s.[3]

I begin with Staley and examine how he elaborated Truman's spatiotemporal designation of the postwar geopolitical environment and staked a claim on the future of the periphery. I then consider how Millikan and Rostow situated the future of the periphery within American foreign policy and implicated that future in the nation's conflict with the Soviet Union. Finally, my analysis of Lerner's contribution to MT examines how the process of modernization was conceptualized in terms of agency and causality and demonstrates how that conception served to remove it from the local space-time of the Cold War and transform what was a historically specific American vision of the future into a universal, inevitable future.

Staley: The "Vital Matter" of Their Future

As explained in Chapter 3, the aftermath of World War II saw the emergence of a sociopolitical temporal scheme in which juxtaposed "developed" and "underdeveloped" societies assume a prominent role in foreign policy discourse. President Truman introduced this scheme by noting that because "more than half the people of the world" are "outside the mainstream of world technological progress," aiding their development will require that the United States make "the benefits of our scientific advances and industrial progress" available to these "underdeveloped areas" (Truman 1949, January 20; Committee on Foreign Affairs 1949: 1).[4]

In *the Future of Underdeveloped Countries* Eugene Staley echoed the president's construal of global space-time when he explained that

[80] *The Great Nation of Futurity*

1. Peoples outside the Western World, however—and they are the great majority of mankind—have shared only in a minor degree in the material and social *progress* of these centuries. *Ancient ways* of making a living and *ancient poverty have remained.* . . . They know little of the West's home achievements in personal freedom, self-government, human dignity, and respect for individual personality. (1–2)

Through the temporal lexis of "progress" and "ancient," Staley construes the global environment as comprising societies that occupy different places on a linear timescale of past–present–future and, thereby, creates a relationship of temporal difference between them. At issue for Staley is what this lack of coevalness, the fact that We occupy a future about which "they know little," means for the security and prospects of the West. For Staley, the fact that They occupy a space-time untouched by Western progress presages the possibility of global upheaval and danger. Specifically, through the perfective aspectual profile of "have remained," Staley construes ancientness as a condition of non-Western peoples that is relevant to the present moment. This construal is reinforced and amplified in a subsequent statement in which Staley declares that

2. the hitherto "backwards" people are in ferment. (2)

The temporal adjunct "hitherto" indexes a changing environment in the non-Western world, an environment that has existed up to this point but that may not continue in the postwar era. This change is rendered potentially threatening through the relational process clause that assigns the attribute "in ferment" to the " 'backwards' people," thereby rendering them as agitated or in a state of heightened excitement. Consequently, Staley warns that the "extreme contrasts" between "Our" progress and "Their" stagnation are becoming "less and less tenable" (2).

Staley's assessment of the geopolitical environment is grounded in "the socially ratified power of prediction" (Fairclough 2003: 167) through which he divines in the present conditions of the postwar era the possibility of a volatile and politically consequential future. As can be seen in the following excerpts, he draws on the alternative-futures trope to juxtapose two diametrically opposed scenarios for the postwar geopolitical environment. Through a moral lexis, he privileges the Western-designed future over a non-Western future: while the former could bring "benefits," "pioneering contributions," "freedom," "human dignity," and "material welfare" to the non-Western world, the latter would lead to the loss of Western benefits and the ruin of Western civilization.

3. *Either* the benefits of modern civilization in living levels and human dignity are generalized so that they no longer will be almost exclusively enjoyed by

the peoples of the West where they originated, *or* they will be lost even to the peoples of the West. (2)

4. *If* the present efforts of the underdeveloped countries to develop themselves go forward with Western cooperation, *then* it is possible—though not certain—that a world civilization may gradually evolve in which the West's pioneering contributions to such human values as freedom, individual dignity, and material welfare are preserved and combined with the cultural heritages of non-Western peoples. *The alternative*, over the long run, is a real "Decline of the West." (4)

In excerpt 3 Staley presents a Manichean projection of the postwar future that comprises two alternative scenarios, each of which is coded as highly certain. "*Either* the benefits of modern civilization" are "generalized" so that they "will" extend beyond the West "*or* they will be lost" to all. In excerpt 4, we see a conditional statement whereby Staley projects an imaginary world (James 1982) in which the continued evolution of Western civilization and its "pioneering contributions" are dependent upon decolonized societies developing in accord with a Western model. This imaginary world offers the possibility, though not the certainty, that Western advances of "freedom, individual dignity, and material welfare" could be assimilated by non-Western peoples and, thereby, "preserved" well into the future. Although Staley hedges on whether the decolonized people will actually experience the benefits of Western civilization ("though not certain"), he is unequivocal concerning the future consequences of postcolonial societies following a non-Western model of development: a future defined by "a real 'Decline of the West.'"

Taken together, these excerpts align the future of the underdeveloped countries with a Western theory of modernity by introducing a development scheme whereby Their ancient ways would be—indeed, must be—modernized by Our techniques and values. This scheme is grounded in a space-time according to which Their future resides in Our past and present. Staley doesn't merely align Their future with Ours, however; he stakes a claim on it by implicating the future of Western civilization in the success or failure of Their development. Either Our benefits are enjoyed by Them, or those benefits will be lost "even to us;" either the "West's pioneering contributions to human values" are "combined" with and "preserved" in Their "cultural heritage," or the world will likely witness the demise of Western civilization.

This contingent global environment, its "unfinished" and volatile state, gives rise to Staley's "first major thesis," which further renders the future of the decolonized societies as the province of the West:

5. [T]he future of the underdeveloped countries in Asia, Africa, and parts of Europe and the Americas *is a vital matter* to the future of Western

civilization, including, of course, the security and way of life of the American people. (3)

By declaring that the "future of the underdeveloped countries . . . is a vital matter" to the future of the West, this relational process clause identifies the future of the decolonized societies in terms of its implications for and value to the "future of West civilization," generally, and the future "security and way of life of" the United States, specifically. This process of linking Their future to Our future redounds in subsequent statements through which Staley elaborates his thesis:

6. Economic development in cooperation with the West *is a necessary part* of the conditions for Western survival and the survival in the world of some of the West's most important contributions to human progress. (3)
7. Concern for the economic and social progress in the lands where archaic production and chronic poverty are still the rule . . . *is therefore a concern* that the distinctive values which Western civilization has fostered shall remain viable in the world and viable in our own country. (4)

As Thompson (2004) explains, identifying relational process clauses in political discourse signify the "wider ideological beliefs" embedded within particular texts (98). Drawing from Halliday (1994), he uses the terminology "Value" and "Token" to conceptualize the way a clause creates a relationship of identity between a general category—Value—and its specific realization—Token. Analyzing the construal of Value and Token, he explains, can "guide us toward the broader concerns and values" of a text (98). Table 4.1 presents the Value Token analysis of excerpts 5–7.

For Staley, Value is the future of the West and the United States, and Token is the development of the "underdeveloped countries." The future of these countries, consequently, is rendered as the space in which the future of Western civilization will be further "realize[d] or embodie[d]" and, thus, ensured (Thompson 2004: 98). In other words, Their value, why they are "important in the world," derives from the role they could play in ensuring Our survival and viability (Thompson 2004: 98).

In addition to identifying and linking Western and non-Western space-times, excerpts 3–7 reveal a texturing of space-times that entails a movement from value-laden projections of hypothetic futures to present fact. That is, we see Stately moving from projections of alternative futures in excerpts 3 and 4 to assertions about what those projections mean for the present geopolitical moment in excerpts 5, 6, and 7: their future "*is* a vital matter to," "*is* a necessary part of," and "*is* a concern" for Our future. By moving from future projection to present reality in this way, Staley elides the hypothetical nature of the

Table 4.1. VALUE AND TOKEN IN STALEY'S THESIS

Token	Process: relational: identifying	Value
The future of the underdeveloped countries in Asia, Africa, and parts of Europe and the Americas	is	a vital matter to the future of Western civilization, including, of course, the security and way of life of the American people.
Economic development in cooperation with the West	is	a necessary part of the conditions for Western survival and the survival in the world of some of the West's most important contributions to human progress.
Concern for the economic and social progress in the lands where archaic production and chronic poverty are still the rule	is	therefore a concern that the distinctive values which Western civilization has fostered shall remain viable in the world and viable in our own country.

basis of his thesis and suppresses "the value-based dimension" of the policy implicated in that thesis (Alqvist and Rhisiart 2015: 93).

Staley's identification of the future of the "underdeveloped areas" as "necessary" to the "survival" of the West entails the proposition that Their future is a potential threat to or ally of Our future. The possible impact of the "underdeveloped areas" on postwar geopolitics derives not from any particular action they might take against or in support of the United States and the West, however. Rather, as suggested in excerpts 3 and 4, it inheres in the potentiality of the underdeveloped countries—in what they could *become* at some future moment rather than what they could *do*. Staley specifies this threat by juxtaposing alternative postwar futures and siting the battle over those futures in the "underdeveloped countries":

8. The underdeveloped countries in fact *hold the balance of the future* as between the political system and way of life which *have been evolving over several centuries* in the West and *the modern reversion to tyranny* represented by Communism or other totalitarian systems. (15)
9. Whether most of these countries take a democratic or Communist path in their development *is likely to determine the future of civilization* on our planet. (15)

[84]   *The Great Nation of Futurity*

10. Should the Communist power bloc, however, succeed in bringing most of the underdeveloped countries into its orbit ... *the effect on our security would be disastrous.* (3–4)

Again, we see that the value of "underdeveloped" countries' potential is represented as deriving from their role in and implications for the battle between democracy and tyranny: will this potential be realized in a way that helps ensure the continued evolution of the former or the reversion to the latter? In excerpt 8, Staley further construes the value of the newly decolonized peoples by endowing them with agentive capacity vis-à-vis the future (Scollon and Scollon 2000): they "hold the balance of the future" and, thus, are "likely to determine the future of civilization" depending on the "path" they "take." This agency is partially qualified in excerpt 9, as Staley renders the "underdeveloped countries" as potential victims of the "Communist power bloc": rather than choosing to align with the Soviet Union, they would be "[brought] into its orbit." Regardless of whether they act to realize their potential or have it usurped, in this potentiality resides the future prospects and viability of the West.

What the newly decolonized countries will become, consequently, is rendered as contested terrain: it is the site on which democracy and communism will do battle, the space in which the future of "civilization on our planet" will be worked out. And while two modern political-economic systems will vie for this potential, Staley draws on a morally charged temporal lexis of progress/regress to render only one as a legitimate path to the future. If the "underdeveloped countries" choose the Western path, they will "evolve" into modern societies defined by a political system and way of life that have been several centuries in the making. Should they be subsumed by the Soviet Union, however, they will not progress toward the future but, rather, will experience "the modern reversion to tyranny" inherent in the communist system.

Staley's *The Future of Underdeveloped Countries* elaborated on the "underdeveloped" condition of the newly decolonized societies and specified the significance of this condition for the West. That is, he established a relationship between Their space-time and Our space-time that implicated Their future development in Our future existence. In so doing, he identified the future of the periphery as a central concern to the security and prospects of the West and, thereby, staked a claim on that future. The themes linking Staley's work to subsequent articulations of MT are

- characterization of the decolonized societies as transforming, aspirational, and threatening,
- conflicting avenues of development: democratic capitalism versus authoritarian communism,

- aiding and directing postcolonial development as foreign policy goal, and
- the future of the periphery as reciprocally related to the future of the West.

The following analysis examines how the work of Millikan and Rostow contributed to and further developed Staley's thesis on development, modernization, and foreign policy. Specifically, I consider the linguistic means through which they operationalized Staley's thesis and worked out its implications for American foreign policy.

Millikan and Rostow: Instrumentalizing Their Future for Our Security

I begin this section by considering how Staley's declaration that "the future of the under- developed countries is a vital matter" to U.S. foreign policy was recontextualized within Millikan and Rostow's thesis and how this recontextualization, in turn, laid further claim to the future of postcolonial societies. The central thesis of Millikan and Rostow's proposal asserts that

11. A much expanded long-term program of American participation in the economic development of the underdeveloped areas *can and should be* one of the most important means for furthering the *purposes* of American foreign policy. (1)

Through this relational identifying process clause, Millikan and Rostow render Their development as a "Token" of Our foreign policy. That is, the future of the "underdeveloped areas" becomes both the means by which the United States can further its geopolitical goals and the embodiment of those goals. Moreover, by moving from the epistemic modality of "is" to the deontic modality of "can" and "should," the authors transform Staley's assertion about the value of the future of the "underdeveloped countries" into a policy proposal by deriving the "ought" implicated by his "is." Given that Their future "*is* a vital matter" to Ours, it "can and should be" a component of our foreign policy. In so doing, Millikan and Rostow add the concept of "purpose" to the relationship that holds between "modern" space-time and "ancient" space-time (van Leeuwen 2008: 20).

According to van Leeuwen (2008), articulations of purpose are important to acts of legitimation because they explain why an action should be taken or why a social practice exists (113). He further explains that for purposes to serve as legitimations of actions or practices, they must have "an element of moral evaluation" (113). Millikan and Rostow are careful to include this evaluation in their policy proposal both by insisting that American development

[86] *The Great Nation of Futurity*

of postcolonial societies "can" be (i.e., has the capacity to be) an instrument of foreign policy and by imbuing that proposal with moral necessity through the evaluative modal "should" (Palmer 2001: 154). The value of the postcolonial societies, consequently, is an instrumental value as Their future "can and should" be used in service of Our foreign policy goals. In sum, Their future is absorbed by Ours as an instrument that will enable the United States to realize its geopolitical purpose of creating "a world environment in which we ourselves can live freely, secure from both the menace of hostile states and from the distraction of chaotic ones" (Millikan and Rostow 1957: 7).

Millikan and Rostow further legitimate this American claim on the future of the "underdeveloped areas" by rendering it as a threat to the nation's security and prosperity. That is, they contend that in the postcolonial moment, the United States is confronted by "dangers and opportunities" in its "relations with the rest of the world" (2). Of interest here are the dangers, which manifest as two distinct Others: menacing "hostile states" that have the capacity and intention of engaging in "overt military aggression" against us (i.e., the Communist Bloc) and distracting "chaotic" states in which threats to our security and way of life could potentially "arise" (i.e., the underdeveloped countries; 2). As is typical of the discursive construction of threats, Millikan and Rostow's iteration draws upon the Self/Other trope to position the nation as the target of a threatening Other and, accordingly, to legitimate the means by which that threat will be addressed.

In what follows I demonstrate how Millikan and Rostow construed these threats in temporal terms. In brief, they render the threat of the "underdeveloped areas" as owing to their temporal location of past relative to the United States and the Soviet threat as stemming from its capacity to shape the future of newly decolonized societies in ways that run counter to American geopolitical interests. In this way, their articulation of danger, similar to Staley's, can be understood as engaging in the "an 'evangelism of fear' that emphasizes the unfinished and endangered nature" of portions of the postwar world (Campbell 1998: 61).

Millikan and Rostow draw on a future-oriented temporal lexis of aspiration, expectation, and hope to characterize the newly emerging states as currently lacking, yet desiring, a modern way of life. That is, Millikan and Rostow insist that, because they occupy a space-time that is past relative to that occupied by the West, the "underdeveloped areas'" desire and aspiration to move from past to future poses a geopolitical problem. As can be seen in the following excerpt, Millikan and Rostow construe global society as being, at present, "in the midst of a great world revolution" whereby the "bulk of the world's population" is transitioning from a state of political and economic stagnation to a process of active engagement with and control over their political and economic lives:

12. For centuries the bulk of the world's population has been *politically inert*. Outside America and Western Europe . . . until recently the pattern of society remained *essentially fixed*. . . . *The possibility of change for most people seemed remote*, political activity was confined to an extremely small elite. . . . This revolution is rapidly exposing *previously apathetic peoples to the possibility of change*. It is creating in them *new aspirations*. (4–5)

Millikan and Rostow draw on spatiotemporal concepts that render the "bulk of the world's population" as unable to progress through time and space: "politically inert" and "essentially fixed" in a social "pattern," they have been, heretofore, unable to imagine the "possibility" of change and grasp that their future could be different from their present. This perspective, the authors warn, is changing due to "previously apathetic peoples" experiencing "new aspirations" and understanding that a future different from the past and present is, in fact, possible. This realization, in turn, is transforming them from being passive and inert to aspirational and active. "The bulk of the world's population" is, indeed, "in ferment." This change in political disposition and consciousness is further construed through a texturing of tense and aspect that represents the political environment as in flux, as transitioning from a past state of stagnation—"remained," "seemed," "was confined"—to a dynamic present of generative processes—"is exposing," "is creating."

Emboldened by their "new aspirations" and the "possibility of change," the decolonizing societies are deemed a danger for U.S. foreign policy. This danger stems from the different space-times comprising the postwar moment, specifically the relationships that hold between the temporal status of the "underdeveloped areas" and that of the United States and the Soviet Union. That is, Milliken and Rostow render the "underdeveloped areas" as a problem for the United States by situating them in the temporal domain of past relative to both the United States and the Soviet Union.

As can be seen in the left-hand column of Table 4.2, Millikan and Rostow render the danger posed by the "underdeveloped areas" as a temporal threat centered on which future the "newly awakened" people in the "uncommitted areas" will orient themselves toward: a future of democratic capitalism or authoritarian communism. In Millikan and Rostow's formulation, this threat resides in the possibility that the "new" and "emerging aspirations," "rising expectations," "current hopes," and "awakening" of "formerly static peoples" will be realized "along lines hostile" not just to the United States but to the "West and Western tradition." Moreover, it derives from a lack of identification between the United States and the newly decolonized peoples who "no longer" identify their "aspirations" with the United States or see in America a "Utopian image of a society designed to satisfy those aspirations."

[88] *The Great Nation of Futurity*

Table 4.2. POSTWAR THREATS AND DANGERS

Underdeveloped areas	Soviet Union
"*The danger* is that increasing numbers of people will become convinced that *their new aspirations* can be realized only through violent change and the renunciation of democratic institutions." (5)	"[T]he Communists have recognized their opportunities to exploit the revolution of *rising expectations*." (5–6)
"[*T*]*he dangers* of instability inherent in *the awakening of formerly static peoples*." (6)	"All this is well-understood by the Communists, who concentrate their efforts not among those who are hopeless but *among those in whom expectations have been already aroused*." (20)
"The United States has come to be regarded increasingly in the uncommitted areas of the world as a power . . . which has no meaning for the *newly awakened* ordinary citizen." (6)	"The Communist line is *that these newly aroused expectations* can never be satisfied except under revolutionary Communist leadership." (20)
"We are no longer identified . . . with the *aspirations* of people for social and economic improvement or with their Utopian image of a society designed to *satisfy those aspirations*." (6)	"This line is carefully tailored to *whatever expectations and aspirations* turn out to be most powerful in the particular people they are trying to influence." (20)
"The constructive tasks . . . must relate to the *emerging aspirations* of all classes and all regions in the society." (27)	"[T]he Communist movement . . . *provide[s] outlets for the awakening energies* of young men previously denied opportunity by the rigid feudal class structure of their societies." (29)
"The fight against international communism is neither sufficiently meaningful nor sufficiently related to the *current hopes* of most of the peoples of the underdeveloped areas." (27)	"Moscow's method is to *associate itself ostensibly with the aspirations of the people* of the Free World for peace, economic progress, and political independence." (139)
"When one looks ahead over the next fifty to one hundred years . . . the danger is that the *underdeveloped countries develop along lines hostile to the West and Western tradition*." (141)	"In the Middle East *the association with unsatisfied national aspirations* is linked to credits, technical assistance, and trade . . ." (140)
"[T]he United States would confront a very grave set of problems *as the presently underdeveloped societies were modernized and strengthened*." (141)	"The present Soviet policy in the underdeveloped countries is based on a failure of the United States to associate itself with the *constructive aspirations of the peoples* in these areas." (145–146)

This danger, Millikan and Rostow insist, can be addressed through "efforts to produce political, social, and psychological results" among the peoples of the "underdeveloped areas" that will serve "the national interest" (1–2). Specifically, by aligning Their future with Ours, the United States can appropriate that future and, in so doing, "promote the evolution of stable, effective, and democratic societies abroad that can be relied upon not to generate conflict because *their own national interests parallel ours*" (4). Indeed, the successful pursuit of American interests in the postwar era lies in the "underdeveloped areas" having "aspirations for the values of individual dignity, national independence, and material welfare" (142). In Millikan and Rostow's scheme, such efforts, if successful, will transform the relationship between the United States and the "underdeveloped areas" from a relationship of conflict, "Them versus Us," to a relationship of identity, "Them as Us." Or, in Millikan and Rostow's terms, the relationship between the United States and the "underdeveloped areas" will be governed by "lines of association rather than conflict" (142).

Millikan and Rostow also render the Soviet threat in temporal terms by granting it coeval status with the United States. They invoke the alternative-futures trope by characterizing the Soviet Union, another modern industrial state, as threatening the future of the American system by offering a counter modernity that could meet the aspirations of the "underdeveloped areas." As can be seen in the right-hand column of Table 4.2, the Soviet Union is represented as able to make—indeed, as making—a claim on the future of the "underdeveloped areas" by associating itself with and "provid[ing] outlets for awakening energies," "newly aroused expectations," and "constructive" yet "unsatisfied" "national aspirations."

Millikan and Rostow insist, however, that although the United States and the Soviet Union are coeval, their underlying motives and the futures they offer are not in any way equivalent. Their morally evaluative lexis represents the United States as operating according to enlightened self-interest and, thereby, as offering a mutually beneficial future to the "underdeveloped areas." The Soviets, in contrast, are delegitimized by being characterized as exploitative, unprincipled (i.e., "whatever expectations and aspirations turn out to be most powerful"), and cynical ("this line is carefully tailored," "associate itself ostensibly"). According to the logic of the ideological square, if Their claim on the future of the newly decolonized peoples is imperialistic and self-interested, then Our claim must be democratic and altruistic. This contrast redounds in statements concerning the type of future each system offers, the means by which those futures will be realized, and their authenticity.

As can be seen in Table 4.3, the American future is rendered in wholly positive terms while the Soviet future is construed as unequivocally negative. Millikan and Rostow make this contrast by drawing on the "building metaphor," which, as noted in Chapter 3, conceptualizes "good governing" as

Table 4.3. ALTERNATIVE FUTURES FOR THE "UNDERDEVELOPED AREAS"

U.S. future	Soviet Union future
• "upward spiral of economic, political, and social development" (56)	• "downward spiral of stagnation and decay" (56)
• "viable, energetic and confident democracies throughout the Free world" (1)	• "violent change and renunciation of democratic institutions" (5)
• "healthy and mature" (4)	• "exploitation, compulsion, social disorganization" (5, 8)
• "building a better world" (7)	• "degenerative processes, destructive direction" (141, 8)
• "newly aroused energies steered in constructive directions" (8)	• "retrospective, focused on the battle symbols of the past" (27)

"creating" and bears temporal coding (Charteris-Black 2011: 205). Given that the United States is dedicated to "building a better world," it offers the "underdeveloped areas" a positive future that will lead in "upward" and "constructive directions" and comprise "viable, energetic and confident democracies" that are "healthy and mature." The Soviet future, however, is "degenerative" and "destructive" and will lead the "underdeveloped areas" "downward" to a state of "stagnation and decay," "violent change," and "exploitation." Moreover, the prospective outlook of the United States stands in stark contrast to the retrospective outlook of the Soviet Union, which, in fact, is not focused on the future but on "symbols of the past."

Despite the Their current infatuation with communism, it is the American system, Millikan and Rostow insist, that will lead the "underdeveloped areas" to the future they seek. They explain that the economic development plan they have developed will "pose" for "the leadership and the people of each country challenging and constructive internal tasks which *look to the future of their societies*" and will encourage them to "turn their constructive energies . . . to the *real problems of their own internal future*" (26–27). In making this argument, Millikan and Rostow have to reconcile the fact that their proposal is ultimately designed to serve the national interests of the United States with their insistence that it is not intended to create "societies abroad built in our own image" (131). As I will demonstrate, they do so by aligning the values, aspirations, and destinies of the "underdeveloped areas" with those of the United States, specifically, and the West, generally. This alignment, in turn, warrants the authenticity of Our system as the model for Their future.

Although Millikan and Rostow create a relation of difference between the United States and the "underdeveloped areas" by placing them at different points along the temporal trajectory of past/present/future, they also create a relation of identity by orienting them to the same future. This relation of identification is realized through a rhetoric of commonality and authenticity:

13. [T]he goals, aspirations, and values of the American people are in large part the same as those of peoples in other countries. (1)
14. [T]he authentic human striving for the values of democracy which ... characterizes virtually all the new nations (35)

Through the relational process clause in excerpt 13 Millikan and Rostow create a relationship of identity that equates the "goals, aspirations, and values of the American people" with "those of peoples in other countries." While this statement localizes and particularizes these values by linking them to the American people, excerpt 14 abstracts and universalizes them, first, by rendering them as "authentic human values" and, second, by associating them with "all new nations." In this way, Colonial America of the 18th century and postcolonial societies of the 20th century are identical in terms of the future they seek. The difference resides in the fact that America was the first "new nation" to realize this future.

Millikan and Rostow further note that the democratic values of "national independence and human liberty under law" are "fundamental principles" that, although it did not create them, the United States has been dedicated to throughout its history (8). They are values that have given America "a meaning and purpose which transcend" the nation's idiosyncratic needs and concerns (150). Consequently, the authors render the United States not as the creator of these values and principles but merely their servant. Although not the sole province of the United States, the vitality and perpetuation of democratic principles, nevertheless, depend upon the exceptional character of the United States, the nation that "represents a continuing, unique experiment in the development of free societies" (150–151). As such, the future of the "underdeveloped areas" rests ultimately with "the historic American sense of mission—a mission to see the principles of national independence and human liberty extended on the world scene" (8). For Millikan and Rostow, the American mission, and, by extension, their proposal, is grounded in a "sense of the community of human destiny," the belief that, in the words of Walt Whitman, "All peoples of the globe together sail, sail the same voyage, Are bound to the same destination" (as quoted in Millikan and Rostow: 151).

While Staley identified the future of the periphery as a central concern of the West, Millikan and Rostow placed that future at the heart of American foreign policy by rendering it as an instrument via which the nation could wage its battle with the Soviet Union. Their development scheme construed the geopolitical environment as comprising two Others that they identified as threats based on their temporal relationship to the United States. The threat posed by the "underdeveloped" countries stems from their occupying a space-time

[92]   *The Great Nation of Futurity*

of past relative to the United States; the threat from the Soviet Union derives from its coeval status with the United States and, thus, its offering an alternative future for the peoples of the periphery. Millikan and Rostow's proposal for how to counter these threats is rooted in the conviction that the American future represents the only authentic future for global society. They construe this authenticity by aligning the aspirations and desires of the periphery with American history, values, and experience, thereby identifying the American system as best able to meet those aspirations and desires. The Soviet claim on the future of the periphery, in contrast, is deemed inauthentic as it seeks only to exploit this future for its own geopolitical goals and interests. In the final part of my analysis, I examine how MT further established the legitimacy of the American future by examining how its historically and politically situated conception of societal development was rendered as inevitable and universal.

Lerner: Naturalizing and Universalizing the Future

The preceding analysis illustrated the linguistic means by which Millikan and Rostow constructed contrastive space-times and Self/Other pairings for the postwar geopolitical environment and used them to legitimate their proposal for the United States to direct the development of the newly decolonized societies. Another consequential spatiotemporal construct embedded in and deployed by MT involves a movement from the localized, contextualized space-time of policy to the universalized space-time of history. That is, Millikan and Rostow presented an explicitly contextualized account concerning the place and purpose of the "underdeveloped areas" in the postwar era, which construed their identity, meaning, and significance wholly from the vantage of the West, generally, and the United States, specifically. Moreover, their proposal instrumentalized the "underdeveloped areas" by rendering their future as a key means by which the goals of American foreign policy could be realized.

Lerner took a different tack. Rather than deploy Self/Other contrasts to legitimate the American future, he deployed the morally evaluative tactic of *naturalization* to construe a particular sociopolitical temporal order as "the natural order" (van Leeuwen 2008: 111). In so doing he removed the "underdeveloped areas" from the realm of geopolitics and placed them in the realm of history, at a particular moment in the natural, historical development of societies—that of "tradition." Concomitantly, earlier calls for Western-led development of the "underdeveloped areas" gave way to Lerner's effort to establish "modernization" as an autonomous historical process. The programs and agendas advocated by the antecedents to Lerner's work, consequently, were supplanted by "modernization," a historical fact that can be gleaned from a society's inevitable progress along a unilinear, universal temporal path that begins at "tradition" and culminates in "modernity." In Lerner's scheme, concerns over whether "traditional" societies would follow the United States or Soviet Union to the future were replaced by a conception of natural, inevitable progress that eventually moves all societies and peoples toward "a perfect state of things" (Alqvist and Rhisiart 2015: 97).

The following analysis examines the linguistic means by which Lerner objectified and reified the modernization process and, thereby, legitimated the American conception of the geopolitical future. He did so, I contend, by representing modernization "as a thing that has come about" on its own rather than as "a thing that is the effect of causal agents" (Fairclough 2003: 144). I begin by demonstrating how Lerner lexicalized the modernization process and then consider how he construed the causal factors underlying it.

Lerner opened his account by explaining what we "well ... know" about the past of the West, specifically how it became "modern":

15. Western men need only reflect on the titanic struggles whereby ... medieval lifeways *were supplanted by modernity* ... we know that *this historical sequence worked itself out* through millions of individual lives; that many suffered, others prospered, while their world *was being reshaped* in the modern image. In the end—and the end is not yet—all men of the West *had acquired a new style of life*. (43)

This statement provides a snapshot of how Lerner conceptualized the modernization process: in terms of an autonomous, nonhuman entity ("modernity," "this historical sequence") endowed with agentive capacity to engage in various material processes ("supplanted," "worked out," "reshaped") that have both negative ("suffered") and positive ("prospered") effects on people's lifestyles and worlds. Moreover, it is a "new style of life" that people can "acquire" but not create. What we don't see in this account is a rendering of modernization as a process undertaken and directed by human agents acting in a geopolitical context in pursuit of specific political and security goals. This synopsis of how the West modernized typifies Lerner's representation of the modernization process: objectified and reified representations that obfuscate agency and causality.

This construal of modernization was realized through Lerner's extensive use of the nominalization "modernization" and its cognates (i.e., "the process," "the model," "the sequence," "the larger historical order," "the modernizing sequence"). For example, in several statements the nominal "modernizing" is used as a participle modifying some entity or phenomenon: "modernizing Middle East," "modernizing societies," "modernizing trends," and "modernizing peasants." Lerner's account also contains numerous statements constructed as relational attributive process clauses in which "modernization" is reified as an entity that exhibits discernible features: "Modernization is a tangible fact"

[94] *The Great Nation of Futurity*

(44); "Modernization is the unifying principle" (45); "Modernization is out of phase" (401). As several discourse analysts have noted, representing processes through nouns (e.g., "modernization") rather than verbs (e.g., "modernize") has significant semantic and ideological implications for texts and discourses (Fairclough 2003; Kress 1995). In sum, nominalization obfuscates agency, responsibility, temporality, causality, and social divisions.

Lerner further reifies the process of modernization by positioning it as an actor engaged in a range of material actions. As a noun, "modernization" can take on the role of actor in the transitivity structure of a sentence and, thereby, function as an autonomous, animate agent that acts on a variety of objects and has a range of effects (Kress 1995). As can be seen in the following excerpts, "modernization" engages in a variety of material actions (supplanting, bringing, remedying, spreading, promising, and infusing) and acts on a variety of entities and phenomena (medieval life ways, questions and answers, pleasures and pains, disorder and poverty, vivid images, people, and new perceptions):

16. Western men need only reflect on the titanic struggles whereby, over the course of centuries, medieval lifeways *were supplanted by modernity*. (43)
17. [T]he varied questions and answers, pleasures and pains, *which modernization brings* into the lives of the people (44)
18. The disorder and poverty which rage in the Middle East . . . seem incapable of being *remedied* except . . . *by a general modernization* of these countries. (44)
19. [S]*preading* among a large public vivid images of its own New Ways *is what modernization distinctly does*. (45)
20. That some millions of Turks now live in towns, work in shops, wear trousers and have opinions . . . *is what modernization has already done* to some people. (46)
21. That other millions throughout the Middle East are yearning to trade in their old lives for such newer ways *is what modernization promises* to most people. (46)
22. The *values of modernity have infused* into the area a new perception of a desirable future. (405)

Moreover, Lerner's theoretical account mystifies the causal forces motivating and underlying modernization by making minimal use of causatives such as "make," "create," or "cause" that explicate the agency and causality of a process (Thompson 2004: 138). The following are the only instances in which a causative, or some variant thereof, is used:

23. Cities *produce* the machine tools of modernization. (61)
24. Cities *create* the demand for impersonal communication. (61)

25. When most people in a society have become literate, they tend to *generate* all sorts of new desires and to *develop* the means for satisfying them. (62)

Although they contain causal verbs, these statements do not clarify the causal dynamics of the modernization process. Statements 23 and 24, for example, identify the amorphous entity "cities" as agents that "produce" and "create" not modernization itself, but some of its key components—"machine tools" and "the demand for impersonal communication." In excerpt 25, we see literate people generate new desires and develop ways of realizing them; it's unclear, however, what agents and forces are acting on these people.

In excerpts 26–32, we see that Lerner's theory does include several material process clauses in which an agent is represented as taking (or as able to take) material actions associated with the modernization process:

26. [T]*he secular process of change*, which *brought* modernization to the Western World. (46)
27. *The experience of mobility* through successive generations gradually *evolved* participant lifeways which feel "normal" today. (49)
28. *The secular evolution of a participant society* appears *to involve* a regular sequence of three phases. (60)
29. Out of this interaction *develop* those *institutions of participation* which we find in all advanced modern societies. (60)
30. It is *the transfer of populations* from scattered hinterlands to urban centers that *stimulates* the needs and provides the conditions needed for "take-off" toward widespread participation. (61)
31. Take *the factor of physical mobility*, which *initiated* Western take-off in an age when the earth was underpopulated in terms of world man–land ratio. (65)
32. We have seen that *its [urbanization]* historic function is to *stimulate* take-off. (65)

For example, we see that the "secular process of change" "brought" modernization to the West and that "urbanization" can "stimulate take-off." Of interest here is that the majority of these statements imbue abstract phenomena with agentive capacity, namely, the "secular process of change," "the experience of mobility," "the secular evolution of a participant society," "institutions of participation," "the transfer of populations," "the factor of physical mobility," and "urbanization." Moreover, two of the abstractions, "the experience of mobility" and "the transfer of populations," are nominalizations of processes that would have had agents assigned to them had they been construed through a verb (e.g., people experienced mobility; populations were transferred to new areas). In the nominalized forms the people who "experienced" "mobility," the actors causing populations to transfer from the "hinterlands" to "urban

[96]   *The Great Nation of Futurity*

centers," and, most importantly, those people who were "transferred" are all omitted.

I want to close this portion of my analysis by considering Lerner's use of the journey metaphor to construe the modernization process. This rhetorical move coheres with and reinforces his representation of modernization as an autonomous, natural process. Moreover, it invokes a discourse about the future that posits the "teleological idea of an endless progress and a perfect state of things" (Alqvist and Rhisiart 2015: 97). In the statements in Table 4.4 we see that both the modernization process and the people and societies caught up in it are construed as being on a journey.

For Lerner, modernization is a phenomenon that travels across time and space, impacting the people and societies it encounters along its journey. Once modernization "takes off" and gets "underway" it makes "appearances" in "virtually all modernizing societies." Modernization doesn't travel alone, as it has a traveling companion, namely, the "characterological transformation" accompanying it. Moreover, the journey to modernization is not risk free, as

---

Table 4.4. LERNER'S JOURNEY METAPHORS

"A balanced process of modernization is *underway*." (401)

"the *coming* of modernization to the west" (44)

"old ways must *go*" (44)

"The same basic model *reappears* in virtually all modernizing societies." (46)

"the secular process of change, which *brought* modernization to the Western World" (46)

"But these *societies-in-a-hurry* have little patience with the historical *pace* of Western development." (47)

"These historical regularities some Middle East leaders now seek to obviate, trying instead *new routes* and *risky by-passes*." (47)

"Physical mobility so experienced naturally *entrained* social mobility." (48)

"This is an indispensable skill for people *moving out* of traditional settings." (50)

"They had to *learn their way* in these new settings." (50)

"It is the transfer of populations from scattered hinterlands to urban centers that stimulates the needs and provides the conditions needed for '*take-off*' toward widespread participation." (61)

"We have seen that its historic function is to stimulate *take-off*." (65)

"the enormous *hurdles in the path* to modernization" (65)

"how a country *moved* from one phase to the next" (69)

"the characterological transformation that *accompanies* modernization" (69)

"The Transitionals, at various phases of modernization, are *making their way toward* an unclear future via *a path replete with hard bumps and unsuspected detours*." (73)

"Their *voyage* entails a sustained commingling of joyous anticipations with lingering anxieties, sensuous euphoria with recurrent shame, guilt and puzzlement." (73)

"From their *changes of pace and shifts in direction*, we learn how to they perceive the *terrain*, its pitfalls and its promises." (73)

the path leading to it is fraught with "hurdles," namely, "societies in-a-hurry," which, frustrated by the "pace" of Western development, attempt to "obviate" the "historical regularities" by "trying new routes and risky by-passes." The journey is also precarious for those caught up in modernization's wake, as people "moving out of traditional settings" have to "learn their way" in more modern venues. "Transitionals," that is, people occupying the space between "traditional" and "modern," are themselves on a journey to an "unclear future." Indeed, the "path" they are on is "replete with hard bumps and unsuspected detours." While on this journey they experience a range of conflicting emotions and will change their "pace" and shift their "direction" as they traverse the "terrain" of modernization.

In Lerner's account, modernization is not created or caused to happen; it is a "fact of history," the inevitable outcome of societal development. At various moments and tempos, societies travel along a temporal path that has "tradition" as its starting point and "modern" as its endpoint. This trajectory has a "basic logic all its own: it presupposes that a destination is in view or in mind, and necessitates that it be reached by passing through certain points or stages" (Chilton 1996: 52). It's a trajectory that assumes that "history and time are linear paths" and that "the future is on this path" (Chilton 1996: 336). Finally, it is a process that grants very little agency to those it impacts: they are merely the "subjects of some force" who have been sent on a "mission" toward "some specified goal" (Chilton 1996: 52).

Lerner's use of the journey metaphor and his linguistic obfuscation of the causal and agentive aspects of the modernization process work together to mystify the Western approach to social and economic development—to elevate it beyond the political and ideological domain of postwar geopolitics and place it in the transcendent realm of history, fact, and truth. In sum, modernization, in Lerner's words, is a phenomenon that "follows an autonomous historical logic—that each phase tends to generate the next phase by some mechanism which operates independently of cultural or doctrinal variations" (61).

CONCLUSION

America's identity as the nation of the future was in full force in the Cold War policy of modernizing the "underdeveloped areas." My analysis of Staley's, Millikan and Rostow's, and Lerner's contributions to this effort demonstrates how this identity was used to justify an American claim on the future of the periphery and, thereby, on the postwar future.

Elaborating on President Truman's spatiotemporal designation of the newly decolonized societies as the "underdeveloped areas," Staley mapped out a sociopolitical temporal scheme that came to frame Cold War conceptions of postwar geopolitical development. This scheme embeds an ideology of time that construes Self and Other differently in terms of progress and modernization and, thereby, participates in "an economy of representation in which the modern is prized over—and placed over—the non-modern" (Gregory 2004: 4). By juxtaposing the "modern" and the "ancient" he identified a lack of coevalness as a threat to the West, broadly, and the United States, specifically. Mitigating this threat would require the nation to stake a claim on the future of the "ancient" peoples in order to ensure that they develop in ways amenable to Western interests and values. Consequently, the future of the "underdeveloped countries" was identified as the terrain upon which the Cold War battles would be waged. Through various linguistic and rhetorical devices—that is, the alternative-futures and Self/Other tropes, clause structure, moral lexis—Staley's discourse both aligned the future of the decolonizing societies with a Western political-economic system and implicated the future of that system in the development of the societies within the periphery.

For their part, Millikan and Rostow recontextualized and operationalized Staley's thesis about the geopolitical significance of the future of the decolonizing societies into a policy proposal and, thereby, instrumentalized that future. In so doing, they participated in the "colonizing of future times" by insisting that the primary value of the future of postcolonial societies resides in what it means for the United States rather than in what it means for the periphery (Andersson 2006: 281). Their policy discourse identifies two temporal Others—"chaotic" and "hostile" states—that, they asserted, would require the United States to take an active role in shaping the postwar future. Through spatiotemporal lexis and concepts, Millikan and Rostow represent the periphery as transforming from being stagnant and inert to being dynamic and aspirational. This transformation, in turn, rendered the periphery as a particular type of threat: a threat deriving from its *potentiality*, from what the people and societies of the periphery could *become*. They also construed the threat posed by the Soviet Union in temporal terms by identifying it as coeval with the United States and, thus, as offering an alternative future for the periphery. Millikan and Rostow's moral lexis and rhetoric of authenticity and commonality legitimated the American future as the postwar future. At the same time, purported efforts by the Soviet Union to aid the newly decolonized societies were deemed illegitimate through a moral lexis that rendered those efforts as regressive and authoritarian.

Lerner further legitimated America's claim on the future by construing modernization not as a process brought about by political actors driven by geopolitical interests and goals but as a natural, universal process that impacts all societies. He did so through linguistic and rhetorical devices that obscured agency and causality and reified and naturalized the modernization process. That is, his theory of modernization provided a narrative of the future that was "hermetically sealed within a causal matrix" deemed to be "beyond individual and social agency," a narrative that foretold the "inevitable developments on the historical horizon" (Bussey 2007: 56). By representing what was a geopolitically interested development scheme as a natural, inevitable process, Lerner provided a spatiotemporal framework that rendered the United States as the steward of a universal and mutually beneficial global future.

As noted earlier, MT held great appeal for policymakers in the context of postwar uncertainty, as it provided a metalanguage they could draw upon in developing the nation's foreign policy. This metalanguage was particularly helpful, Gilman (2003) argues, in addressing the "peculiar combination of anxiety and confidence about American ways of organizing the world" that circulated during the postwar moment (4). That is, while it was generally held that America should present itself as a model for others to follow, there was less clarity concerning how the nation should define itself, particularly in light of the challenges arising from its "geopolitical ideological competitors" (Gilman 2003: 4). MT offered both a means for fulfilling the nation's geopolitical role and an identity for rationalizing and justifying the necessity of that role. That is, by grounding its policy proposals in seemingly scientific "modern forms of divination," MT offered a strategy for "governing from the future" (Connelly et al. 2012: 1459; Andersson and Rindzeviciute 2015: 93). It rendered the future as knowable and controllable and, thus, as a "distinct temporal field . . . of human action, political will, and scientific rationality" (Andersson and Rindzeviciute 2015: 1–2). The future, then, was presented as a space in which and through which the United States could, at one and the same time, work to shape the geopolitical future and position itself as uniquely qualified for that global task.

In the early 1970s the relationship of radical difference embedded within MT and that underwrote American claims on the global future was being reimagined as a relationship of possible cooperation through the policy of detente. The possibility of a future of diminished hostility between the two superpowers was undercut, however, by a rhetorical and political campaign focused on reidentifying the Soviet Union as an existential threat to the United States and its geopolitical status and mission. The following chapter examines the discursive means by which this campaign was realized and how, by "resecuritizing" the Soviet Union, it reclaimed and reaffirmed America's privileged position vis-à-vis the global future.

[100]   *The Great Nation of Futurity*

CHAPTER 5

"Alerting America"

The Committee on the Present Danger and the

Re-Securitization of the Soviet Union

INTRODUCTION

This chapter focuses on the discursive efforts undertaken by the Committee on the Present Danger (CPD) during the period of detente to reposition the Soviet Union as the nation's radical Other and, concomitantly, to sustain America's global preeminence. The CPD project was a carefully orchestrated, highly consequential disciplining of the detente security environment that involved resituating the Soviet Union at the center of the nation's security policy and practice. Moreover, it involved reasserting the relationship of radical difference that the Committee insisted be held between the two superpowers and the fundamental identities from which that difference derived. This task involved two Self/Other contrasts: a less-than-radical Soviet Other / radical Soviet Other and American Self / Soviet Other. A central premise of the CPD's disciplining discourse was that the nation's leaders were relinquishing America's geopolitical role to the Soviet Union and, consequently, were placing the nation's, and the global community's, future at risk. By re-establishing the Soviet Union as America's radical Other, the Committee also sought to reaffirm the nation's exceptionalist identity and geopolitical purpose.

The first part of my analysis focuses on the spatiotemporal dimension of the CPD's discourse, specifically its projection of alternative futures to create relations of identity and difference between the two superpowers and its management of temporal distance to render the Soviet Union as an imminent threat. The second part examines the iterative nature of the CPD's "securitization" project by analyzing its antecedent articulation in NSC 68 and its

The Great Nation of Futurity. Patricia L. Dunmire, Oxford University Press. © Oxford University Press 2023.
DOI: 10.1093/oso/9780197658222.003.0005

contemporaneous rhetorical performance by Ronald Reagan. I argue that the CPD discourse construed the Soviet Union as a threat by re-identifying it as a radical Other capable of usurping the America's role vis-à-vis the geopolitical future. This threat, in turn, was used to legitimate a recommitment to an activist and interventionist approach to foreign policy. In what follows I contextualize the CPD and its work and then provide an overview of the concept of securitization that underlies the subsequent analysis.

DETENTE AND THE REASSERTION OF DIFFERENCE

As noted in Chapter 1, declarations of danger within foreign policy discourse are a key means by which the identity and legitimacy of the state is asserted, legitimated, and sustained (Campbell 1998: 13). That is, a state's existence and legitimacy depends upon a relentless, dynamic performance of identity that juxtaposes the identity of Self to some radical, threatening Other (Campbell 1998: 12). Because such performance is essential to the continued existence of the state, the security of the state, paradoxically, requires that it be seen as being in a perpetual condition of insecurity (Campbell 1998: 12). The accomplishment of "pure security" would mean that the state had achieved "stasis" and, thus, that "all identities would have congealed, all challenges evaporated, and all need for disciplinary authorities . . . would have vanished" (Campbell 1998: 12).

The 1970s were a period when the mainstream of the foreign policy establishment deemed the United States to be nearing a type of stasis: the relaxation of tensions with the Soviet Union. This period of "detente" ran from 1969 to 1979 and was embraced by the Nixon, Ford, and Carter administrations (Gaddis 2005: 286; Dalby 1990: 46). It saw the fading of the "Cold War vision" of an aggressive Soviet Other seeking global expansion as the nation's leaders sought to reset relations with America's superpower rival (Sanders 1983: 4). With the onset of detente came the transformation of how the relationship between the United States and Soviet Union was conceived. While the Cold War containment policy construed the relationship as one of divergent polarity, proponents of detente conceptualized it as one of convergence marked by cooperative engagement whereby both superpowers would work together toward a future of peace and stability (Sanders 1983: 163; Westad 2007: 415).

The diminishing of difference between the United States and the Soviet Union was seen by the CPD as a "clear and present danger" that imperiled not only the nation's security but also its geopolitical status, its mission of assuring global "peace with freedom," and, importantly, its exceptionalist identity (Tyroler 1984: xvi).[1] The Committee was adamant that the claims of detente were based on the "illusion" that the Soviet Union had changed,

[102] *The Great Nation of Futurity*

an illusion that had put the United States at risk of "becoming number 2" (Tyroler 1984: xx). Contrary to what others had asserted, the CPD held strong to the conviction that the Soviet Union continued to be "driven" by an "internal logic" that impelled it to seek global hegemony (Tyroler 1984: 14, 25).

The CPD was formed after President Carter's election and served as a "virtual shadow government" during his term in office (Sanders 1983: 8, 17). Its membership comprised opponents of detente who wanted to shape the nation's arms policy by re-establishing "a militarized doctrine of containment" as the foundation of the nation's foreign and security policy (Johnson 1983: 951; Sanders 1983: 8). Many CPD leaders and members subsequently joined the Reagan administration and served as the "architects and engineers" of his foreign policy (Sanders 1983: 8). The Committee described its purpose as primarily educational: to "facilitate a national discussion of the foreign and national security policies of the United Stated directed toward a secure peace with freedom" (Tyroler 1984: 1). Its work was guided by the conviction that "international stability and peace with freedom required a strong America— one that could and would deter Soviet adventurism and aggression" (Tyroler 1984: xvi).

As such, the CPD set about "alerting" Americans to the continued Soviet threat posed by its "alarming" military buildup—a threat that, in the Committee's view, proponents of detente had obscured and relegated to history. It viewed detente as an "aspiration" rather than a reality that could only be realized through a vigorous and rapid strengthening of the nation's strategic and conventional military forces. Such a military program, however, would require that the public and political leaders "see the world as it is": a world in which an expansionist Soviet Union was increasing its military and political power while America was neglecting its geopolitical responsibilities and ceding the geopolitical future to the Soviets (Tyroler 1984: xx). The overriding purpose of the Committee was to provide this clarity of vision by "alert[ing] American policymakers and opinion leaders and the public at large to the ominous Soviet military buildup and its implications, and to the unfavorable trends in the United States–Soviet military balance" (Tyroler 1984: xv). It did so, as I demonstrate, by reconstituting Cold War relations of identity and difference between the two superpowers.

THE TEMPORALITY OF SECURITIZATION

The identity/difference work of the CPD took place through the discursive process of "securitization." As defined by Buzan and Wæver (2003), securitization is a constitutive, rather than referential, communicative act "through which an intersubjective understanding is constructed within a political community to treat something as an existential threat to a valued referent object, and to enable a call for urgent and exceptional means to deal with the threat" (491). Rooted in speech act theory, the concept of securitization is based on the premise that the articulation of security constitutes a "crucial form of security action" because such articulations "structure the social practices that follow" (Stritzel 2007: 360). The mission of the CPD, then, can be understood as an effort to securitize, or, perhaps more accurately, re-securitize, the Soviet Union as the principal threat to the nation and to use that threat to legitimate particular foreign policy proposals and actions.

Securitization is at once a semiotic and disciplining process, as it serves to give meaning and clarity to the inherent ambiguity of sociopolitical life. For the CPD, such disciplining was needed to counter the broadening of the nation's security concerns ushered in by detente. Whereas Cold War security policy was keyed solely to Soviet actions and policies, detente put the focus on an amorphous array of issues and problems such as human rights, the environment, food, energy, and North–South relations. As Eugene Rostow,[2] a leading member of the CPD, explained in 1976, "the pressure of Soviet policy is increasing steadily, but the perception of the threat . . . has been diminishing" (as quoted in Sanders 1983: 162). This diminished perception, he warned, was at the "heart of our foreign policy problem today" (as quoted in Sanders 1983: 162). In short, through its wide-ranging "Soviet Threat Campaign" (Sanders 1983: 163), the CPD worked to re-securitize the Soviet Union by constituting Soviet capabilities, actions, and intentions as posing a "clear and present danger" to United States security.

My analysis of the CPD's securitization project assumes temporality to be a key modality through which this discursive practice operates. Temporality figures in the CPD project in three key ways: in the temporal orientation of its securitizing acts, as an axis along which relations of identity and difference are configured, and through the intertextual, iterative nature of securitizing practice.

As Balzacq (2011) explains, securitizing acts are temporally oriented in that their goal is to shape future behavior by setting up relationships between different temporal moments (24). They mediate the present through projections of the future and, concomitantly, mediate the future through depictions of the present. Securitizing actors essentially ask: What happens in the future if we do or do not take a particular action or pursue a particular policy in the present? (Buzan et al. 1998: 32). They answer this question both by projecting images of the future that render a given present action or policy as necessary and by offering up representations of the present that implicate a particular future as inevitable.

As explained in Chapter 1, temporality is also a factor in the construction of the relations of identity and difference essential to securitization. The CPD draws upon each of the "big concepts"—ethics, space, time—in its

[104]   *The Great Nation of Futurity*

construal of the Soviet Union as threat and the United States as the object of and counter to that threat (Hansen 2006: xx). Spatially, it renders the Soviets as violating both behavioral and territorial boundaries by insisting on its lack of self-restraint and noting its incursion into specific spaces. The United States, meanwhile, is represented as a disciplined, self-restrained global actor mindful of others' territorial integrity. In terms of ethical identity, the CPD consistently imputes suspect motives and goals to Soviet action and characterizes its behavior as exploitative and amoral. The United States, on the other hand, is rendered as a global actor that acts in the interest of universal human values.

As its name suggests, however, the Committee on the *Present* Danger draws heavily on the temporal axis to construe the Soviet threat. That is, the key rhetorical task facing the CPD is to create a symbiotic relationship between the present and two future moments, a distal future of "reality" and a proximal future of action. It must render the present as a moment of grave danger and the distal future as a moment in which that danger, if left unchecked, will become a reality. This projection of a catastrophic future, in turn, serves to compel and legitimate action in the proximal future. As we'll see, the CPD approached this task in two key ways: creating relations of identity and difference by juxtaposing the two superpowers vis-à-vis the future and construing present-ness in such a way that melds present and future and, thereby, renders the Soviet Union not just as a threat but as an *imminent* threat.

Temporality further enters into the CPD discourse through the intertextual, iterative nature of securitizing practice. As a discursive practice, a given securitizing act is not a one-off affair that occurs within the bounds of a particular moment; it is an iterative process that, if it is to take hold, must be enacted and sustained by multiple securitizing actors at different historical and discursive moments (Stritzel 2007: 366). It is a process that draws upon "the distinct linguistic reservoir" of prior and co-present discourses and texts and relies upon and perpetuates a series of "accepted visions" of what is to be secured, against which threats, and for what reasons (Stritzel 2007: 369; Kraus and Williams 1997: x). The discursive construction of threats, then, is a multiply articulated process that unfolds across time. Moreover, while a given threat articulation takes place within the context of its present, it also has a history and a future, as it exceeds the boundary of the present by drawing upon prior articulations and shaping subsequent ones. The second section of my analysis examines the iterative and intertextual nature and function of the CPD project by identifying the intertextual links between the CPD's securitization discourse and the prior securitizing effort made through NSC 68. I then examine the ways in which Ronald Reagan served to legitimate the CPD project through his rhetorical performance of the nation's exceptionalist identity.

THE RE-SECURITIZATION OF THE SOVIET UNION
Mediating Identity and Difference Through Projections of the Future

Contrasts between American and Soviet space-times are a central component of the CPD's securitizing discourse. These contrasts draw on the alternative-futures trope to render the Soviet Union as an existential threat and underline the need for the United States to take action against it. Moreover, the Committee contrasts the United States' and Soviet Union's competing claims on the future and the futures implicated in those claims in a way that legitimates the American claim and undermines the Soviet claim.

As noted earlier, proponents of detente saw the interests and goals of the United States and Soviet Union as converging and, thus, as moving toward a mutually compatible future. From this perspective the Soviet Union had become a "less-than-radical" Other (Hansen 2006: 49). The CPD, however, insisted that this purported convergence was "a figment of political imagination" that risked the very survival of the free world (Tyroler 1984: 36). In short, it warned against the United States "mortgaging our security and our future to hopes of fundamental change in the Soviet Union" (Tyroler 1984: 25). This insistence that the Soviet Union had not, indeed, could not, change is emphasized throughout the CPD documents:

1. *It continues, with notable persistence,* to take advantage of every opportunity to expand its political and military influence throughout the world. (3)
2. Its objectives are global . . . and its ability to pursue long term objectives while exploiting short term opportunities *remains unchanged.* (14)
3. The ideological members of the other committee [Team A] . . . believe that the Soviet Union . . . has undergone a very fundamental change which makes our . . . old views of the Soviet Union no longer realistic. *No such constitutional changes have occurred* in the Soviet Union since the death of Stalin . . . *we do not see a changed structure.* (25)
4. *The notion that there has been a change* for the better in Soviet–American relations since 1972 *is persiflage, or worse—a figment of political imagination.* (30)

I want to consider here how the concept of change figures in the Self/Other dynamic embedded in the CPD documents. As explained in Chapter 3, relations of identity and difference aren't construed solely between Self and a co-present radical Other (Buzan et al. 1998; Hansen 2006; Wæver 1996); they can also involve contrasts between different temporal versions of Self and Other. In that chapter, we saw the Self/Other trope take shape as a difference between two American Selves: an active Self identified by its proactive posture toward the geopolitical future and a passive Other that rejected that

[106]   *The Great Nation of Futurity*

identity. In its efforts to re-securitize the Soviet Union, the CPD juxtaposes two temporal Soviet Others: a past Soviet Union that threatened the United States and a present Soviet Union that no longer poses that threat. Through its declaration that the Soviet's "long term objectives remain unchanged," The CPD rejects the idea that the Soviet Union of the 1970s is America's less-than-radical Other, insisting that it must be understood to be the same Soviet Union that animated the Cold War. By insisting on the immutable character of the Soviet Union, the CPD sought to restore the American Self / Soviet Other dynamic to its original Cold War form. In this view, the relationship between the two superpowers was a relationship of radical, irreconcilable difference owing to the Soviet "ideology which views the modern age as the time of a life and death struggle between 'capitalism' and 'socialism'" (167).

By rejuvenating this Self/Other dynamic, the CPD also reoriented geopolitical space-time away from a future of cooperation between East and West back to a future of antagonism and conflict. As we'll see below, the Committee deploys the future as the domain of contest in which the legitimacy of the two superpowers' geopolitical goals and character are presented, contrasted, and vetted (4). Specifically, it presents contrasting construals of American and Soviet claims on the global future, their different visions of that future, and their divergent positions concerning a particularly catastrophic future.

In the following excerpts, the CPD presents both the Soviet claim that it is the true nation of the geopolitical future and the purported objectives for and consequences of that future:

5. The Soviet leadership asserts that it is *the vanguard* of a revolutionary society which has discovered *the fundamental laws of history.* (11)
6. Soviet theory holds that the Soviet Union is *the vanguard* of *"progressive"* socialist forces of the world. (43)
7. The Soviet Union *is consciously seeking* . . . a "visible preponderance" for the Soviet sphere. Such a preponderance . . . will permit the Soviet Union *"to transform the conditions of world politics" and determine the direction of its development.* (4)
8. The ultimate Soviet objective is *the worldwide triumph of Communism.* This triumph would . . . *do away with* . . . *all alternative political and social systems.* (11)
9. Soviet pressure . . . would be aimed at forcing our *general withdrawal from a leading role* in world affairs, and *isolating us* from other democratic societies, which *could not then long survive.* (14)

According to the CPD, the Soviet threat stems, in part, from its claiming the "vanguard" mantle and the geopolitical consequences of that claim going unchecked. Moreover, the threatening nature of this claim derives from the fact that it represents a direct challenge to the claim on the future made by the United States. Indeed, if allowed to occupy this role and pursue its objectives, the Soviet Union would "transform . . . world politics and determine" the "direction" of the geopolitical future, a future that would be devoid of "all alternative political and economic systems." Furthermore, by marginalizing and isolating the United States, this Soviet future would create a geopolitical environment in which the world's democracies "could not then long survive." The future viability of democracy around the world is thus construed as dependent upon the United States continuing in its role as the exemplar of democracy.

While the Soviet's designs on the future are rendered by the CPD as specious, imperialistic, and hegemonic, American claims are presented as genuine, universal, and democratic:

10. There is a crucial moral difference between the two superpowers in their character and objectives. The United States—imperfect as it is—*is essential to the hopes of those countries who desire* to develop their societies in their own ways, free of coercion. (4)
11. American strength holds the key to *our quest for peace and to our survival* as a free society in a *world friendly to our hopes and ideals*. (15)
12. The foreign policy of the United States . . . draws its substance from *taproots deep in the American earth*, from the *principles and ideals* which make this nation what it is. (173)
13. America is more than a superpower. The idea of the United States is *a living part of Western civilization*, with a *compelling and altogether special history which belongs to all who cherish human liberty*. (173)

The Committee grounds the nation's claim on future in the discourse of American exceptionalism by noting that the nation's foreign policy has "taproots deep in the American earth" and that the values guiding its foreign policy are grounded in its foundational "principles and ideals." "America," the Committee emphasizes, isn't "just a superpower"; it is an "idea . . . a living part of Western civilization" that has a "compelling and altogether special history that belongs to all who cherish human liberty." The CPD also draws on a lexis of hope, desire, and survival to align American ideals and history with those of global society, insisting that the nation's "special history" is "essential to the hopes of those countries which desire to develop . . . free of coercion." Moreover, it is the nation driven by a "quest for peace" that will ensure "our survival" by creating a world "friendly to our hopes and ideals." Consequently, America "holds the key" both to global society's "quest for peace" and to the nation's "survival as a free society in a world friendly to our hopes and ideals." America, in short, is the democratic society without which "other democratic societies . . . could not then long survive."

[108]   *The Great Nation of Futurity*

The CPD further construes the "crucial moral differences" between the United States and the Soviet Union through assertions about the future each "sees" emerging from the present:

14. The two superpowers have utterly opposing conceptions of the world order. The United States, true to its traditions and ideals, *sees a world moving toward peaceful unity and cooperation* within a regime of law. The Soviet Union, for ideological, as well as geopolitical reasons, *sees a world riven by conflict and destined to be ruled exclusively by Marxist-Leninism.* (40)

Through evaluative lexis, the CPD offers a projection of a Soviet future that directly opposes that of the United States. While the United States sees "peaceful unity and cooperation," the Soviet Union sees "a world riven by conflict." While the United States sees a future developed and governed "within a regime of law," the Soviets see a future "destined to be ruled exclusively by Marxist-Leninism." Finally, while the American future is devoted to the nation's "traditions and ideals," the Soviet future is rooted in "ideological" and "geopolitical" expediency.

The fundamental difference between the two superpowers is put into full relief through the CPD's positioning of each relative to an unimaginable future, namely, a future in which nuclear war is not only waged but won and survived. The CPD explains that the two global powers "do not share" the same position regarding this devastating future (207). For the United States, a future in which a nation would fight a nuclear war in the belief that it could both survive and win is unimaginable.[3] The Soviets, however, "look at the world quite differently" (207). In the following excerpts, we see the CPD using a catastrophic projection of the future to mediate and dramatize the stark contrast between Us and Them, as well as the continued role the Soviet Union occupies as America's, and the free world's, radical Other:

15. Soviet literature tells us that the Soviets *do not agree* with the Americans *that nuclear war is unthinkable and unwinnable.* (42)
16. They believe that the best deterrent is the capacity *to win and survive*, were deterrence to fail. (42)
17. The crucial difference . . . lies in the Soviet recognition that . . . the Soviet Union must prepare *to fight, survive and win, even in nuclear conflict.* (42)
18. The Soviets must prepare for *nuclear war-fighting, war-surviving, and war-winning.* (207)
19. The Soviets therefore plan on the assumption that *war is quite possible, and they are prepared to resort to any means, including nuclear, to win a war.* (207)

The danger facing the United States and its allies does not reside solely in the future the Soviet Union is oriented to and can imagine, however. The alternative futures identified in the preceding analyses are, after all, relatively remote from the present, as they represent the goals, objectives, and aspirations each superpower is working toward. The real danger lies in the present-ness of the Soviet future, in its proximity to the "now" of the 1970s and the progress the Soviet Union is making toward it. In what follows, I examine how the CPD's securitizing discourse construes the present-ness of the Soviet threat and manipulates the temporal space between present and future in order to reinforce the imminence of that threat.

The Future-in-the-Present: Constructing Present-Ness, Implicating the Future

In its 1977 paper "What's the Soviet Union Up To?" the CPD acknowledges that "To be sure, *at present* the Soviet Union lags behind the United States in both productive capacity and many areas of weapons technology" (13). It qualifies this assessment, however, by warning that "our lead in these particulars may not last forever" (13). In this statement we see a construal of geopolitical space-time according to which the present is defined by American global dominance and the future as a moment when that dominance could be lost to the Soviets. The following analysis focuses on how the CPD transforms this *moment* of dominance into a "*period* of peril." It does so, I contend, by construing the present in such a way that presages an ominous future, a point at which the United States would have forfeited its military and political advantage to the Soviet Union. Of further interest is how the CPD animates and amplifies this precarity. How does it "alert" the nation's leaders and citizens of the impending threat, to a danger that "is increasing?" This rhetorical effect is realized, in part, through contrastive construals of Soviet and American present action and projections of the future implicated in those actions. In brief, the CPD renders the present moment as defined by a highly determined Soviet Union actively working to increase its military and political power and a moribund United States seemingly willing to forfeit its position as the world's dominant military and political power.

The CPD documents are rife with statements depicting the material actions the Soviet Union is pursuing. In these statements the Soviets are rendered as engaging in a host of material processes intended to expand its military capacity and strengthen its global status. Table 5.1 presents a sampling of these statements. By construing these actions through the present progressive aspect the CPD depicts a "situation in progress" (Comrie 1976: 33). Soviet action is presented from "within, as the action unfolds" and as continuous rather than as a "completed whole" ("sought," "pursued"; Comrie 1976: 51). This

[110]   *The Great Nation of Futurity*

Table 5.1. PRESENT PROGRESSIVE SOVIET ACTIVITY STATEMENTS

- "The Soviet Union *has been acquiring* a network of positions . . . which support their drive for dominance." (4)
- "Soviet Union *has been enlarging and improving* both its strategic and conventional military forces." (4)
- "The Soviet Union *is consciously seeking* . . . visible preponderance for the Soviet sphere." (4)
- "The pressures of Soviet imperial ambition . . . *are threatening* the world balance of power." (29)
- "The Soviet military budget *is growing*." (29)
- "*are vigorously* pursuing ABM [anti-ballistic missile] research and development" (43)
- "[T]hey *are moving* toward a counterforce damage-limiting capability." (43)
- "[T]hey *are developing* larger bombers, submarines and submarine missiles." (47)
- "*is significantly increasing* the capabilities of its phased-array ABM 'early warning' radars." (135)

- "Some 1200 of these missiles *are being produced*." (52)
- "These air defenses *are continually being modernized*." (56)
- "*is continuing to build and modernize* its strategic nuclear missile force at an alarming rate (59)"
- "[T]he Soviet ability to do this . . . *is increasing rapidly*." (63)
- "*are substantially outspending* us in research and development" (82)
- "*are catching up* in some areas and forging ahead in others" (69)
- "*are succeeding* in closing the military technology gap" (83)
- "[T]he rate at with the Soviet Union *is increasing and improving* its nuclear arsenal." (87)
- "*is willing to devote* the resources necessary to maintain military superiority" (208)

sense of continuousness ("has been acquiring," "is consciously seeking") is reinforced through a lexis of determination and persistence as the CPD explains, for example, that the Soviets "will *continue* their military build-up with *no diminution of effort or determination*" (206).

Although continuous and persistent, Soviet actions will not necessarily continue indefinitely. That is, the present progressive aspect renders action as contingent upon situational factors and, thus, as potentially temporary (Comrie 1976: 38). The Committee makes this very point, explaining that "USSR will continue its program of expansionism *unless and until we are able to confront it*" (172, emphasis added). Had Soviet action been represented as a completed past action—"forged ahead," "increased," "expanded"—it would have been rendered as an accomplishment realized in the past that, although it can be responded to, can no longer be prevented or stopped. The use of the present progressive, however, depicts activity as it is happening and, thereby, allows for the possibility that something can be done to hinder or prevent the unfolding process coming to fruition. Consequently, the present moment is represented as one in which the Soviet Union is engaging in ominous actions that it will continue pursuing unless something is done to challenge or stop it. In this way, the use of the present progressive adds a dynamic dimension to the present moment, thereby, amplifying and underscoring the necessity of the CPD's proposals.

The representation of Soviet action contrasts markedly to that of U.S. action. The left-hand column of Table 5.2 contains all the statements in the CPD documents in which the nation's material activity is rendered through the present progressive aspect. These statements, which have a primarily negative gloss, emphasize that the ability of the United States to check the Soviet Union's growing domination is being compromised through actions that undermine its own military strength. Moreover, as can be seen in the right-hand column, the United States has completed actions in the past that have severely compromised the present state of the nation's security.

The use of the present progressive doesn't just depict the present moment, however. It also provides a window onto a future in the making, a projection of where the world is currently headed and where it will end up if its trajectory is not altered. Indeed, according to the CPD, the actions the Soviets are pursuing, and those the United States is not, point to ominous "trends" regarding the geopolitical future:

Table 5.2. UNITED STATES ACTIVITY STATEMENTS

Present progressive	Present perfect
• "[W]e *are spending* . . . ⅓ as much as during the six years from 1958–1964." (32)	• "[W]e *have frozen* our ICBM forces." (25)
• "[T]he United States appears *to be retreating* to a posture of 'finite deterrence,' perhaps even to a 'fortress America.'" (43)	• "[W]e *have deactivated* and partially dismantled our sole permitted ABM site." (43)
	• "*have closed* our Minuteman production line" (47)
• "[A]new generation of United States tactical aircraft . . . *is currently being built and deployed.*" (69)	• "*have delayed* the development of the . . . mobile MX" (47)
	• "[W]e *have cancelled* the B-1." (47)
• "*is just starting deployment* of anti-ship cruise missiles" (80)	• "[T]he United States *has cancelled* the B-1." (54)
• "[T]he United States economy *is operating* well below capacity." (87)	• "[T]he number of United States ships *has declined* precipitously." (78)
• "a United States strategic program that *is struggling* with production" (90)	• "[T]he United States *has phased out* most of its continental air defense capabilities." (135)
• "[W]e *are pursuing* a policy built on illusion, adrift and uncertain." (174)	• "[T]he Congress *has forced* the virtual deactivation." (135)
• "[T]he United States *is just beginning to produce* sea-launched cruise missiles." (212)	• "[T]he number of U.S. ships *has declined.*" (78)
	• "[M]ilitary expenditures *have declined.*" (87)
	• "[T]he United States *has continued to retreat.*" (171)

[112] *The Great Nation of Futurity*

20. The *unfavorable trends* in the United States—Soviet Union military balance (xv)
21. If, then, we permit *these clear trends* to materialize, we may expect to lose the "battle of perceived capabilities." (63)
22. *Trends* are running in their favor. (83)

What we see in the CPD's rendering of the present moment is the potential forfeiting of the global future by the United States to the Soviet Union. That is, the Committee's securitizing discourse construes the present moment in such a way that it serves as warning about the future of the nation's geopolitical role and identity: if the nation's leaders do not change course, they will relinquish America's identity as the nation of the future to the Soviets. In the following section, I consider how the urgency of the present moment is further amplified through metaphorical construals of U.S. and Soviet activity.

Time as Resource: Managing Temporal Distance

Research on language and cognition has long recognized that time is conceptualized spatially with *space* serving as the source domain and *time* as the target domain (Lakoff and Johnson 1980). Accordingly, the passage of time is rendered as movement through space. Nunez and Sweetser (2006) argue that this metaphorical conception of time implicates two "reference points": Time Reference Point and Ego Reference Point. The latter is of particular relevance here. Specifically, the CPD draws on the conceptual metaphor TIME PASSING IS MOTION both to conceptualize the nature of the present danger posed by the Soviet Union and to amplify its calls to action.

In the Ego Reference Point metaphor, time passing is conceived of as the relative motion between "ego," that is, an observer or experiencer of time, and "the times" (Nunez and Sweetser 2006: 409). This metaphor manifests as two variants, the "moving-time variant" and the "moving-ego variant" (Nunez and Sweetser 2006: 411). In the moving-time variant, time moves relative to a static observer (e.g., January is fast approaching), while in the ego-moving variant, the observer/experiencer moves relative to temporal moments located along a linear path of past, present, future (e.g., "We are approaching the end of the season"; Nunez and Sweetser 2006: 409). The authors further explain that regardless of whether a given temporal moment is construed as approaching the observer or an observer is construed as approaching a temporal moment, the "metaphorical distance" between the observer and a given temporal moment "gets shorter as the action 'approaching' takes place" (Nunez and Sweetser 2006: 411).

Key to the CPD's rhetorical strategy of alerting the nation to the "present" danger is transforming this metaphorical distance from a neutral, empty space between two temporal moments into a highly consequential space in which the fate of the world will be determined. This transformation is accomplished through two rhetorical moves: conceptualizing time as a resource in such a way that lessens the distance between now and future and contrasting the ways the two superpowers are moving through that space.

The CPD creates a sense of urgency by conceptualizing time as a diminishing resource and, thereby, lessening the distance between the present moment in which the United States is the world's leading superpower and the future moment when it will have become "second best." As can be seen in Table 5.3, the Committee notes that while "there is still time," "time is growing short." Indeed, it cautions against the belief that time is an infinite resource—"there is always time"—and false assurances that there is "plenty of time." The problem, as the CPD sees it, is that although the nation has enough time in the mid-1970s, its supply is dwindling. The Committee points out that in 1976 "there is still time for effective action" (3). It warns, however, that the "factors of time and timing in a nuclear exchange" have put added pressure on the nation's temporal stocks; consequently, "'enough' may not be 'enough' and 'time' may run out" as the nation's temporal stocks near depletion (37, 15).

The notion that the distance between now and future is decreasing has implications for the possibility of action; that is, temporal distance can be understood as providing a space in which action can be taken to ward off a potentially negative future. We can understand time and temporal distance, then, as a resource and a space, respectively, for action and, as such, as very much tied to security. When time is "on our side" or when we have "enough" time, the ability to affect the future is possible. Effective action becomes increasingly less likely when time is deemed to be "running out," that is, when the space between now and future narrows. If one has enough time, one is secure; one becomes increasingly less secure if they are "short" on time. Concomitantly,

---

Table 5.3. TIME AS RESOURCE

• "[T]here *is still time* for effective action." (3)	• "*still have time* . . . but that *time is growing short*" (177)
• "[O]ur lead . . . may not *last forever*." (13)	
• "[T]he erroneous conviction . . . that *there is always 'time'* . . . could prove to be fatal shortsightedness." (14)	• "[W]ill their leaders chart an adequate course . . . *in time*?" (177)
	• "[T]he Carter program would provide *too little, too late*." (203)
• "[I]n the nuclear age 'enough' may not be 'enough' and '*time*' *may run out*." (15)	• "turn it [the decline] around *in time*" (208)
• "while there *is still time*" (29)	• "[T]here *is still time*." (175)
• "[A] point *has now been reached*." (172)	• "should be wary also about the assurance of there being *plenty of time*" (111)
• "[T]he *time has come*." (174)	

---

[114]   *The Great Nation of Futurity*

crisis ensues when temporal resources are deemed to be dwindling; crisis can be averted, however, if the necessary and appropriate actions are taken to restock supplies.

In its efforts to create a sense of "urgency of action" among politicians and policymakers, the CPD further manipulates the distance between present and future by invoking the concept of a "window of vulnerability" (Johnson 1983: 956). As can be seen in the following excerpts, it repeatedly urges action that would "close" the window of vulnerability "firmly and without delay" and insists that doing so will prevent the Soviets from taking advantage of the "window of opportunity" current inaction by the United States was providing them:

23. [T]he trends can be reversed and the window of vulnerability closed. (206)
24. The Soviets might perceive a time-limited window of opportunity. (206)
25. close the window of vulnerability before it opens any wider. (202)
26. The window of vulnerability is really being expanded by (the [Carter] administration's strategic) programs. (202)
27. a strategic "window of vulnerability," which, under the Carter program, would extend from the early 1980s well into the late 1980s (203)
28. [T]his window must be closed firmly and without delay. (203)
29. failure to close the window of vulnerability firmly and rapidly (235)

The idea of a window of vulnerability is grounded in the CPD's belief that "historical precedent" no longer provides a viable guide for predicting future Soviet behavior; assessing "current Soviet actions" is the only way to evaluate the "prospects of war" between the United States and Soviet Union (Johnson 1983: 951, 953). While the phrase "window of vulnerability" was first used by a Pentagon analyst in 1978, the Committee deployed the concept as a means for compelling a pro-detente "complacent Administration" from "lethargy" to "action" (Johnson 1983: 965, 967). The concept's rhetorical force involves projecting a future "period of peril" during which the strategic balance of power will have shifted in the Soviet's favor (Johnson 1983: 956).

The period, which is "near at hand," begins at the moment when the Soviet Union is estimated to have achieved "a significant new [nuclear] capability" that leads to American vulnerability; it ends when the United States eliminates this vulnerability by regaining its military preeminence (Johnson 1983: 956). Thus, while this time period represents a window of vulnerability to the United States, it provides a window of opportunity during which a "confident, bold, venturesome" Soviet Union can pursue "programs of expansion" throughout the globe (Johnson 1983: 955). According to the CPD's "prediction of future danger," the window of vulnerability facing the nation would "extend from the early 1980s well into the late 1980s" (Johnson 1983: 967). As Johnson (1983) argues, the rhetorical and material power of this temporal construct lies in its creating "timetables of future dangers" that transform "a false precision" into "undue alarm" (961).

Conceptualizing time as a dwindling resource implies that there is a point in the future when the nation's temporal stocks will be fully depleted. As noted earlier, from the vantage of the late 1970s, this moment is quickly approaching with the inception of the 1980s, the new decade in which the United States will enter "a period of danger" created by a change in the balance of strategic nuclear weapons (3). Looking forward from 1978, the CPD sees a moment when the Soviets will have "exploited their advantage in the international balance of power against the United States and its allies" (87). Although perilous, the coming decade is not totally devoid of hope, as it is "the period in which the effects of present programs can reasonably be foreseen and also the earliest time at which near-term changes to the defense program could influence the balance" in military power (41).

As the preceding analysis demonstrates, the CPD narrowed the metaphorical space between now and future and, concomitantly, the amount of time needed for actors to move through that space: America in the 1970s was quickly approaching its future as a secondary world power. The lessening of the distance between now and future is given added urgency through contrasts the CPD sets up between the pace and direction of Soviet movement relative to that of the United States. To begin with, it renders the nation's temporal inventory as being further taxed by the "tempo" and "momentum" of Soviet activity. Not only are the Soviets engaging in persistent, continuous activity; they are doing so at an "alarming rate":

30. The scope and sophistication of the Soviet campaign have been increased in recent years and *its tempo has quickened*. (3)
31. We know that the Soviet Union is continuing to build and modernizing its strategic missile force *at an alarming rate*—150–200 ICBMs a year as compared to *a rate of zero* for the United States. (59)
32. The trends in Soviet policy . . . have continued with *accelerating momentum*. (170)

In light of the Soviets' frenetic pace, the Committee warns that if the nation were to "relax," it would be doomed to live in a world in which the Soviets would be in a position to "transform the conditions of world politics and determine the direction of its development" (30, 4).

Moreover, while both superpowers are construed through the ego-moving metaphor and, thus, as actively moving through time, the CPD, as I will demonstrate, characterizes that movement as both differently oriented and infused with different degrees of commitment, determination, and energy. In short, while the Soviet Union is rendered as rapidly driving toward a future in which it will have achieved "ascendancy over U. S. strategic forces" (115), the

[116] *The Great Nation of Futurity*

United States is construed as retreating from its "position of strength" as the world's leading military and political power (30).

According to the temporal models embedded in English, the future is conceptualized as in front of ego, while the past is conceived as behind ego (Lakoff and Johnson 1980). Given this, the statements in Table 5.4 can be understood as rendering the present as a moment in which the Soviet Union, engaging in actions such as "drive," "forge ahead," and "lunge," is on a forward trajectory, actively moving toward the future unimpeded by a foreign

Table 5.4. SOVIET UNION DRIVE, U.S. RETREAT

Soviet Union drive	U.S. retreat
• "is organized on different principles and *driven* by different motives" (10) • "[I]t *is driven* by international, historical, and ideological pressures toward an expansionist policy." (14) • "*its drive* for global domination" (40) • "*driven* both by deep-rooted Russian imperialist impulses and by Communist ideology" (40) • "[T]he Soviet Union is intent to go about as far as it can go in *its drive* for strategic ascendancy." (96) • "the Soviet goal in *the drive* for . . . 'a visible preponderance of military power'" (41) • "the Soviet *drive* for strategic superiority" (89) • "the spreading Soviet *drive* for military and political domination" (176) • "has shown a *determination to forge ahead*" (13) • "[T]he Soviet Union *has moved forward* since 1970 with increasing boldness." (30) • "as the Soviet Union *has moved forward*" (171) • "a world crisis caused by the Soviet Union's *lunge* for dominance" (178) • "The *major expansive thrusts* the Soviet Union supported" (65) • "its *endless, probing quest*" (40) • "*has consistently striven* to attain overwhelming strategic superiority" (168)	• "appears to be *retreating* . . . to a posture of 'finite deterrence,' or perhaps even to 'fortress America'" (43) • "has *continued to retreat*" (171) • "*has turned away* from the foreign policy pursued by Truman" (171) • "an unwillingness to . . . hold its [Soviet Union] *drive* in check" (171) • "is still unwilling . . . *to move forward* with programs capable of arresting and containing *the Soviet drive*" (179) • "[W]e can, of course, *retreat* to fortress America." (26) • "a choice between *retreat* and a nuclear war" (41) • "has . . . by . . . *acts of restraint*, taken one unilateral step after another in the hope that the Soviet Union would accept such a policy of restraint for itself" (172) • "in recent years has appeared *to be retreating* toward a minimal defensive posture" (208) • "Pursuing a policy built on illusion, we *have been adrift and uncertain*." (174) • "If we *continue to drift*, we shall become second best." (235) • "Our *waning* capabilities" (64) • "The United States has *restrained* its research, development and weapons deployment programs." (17)

policy defined by an "unwillingness to . . . hold [the Soviet Union's] drive in check" (171). The Soviet Union is a determined global actor that "has moved forward" and is making tangible progress toward attaining its ultimate goal of a "visible preponderance of military power," "overwhelming strategic superiority," and "global domination." The United States, "adrift and uncertain," is on a backward trajectory, as it "has continued to retreat" away from the future. Having assumed a "posture of 'finite deterrence,'" it is a global actor that is in danger of "becom[ing] second best." In fact, because it has "closed," "cancelled," and "delayed" a host of weapons programs and military installations, the CPD avers that the nation "has already reached that unenviable position" (171). In sum, the Committee declares that in the present moment "the one side"—the United States—is "marking time" and, thus, "retreating . . . to a 'fortress America,'" while "the other forges ahead and upwards" toward its "global objectives" (102, 43).

As the analysis presented in this section demonstrates, the CPD's temporal play serves as an "anticipatory regime" that projects "a future that may or may not arrive . . . yet is necessarily coming" (Adams et al. 2009: 249). This future of "entanglements of fear and hope" is uncertain yet inevitable and, thus, "demand[s] a response" (Adams et al. 2009: 249, 259). Moreover, by cautioning that "things could be (all) right if we only anticipate them properly," the CPD renders the future of the 1980s as a "site for active intervention" (Adams et al. 2009: 259).

As Hodges (2015) notes, although an individual actor can produce a "single authoritative pronouncement" about a particular threat or problem, such pronouncements do not stand on their own (54). The elevation of such claims to "the status of a widely accepted truth" requires a "chain of authentication" (Hodges 2015: 54–55). That is, they must enter into and be bolstered by "a historical sequence of reiterations" that serve to underwrite the authority of the original pronouncement (Hodges 2015: 55). The second part of my analysis focuses on the chain of authentication that helped transform CPD claims about the "present danger" into "a widely accepted truth," a truth that ultimately resulted in the "Second Cold War" of the 1980s (Dalby 1990; Halliday 1983).

THE ITERATIVE AND INTERTEXTUAL NATURE OF THE PRESENT DANGER
NSC 68: The Discursive History of the "Present Danger"

The following analysis examines the iterative nature of the re-securitization of the Soviet Union by tracing the CPD's threat articulation to an antecedent securitizing act. That is, the CPD's re-securitization of the Soviet Union assumes and depends upon a prior articulation of the "present danger" facing the nation. This iterative process is indexed by the Committee's characterization of Soviet behavior as continuous and unchanging, a characterization that raises the questions: What prior state has the Soviet Union failed to evolve from? What actions and objectives are the Soviet Union continuing to pursue? The answers lay in NSC 68 promulgated in 1950. Although formulated at different historical moments and in different geopolitical environments, NSC 68 and the CPD documents worked together to initiate and sustain the securitization of the Soviet Union. NSC 68 is not just the antecedent document upon which the CPD's grounds its case, however; it also provides a rhetorical blueprint for how to temporalize the Soviet threat as present and urgent. That is, as I demonstrate in the following analysis, the iterative nature of the securitization of the Soviet Union manifests at the level of discursive strategy, in the way both manage the temporal dimension of the construal of the Soviet threat. In sum, by simultaneously insisting on the present-ness of the threat and the immutability of the Soviet system, the CPD indexes and participates in the iterative process of securitizing the Soviet Union, a process that flares up at particular moments but extends beyond them.

This process can be seen, first, by comparing NSC 68's statement of Soviet goals with that presented by the CPD:

> NSC 68: The *fundamental design* of those who control the Soviet Union and the international communist movement is to *retain and solidify* their absolute power, *first* in the Soviet Union and *second* in areas now under their control.
> CPD: The Soviet Union *has not altered its long-held goal* of a world dominated from a single center—Moscow. It *continues, with notable persistence*, to take advantage of every opportunity to *expand* its political and military influence throughout the world.

The CPD renders its articulation of "the present danger" as a reiteration of the NSC 68 statement of the Soviets' fundamental design through the verb phrases "has not altered" and "continues to take," the nominal "long-held goal," and the adverbial phrase "with notable persistence." In so doing it construes Soviet objectives and actions of the 1970s as aligning with rather than diverging from those it pursued in the wake of World War II, thereby rendering Soviet action as a continuation of its efforts to realize its "fundamental design." Specifically, the CPD statement that the Soviet Union seeks "to expand its political and military influence throughout the world" presupposes the prior success of earlier efforts, as mapped out in NSC 68, by Soviet leaders to "retain and solidify" their power at home and in "areas now under their control." The present security environment, consequently, is defined by the

Soviet Union, which, having achieved the initial phases of its design, is poised to realize its "long-held goal" of world domination.

Since the Soviets' geopolitical goals have not changed, neither has the future that the realization of those goals will bring about: a future in which the "idea of slavery" would replace the "idea of freedom" (May 1993: 27), a future in which "conflict" and "Marxist-Leninist philosophy" would dominate over a future of "peaceful unity and cooperation," and a future in which democracies "could not . . . survive" (Tyroler 1984: 40, 14). Of particular interest here is that both NSC 68 and the CPD documents draw on linguistic and rhetorical strategies that constrict the temporal distance between present and future to amplify the immediacy of the Soviet threat and, thereby, underscore the necessity of prompt counteraction. That is, both threat articulations involve a "telescoping of the future into the present" such that "the future is inhabited in the present" (Adams et al. 2009: 258, 249). As the following analysis demonstrates, temporal proximity—the closeness of a devastating future to the present moment—is construed as the defining feature of the "present" security crisis facing the free world at both the inception of the Cold War and its reassertion a quarter-century later.

While NSC 68 was the first full articulation of the Soviet military threat in the post–WWII era, its authors drew on the threat assessment presented two years earlier in the 1948 National Security Council Resolution 20/4 (NSC 20/4). NSC 20/4 declared that "the gravest threat to the security of the United States within the *foreseeable future* stems from the hostile designs and formidable power of the USSR, and from the nature of the Soviet system" (May 1993: 77). Of interest here is that NSC 68 amplifies the Soviet threat by adding language that recontextualizes it from the amorphous, underspecified temporal domain of "the foreseeable future" to the more immediate domain of the here and now.

NSC 68 notes that the threat it has identified "*is of the same character* as that described in NSC 20/4 but *is more immediate* than had been previously estimated" (May 1993: 76). The "immediacy of the danger" stems from the relationship between the "now" of the United States and the "*year* of maximum danger" that lies ahead (May 1993: 77). More specifically, NSC 68 declares that the "disastrous situation" facing the nation in the near term is "the Soviet Union's probable fission bomb capability and possible thermonuclear bomb capability," which "might arise in *1954*" if the United States insists on the "continuation of our present programs" (May 1993: 76). It further points to the "*period* of maximum danger"—an earlier rendition of the CPD's "period of peril"—by warning of "the contingency that within the *next four or five years* the Soviet Union will possess the military capability of delivering a surprise atomic attack" against the United States (May 1993: 76). The immediacy of this apocalyptic future means that the nation's leaders, as they did in the late 1970s, have limited temporal space and resources for averting global disaster.

[120]   *The Great Nation of Futurity*

Indeed, NSC 68 warns that the issues facing the nation "will not await our deliberation" (May 1993: 26). Only if a program that "increase[es] our military power is adopted now" can the nation hope to ward off a Soviet attack (May 1993: 51). Should such action be "too long delayed," the nation will face the risk of falling into a "descending spiral of too little too late" (May 1993: 53).

If the "year of maximum danger" is to be "pushed into the future," the United States must work to maintain its position as the world's leading superpower (May 1993: 76). Recall that in the CPD's construal of 1970s global space-time, the present was marked by American global preeminence and the future by the nation's possible relinquishing of that dominance to the Soviet Union. This construal echoes that embedded within NSC 68 which similarly insists that while the United States has a political, economic, and military advantage over the Soviet Union for "now," that advantage is under threat:

33. [W]hile a large United States advantage *is likely to remain*, the Soviet Union *will be steadily reducing this discrepancy.* (May 1993: 37)
34. When our military strength is related to the world situation . . . it is clear that our military strength *is becoming dangerously inadequate.* (May 1993: 51)
35. *For the moment* our atomic capability is probably adequate to deter the Kremlin. However, when it calculates that it has sufficient atomic capability . . . the Kremlin might be tempted to strike swiftly and with stealth. (May 1993: 55)
36. Although the United States probably *now* possesses . . . a force adequate to deliver a powerful blow . . . it is not sufficient by itself to advance the position of the United States in the cold war. (May 1993: 61)
37. [T]he United States has *a large potential military capability but an actual capability* which, though improving, *is declining relative to the USSR.* (May 1993: 65)
38. [T]he *actual and potential military capability* of the United States . . . *will become less and less effective* as a war deterrent. (May 1993: 65)
39. *For the time being*, the United States possesses a marked atomic superiority over the Soviet Union. (May 1993: 76)

Precarity in these statements is rendered through linguistic devices that limit the nation's advantage to the present and either implicitly or explicitly project a future in which that advantage will have eroded. Several statements use temporal adverbs to signify the present-ness of United States advantage: "for the moment" (35), "now" (36), and "for the time being" (39). In addition to indexing the present, these adverbials point to the future by projecting the possibility that the U.S. advantage may not continue. The future, then, could go one of two ways: either the nation will do what's needed to maintain its advantage, or it will cede its advantage, and thereby, the future, to the Soviets.

Several of the statements (34, 35, 37) explicitly restrict the U.S. advantage to the present through hypotactic clause structures that subordinate this advantage to three key futures: futures in which the nation's overall strength has been reduced relative to that of the Soviet Union (34), the nation's military can no longer fulfill its geopolitical responsibilities (35), and the nation is unable to advance its position in the Cold War (37). A similar contrast can be seen in excerpt 36, which creates a contrastive relationship ("for the moment," "however") between the current superiority of American atomic capability and a future moment in which that superiority will have been nullified.

In excerpts 38 and 39 we see the tension between present and future rendered in terms of the nation's "actual" and "potential" military capability. Excerpt 38 construes the present moment as dire but the future as offering some hope. That is, according to NSC 68, the United States can stem the current decline of its actual military capability by realizing its "large potential" capability. The statement in excerpt 39, however, projects a negative future in which both what the military is actually capable of doing and what it could potentially do prove to be inadequate for warding off war with the Soviet Union.

The U.S. advantage is further called into question through NSC 68's construal, as illustrated in the following excerpts, of "present trends" that, combined with the "dynamism" and "militancy" of Soviet activity, point to a Soviet future in the making. NSC 68 is unequivocal in its assessment that present trends do not favor the United States and the free world, an argument the CPD would continue 20 years later:

40. The capabilities of the Soviet world *are being exploited to the full* because the Kremlin is inescapably militant. (May 1993: 34)
41. The Soviet Union *is developing* the military capacity to support its design for world domination. (May 1993: 37)
42. The Soviet Union *is seeking* to create overwhelming military force. (May 1993: 53)
43. *It is seeking* to demonstrate to the free world that force and the will to use it are on the side of the Kremlin. (May 1993: 53)
44. The Soviet Union *is pursuing* the initiative in the conflict with the free world. (May 1993: 66)

The aspectual profile of these statements presents the Soviet Union as currently engaging in a variety of activities aimed at realizing its fundamental design: its capabilities "are being exploited to the fullest," it "is developing the military capacity" for world domination, it "is pursuing the initiative," and it "is seeking to create an overwhelming military force." A quarter of a century hence, the CPD would similarly render the Soviet Union as engaging in concerted actions to ensure its eventual position as the world's dominant power (see Table 5.1).

[122]   *The Great Nation of Futurity*

NSC 68's construal of a dynamic and militant Soviet Union differs markedly from its representation of the United States, a construal that presages the situation the CPD would contend faces the nation in the 1970s (see Table 5.2):

45. The Soviet Union *is now allocating nearly 40%* of its gross available resources for defense and investment. . . . The United States, on the other hand, *is allocating only about 20% percent* of its resources for defense and investment. (May 1993: 45)
46. There are indications of *a let-down of United States efforts . . . disillusion* resulting from excessively high optimistic expectations . . . and *doubts* about the wisdom of continuing to strengthen free nations . . . in light of the intensity of the cold war. (May 1993: 50)
47. Instead of appearing strong and resolute we are continually on the verge of appearing and being alternately *irresolute and desperate*. (May 1993: 54)

The striking disparity in American versus Soviet efforts represents "the unfavorable trend of our power position" and the "ominous trends in international relations" (May 1993: 61, 65). As such, "It is imperative that [these] trend[s] be reversed by a much more rapid and concerted buildup of the actual strength of both the United States and the other nations of the free world" (May 1993: 79–80).

Ronald Reagan: Legitimation Through Identity Performance

The preceding analysis demonstrated the iterative nature of the securitizing process by identifying the intertextual links between the CPD's and NSC 68's rhetorical strategies. The CPD's project was not complete, however, as another iteration was needed: a contemporaneous public performance of the nation's fundamental identity and geopolitical purpose. This performance was provided by Ronald Reagan, who, although typically credited with ending the Cold War in the late 1980s, was key to reigniting it in the mid-1970s and early 1980s. Reagan's "relentless, dynamic performance" provided "a clear, forceful, reassuringly familiar articulation of American purpose in the world" (Hunt 1987: 186). Furthermore, his rhetoric, which represented a "watershed moment" in presidential assertions of exceptionalism, resonated with "a public longing by the late 1970s for a restored sense of national pride and power and for a reaffirmation of old verities" (McEvoy-Levy 2001: 31; Hunt 1987: 188; also see Neumann and Coe 2011). In sum, Reagan's reassertion and reanimation of America's fundamental identity were key to legitimating the actions and policies entailed in the CPD's program.

Given his close affiliation with the group, Reagan's role in promoting the CPD project isn't surprising: he was a member of the Committee in 1979, and several committee members served in his presidential administration. As Wolfe (1983) states it, "Reagan's election . . . brought the Committee on the Present Danger directly into the government," the "immediate effect" of which was CPD ideas becoming "the basis . . . of actual foreign policy" (4). As such, we see in his foreign policy rhetoric a reiteration of the CPD's rendering of the national security problem facing the United States in the mid-1970s and those that loomed ahead in the 1980s.

The focus of this part of my analysis is not the explicit intertextual links between the CPD's and Reagan's threat discourse; rather, I examine Reagan's role as the public-facing securitizing actor who legitimized the re-securitization of the Soviet Union. As van Dijk (1998) explains, legitimation is a "complex, ongoing discursive practice involving a set of interrelated discourses" (255). It is a particularly necessary and prominent rhetorical act at moments of crisis involving a loss of identification with the shared concepts and beliefs undergirding social institutions that puts the legitimacy of those institutions at risk (Martin-Rojo and van Dijk 1997: 529; van Dijk 1998: 257). As we've seen, the CPD insisted that advocates of detente had created such a crisis for the United States by aligning the nation's interest with those of the Soviet Union and, thereby, calling into question its exceptionalist identity. Indeed, the Committee declared in 1982 that the nation had "become second best" (Tyroler 1984: 235). Reagan's rhetorical task, then, was to remind the nation of its special role in human history and restore that role to its proper place at the center of the nation's foreign policy. He must, in short, remind the nation and the world that "the future is on [the] path" (Chilton 1996: 336) being forged by the America experiment.

Although various legitimation strategies can be seen in Reagan's discourse, taken as a whole, the speeches examined here reveal the strategy of "mythopoesis"—the grounding of legitimacy in stories and narratives (van Leeuwen 2008).[4] His narrative is rooted in the PATH and JOURNEY schemas, as it embeds the structural elements of a starting point, path, and directedness toward a destination.[5] Chilton (1996) explains that the PATH and JOURNEY schemas undergird "important and familiar narrative schemas" and that variants of PATH and JOURNEY—e.g., "national destiny" and "American mission"—are an important aspect of political discourses (52). Reagan's story of America, moreover, is at once a moral and cautionary tale that provides a "look into the future" by foretelling the rewards that await the nation and the world should its leaders act to shape the global future, as well as the dangers should they fail to do so (Charteris-Black 2011: 212; van Leeuwen 2008: 117; Fairclough 2003: 99).

As noted in Chapter 1, construals of futurity "often take a narrative form that ties into familiar modes of storytelling"; such stories, in turn, serve as guides or maps for action (Mische 2009: 701). Storytelling, futurity, and legitimation come together in critical ways in Reagan's rhetorical performances.

The former president narrates the future by telling the "grand story of America" (Oddo 2011: 298) in such a way that draws sharp contrasts between the future entailed in the American system and that entailed in the Soviet system. In this way, he reaffirms the nation's fundamental identity and legitimates its geopolitical policies and actions. That is, a key theme running throughout his speeches is America's legacy of exceptionalism and its providentially ordained geopolitical role of ensuring the destiny of mankind. Statements from these speeches cohere into a narrative of progress with America at the center, a story in which the nation moves ever closer to its glorious, divinely inspired future and, in so doing, lights the way for others. The problem, according to Reagan, is that the nation's leaders have forgotten the nation's story and betrayed its legacy, thereby disrupting the nation's—and the world's—progress toward a divine future.

The following analysis is organized around three rhetorical moments in Reagan's narrative: course correction, reclaiming the future, and projecting the American future. During the course correction moment of his narrative, Reagan tells a story of a fundamentally exceptional nation that, at the current moment, has strayed from its preordained path forged at the nation's inception and urges a return to it. In his move to reclaim the global future, the president directs the nation to renew its commitment to its founding mission by embracing its fundamental identity as an exceptional nation that has a unique relationship to and responsibility for the global future. The denouement of Reagan's narrative comes in his projection of the inevitable global future, which inheres in "American-ism" (Reagan 1980, August 18). He assures the nation that the future is on America's path by invoking the concepts of "destiny" and "national purpose" and by offering assurances that the nation will reach the "pre-determined end" of its journey (Chilton 1996: 52).

Course Correction

As can be seen in Table 5.5, Reagan's call to correct the course of the nation's foreign policy is expressed through the themes of aimlessness and drift, course reversal, and renewal.

As Charteris-Black (2011) notes, journeys can be construed within political discourse as "powerful regenerative experiences" or as "lacking purpose and not generative" (212–213). In his presidential campaign rhetoric, Reagan employs a lexis of aimlessness and drift to construe the nation's journey under the Carter administration as lacking in purpose. In his 1976 campaign speeches Reagan characterizes democratic societies in the second half of the 20th century as "once again wandering without aim," just as they had in the first half of the century (Reagan 1976, March 31). The United States is no exception, as "wandering without aim describes American foreign policy" (Reagan 1976);

Table 5.5. COURSE CORRECTION RHETORIC

Aimlessness, drift	• "wandering without aim" (March 31, 1976)
	• "[W]e have strayed off course many times." (August 18, 1980)
	• "drifts from crisis to crisis, eroding our national will and sense of purpose" (July 17, 1980)
	• "[determine] our course through . . . one of the most perilous decades of our history" (November 3, 1980)
	• "drift and disaster" (November 3, 1980)
	• "dangerous drift" (February 22, 1983)
Course reversal	• "alternative path for America" (August 18, 1980)
	• "reverse a dangerous course America had drifted along for too long" (February 22, 1983)
	• "a new road" (February 22, 1983)
	• "have forged the beginnings of a fundamentally new direction in American foreign policy" (February 22, 1983)
National renewal	• "age of reform" (November 3, 1980)
	• "era of national renewal" (January 20, 1981)
	• "make a new beginning" (January 25, 1984)
	• "a moral renewal" (March 8, 1983)
	• "a crusade for renewal" (January 25, 1984)
	• "the American spirit and sense of purpose; our resolve to preserve world peace and freedom; the American tradition of leadership" (July 17, 1980)
	• "our determination, our courage, our strength; our faith and our" hope (January 20, 1981)
	• "confidence in our country; hope for our future" (January 25, 1984)
	• "faith in the rightness of our system" (February 22, 1983)

just as it had "many times in the past," America in the 1970s has "strayed off course" (Reagan 1980, August 18). Under the stewardship of President Carter, the nation, Reagan insists, "drifts from crisis to crisis, eroding our national will and purpose" (Reagan 1980, July 17). The 1980 presidential election is particularly important, then, because it will "determine our country's course through what promises to be one of the most perilous decades in our history" (Reagan 1980, November 3). Candidate Reagan promises the nation that, if elected, his administration will halt the "drift and disaster in Washington" (Reagan 1980, November 3).

Not surprisingly, President Reagan characterizes the nation's journey as, once again, purposeful and regenerative. He declares that by placing the nation on an "alternative path," his administration has "reversed the dangerous course America has drifted along for too long" (Reagan 1980, August 18; 1983,

February 22). Because the American electorate wanted to "choose a new road," the nation was again able to "progress" in its "quest for peace and freedom in an uncertain world" (Reagan 1983, February 22). Speaking in 1983 the president proclaims that "we have forged the beginnings of a fundamentally new direction in American foreign policy" (Reagan 1983, February 22). In sum, while some claim that "the American spirit has been vanquished," Reagan assures the nation that by electing him president, America has reclaimed a vision of the future animated and guided by that spirit (Reagan 1982, January 26).

The map of the nation's journey along this "new" course is to be found, Reagan insists, by returning to the nation's past, in the path laid out at America's founding. The remedy for the nation's "malaise" will require that Americans "renew our compact with freedom," a compact made in 1620 in Plymouth Massachusetts that "set the pattern for what was to come" (Reagan 1980, November 3; July 17). By renewing this compact, the nation will turn "this perilous decade" into a "new beginning" (Reagan 1980, July 17). Indeed, invoking Thomas Paine, Reagan assures the nation that "we have it in our power to begin the world over again" (Reagan 1983, March 3). Whereas others have relegated the nation to "the dustbin of history," Reagan proclaims the coming decade to be an "age of reform," an "era of national renewal" (Reagan 1980, November 3). The 1980s, he avers, will be a time for the nation to "make a new beginning," a time to "renew" and "restore" the nation's legacy of exceptionalism (Reagan 1980, July 17). Various credos, roles, and commitments are subject to renewal, including: "the American spirit and sense of purpose"; "the American tradition of leadership"; "our resolve to preserve world peace and freedom"; "confidence in our country"; and, importantly, "faith in the rightness of our system" and "hope for our future."

Reclaiming the Future

Getting America back on track, Reagan explains, will require reclaiming the nation's special geopolitical responsibility through a "great national crusade to make America great again" (Reagan 1980, July 17).[6] The necessity, as well as the surety, of this effort is grounded in the fact that America has "a rendezvous with destiny" (Reagan 1980, July 17). As the excerpts in Table 5.6 demonstrate, the temporal aspect of Reagan's exceptionalist rhetoric situates the United States in a rarefied place in the history of humanity, as "separate and different" from nations and peoples that came before, exist presently, or will come after, and, thus, as endowed with a special responsibility to that history.

The unprecedented-ness of the "American experiment" is construed through adjectives ("new," "best"), nominals ("new breed," "entirely new concept"), and adjectival ("who ever lived on this earth") and circumstantial phrases ("than has ever been done before"). Echoing the Founding Fathers,

Table 5.6. REAGAN'S RHETORIC OF TEMPORAL EXCEPTIONALISM

- "The *last* island of freedom" (Reagan 1976)
- "A *new breed* in the world" (Reagan 1976)
- "This *new breed* of people we call Americans" (Reagan 1980, July 17)
- "We gave birth to an *entirely new concept* in man's relation to man." (Reagan 1976)
- "No people *who ever lived on this earth* have fought harder . . . to advance the dignity of man." (Reagan 1976)
- "the *last best hope of man on earth*" (Reagan 1980, November 3; Reagan 1982, January 26; Reagan 1984, January 25)
- "America guarantees individual liberty to *a greater degree than any other*." (Reagan 1981, January 20)

- "The *last* and greatest bastion of freedom" (Reagan 1981, January 20; Reagan 1982, January 26)
- "Here in this land we unleashed the energy and individual genius of man *to a greater extent than has ever been done before*." (Reagan 1981, January 20)
- "Gives others that *last, best hope of a better future*" (Reagan 1983, October 27)
- "An undeniable truth that America *remains the greatest force for peace anywhere in the world today*" (Reagan 1983, February 22)
- "It is our responsibility to preserve world peace because *nobody else can do it*." (Reagan 1980, October 19)
- "give others that *last, best hope* of a better life" (Reagan 1983, October 27)

Reagan proclaims that "Americans" are not descendants with roots in other societies and cultures; they are a "new breed." Accordingly, their actions and accomplishments are also unprecedented, as they "gave birth to an entirely new concept" of human relations, have fought harder for human dignity than any people "who ever lived on this earth," and have enabled individual genius "to a greater extent than has ever been done before." America is also without contemporaries, as it "guarantees individual liberty to a greater extent than anyone," "remains the greatest force for peace anywhere in the world today," and "offers the . . . best hope for man on earth." Consequently, "because nobody else can do it," America must "preserve world peace." Finally, not only did the world's chance for peace, freedom, and dignity begin with America; it also ends with America. America represents the "last island" and "last bastion" of freedom; its "experiment" in liberty and democracy represents "the last best hope for man on earth," the world's "last, best hope for a better future." As such, the nation must "do a better job of exporting American-ism" (Reagan 1980, August 18).

During his presidential campaign, Reagan underscores the significance of the nation's recommitment to its special historical status and purpose by raising the possibility of its neglect. In his election eve speech in which he famously invokes the "shining city on the hill" metaphor, Reagan identifies the question facing the nation: "for the first time in our memory Americans are asking: does history still have a place for America, for her people, for her great ideals?" (Reagan 1980, November 3). Concomitantly, he asks "Is our nation

[128]   *The Great Nation of Futurity*

stronger and more capable of leading a world toward peace and freedom or weaker?" (Reagan 1980, November 3). Through these questions Reagan projects the two "different visions of the future" the nation must choose between in the 1980 election: a future in which America will answer history's call versus a future in which it "shirk[s]" that call, a future in which it will lead the world versus a future in which it will be led (Reagan 1980, November 3). By invoking the alternative-futures trope in this way, Reagan stakes the nation's and global society's future on which of two American Selves arises out of the 1980 election: an America willing to fulfill its preordained global mission—to shape the global future in ways that serve the interests of the nation and, thereby, those of mankind—or an America that eschews that role.

Projecting the American Future

Having elected Reagan president, Americans chose to answer history's call to lead the global community toward a future of peace and freedom. The nation is ready, Reagan declares, to export America's "positive vision of the future, of the world" through a foreign policy grounded in "the unashamed, unapologetic explaining" of our principles and institutions (1983, February 22). The nation's history is, after all, the "story of hopes fulfilled and dreams made into reality" (Reagan 1983, March 8). As can be seen in the following excerpts, as both a candidate and president, Reagan grounds this story in a lexis of exemplar, hope, and change and a space-time that situates America as future relative to the rest of the world. America is the nation that

48. takes *the world as it is* and seeks to *change it* by leadership and example (Reagan 1980, July 17)
49. *show[s]* all mankind that they, too, can be free (Reagan 1980, August 18)
50. will again be the *exemplar of freedom* and the *beacon of hope* for those who *do not now* have freedom (Reagan 1981, January 20)
51. *tell[s]* the world that *a new age is not only possible but probable* (1982, June 8)
52. *give[s]* others that *last, best hope* of a better life (Reagan 1983, October 27)
53. *carr[ies] hope and opportunity* far from our shores (Reagan 1984, January 25)
54. *help[s] [others] realize their aspirations* for economic development and political freedom (Reagan 1982, January 26)

Although America "seeks to change it," the world has nothing to fear because America is "not in the business of imperialism, aggression, or conquest" (Reagan 1983, February 22). Moreover, the "new sense of confidence in America and the universal principles and ideals" underlying its capitalist democratic system "is not an arrogant demand that others adopt our way of life; it is a realist belief in the . . . proven success of the American experiment" (Reagan 1983, February 22). As such, explaining this system to "emerging nations" does not "represent an attempt to impose our way of life" (Reagan 1983, February 22). America's geopolitical interests are temporal, not territorial, as Reagan, echoing Truman, proclaims that Americans "have no territorial ambitions. We occupy no countries. We build no walls to lock people in. *Americans build the future*" (Reagan 1984, January 25). As such, the nation is poised to continue the temporal mission initiated by the Pilgrims, who "dared to cross a mighty ocean to build a future for themselves in a new world": America is ready to work toward "a more peaceful future for all the world's people" (Reagan 1980, July 17; Reagan 1983, January 25).

Implicated by these laudatory statements of the American future are negative assessments of the Soviet future that, as we've seen, would be a future of "global military superiority" in the service of "world revolution" (Reagan 1983, February 22; Reagan 1983, March 8). If We do not "impose our way of life," then They do: They *are* in "the business of imperialism, aggression, and conquest" (Reagan 1983, February 22). The president also contrasts the means by which these divergent futures would come to be by explaining that "our vision of a better life . . . begins with a simple premise: the future is best decided by ballots, not bullets" (Reagan 1984, January 25).

Reagan further legitimizes America's role as the architect of the global future through a space-time contrast that aligns the American future with the natural, inevitable course of human history and, concomitantly, disjoins the Soviet Union from the future altogether. He does so by drawing on a tidal metaphor to naturalize history's "path" and by presupposing the inevitability of its direction. This naturalized future is embedded in the following statements that characterize the Soviet system as antithetical to it:

55. The *greatest fallacy* of the Marxist-Leninist philosophy is that it is *the wave of the future*. (Reagan 1980, August 18)
56. It is the Soviet Union that *runs against the tide of history*. (Reagan 1982, June 8)
57. *The march of freedom and democracy* will leave Marxist-Leninism in *the ash heap of history*. (Reagan 1982, June 8)
58. Marxist revolution is *no longer seen as the inevitable future*. (Reagan 1983, February 22)
59. History is not *a darkening path twisting inevitably toward tyranny*. (Reagan 1983, February 22)

The Soviet Union, according to Reagan, offers only a false, unnatural future: its claims to the future are its "greatest fallacy," as it actually "runs against the tide of history." Indeed, rather than leading emerging nations toward "the

[130]   *The Great Nation of Futurity*

inevitable future" of Marxist revolution, the Soviet system leads its followers down a "darkening path twisting inevitably toward tyranny" and, ultimately, to the "ash heap of history." The Soviet Union, in sum, ensnares its constituents in a "backwash of history. . . . Everything about it is primitive. . . . We have seen nothing like it since the Age of Feudalism" (Reagan 1980, August 18).

According to the logic of the ideological square, if the path of history is not this "darkening path," it must be an enlightened path progressing toward freedom and democracy; indeed, Reagan explains "the one clear pattern in world events . . . is in the opposite direction" (1983, February 22). "The tide of the future," Reagan declares "is a freedom tide" (1984, January 25). In the same vein, if the Soviet Union is *not* the "wave of the future," the American system *is*, as it runs *with* the "tide of history" toward the inevitable future of freedom. Reagan creates a relation of equivalence between the future of America and the "freedom tide" when he declares that "America's best days and democracy's best days lie ahead" (1984, January 25).

While human history naturally and inevitably moves in a given direction and toward a predestined endpoint, it, nevertheless, requires a champion to "carry" its message "far from our shores" and a guardian to ward off threats and challenges to it. In the following excerpts, Reagan draws on a rhetoric of vanguardism to identify America as both the messenger and guardian of the inevitable future:

60. To gain control of their own destinies . . . is the driving aspiration that unites the human family—the burning desire to live unhindered. . . . *America leads the vanguard of this movement.* (Reagan 1983, February 22)
61. The American dream lives . . . in the hearts and minds of the world's people . . . *who look to us for leadership.* As long as that dream lives . . . America has a future, and all mankind has reason to hope. (Reagan 1983, February 22)
62. Our country is a special place, because we Americans have always been sustained . . . by a noble vision—*a vision* not only of what the world around us is today but *what we as free people can make it be tomorrow.* (Reagan 1983, January 25)
63. [T]he United States has *an obligation* to its citizens and *to the people of the world* never to let those who would destroy freedom dictate the future course of human life on this planet. (Reagan 1980, July 17)

CONCLUSION

This chapter has demonstrated the discursive means by which the Soviet Union was re-securitized in the 1970s and 1980s and how that iterative process drew upon the temporal domain of the future and invoked America's purported relationship to the future in construing the Soviet threat. The CPD documents invoked the alternative-futures trope to contrast American and Soviet claims on and visions of the future, projected images of the future implicated in present Soviet activity, and animated and amplified the Soviet threat through temporal metaphors. The Committee also drew upon the shape-the-future trope to raise the specter of the nation's leaders ceding the geopolitical future to the Soviet Union and, thereby, underscored the Soviet threat. In contrast to the active, driven character ascribed to Soviet activity, actions being taken by the United States were characterized as signally a retreat from the world stage, a turning away from the nation's geopolitical mission and responsibilities, and a posture of restraint in the face of an increasingly emboldened Soviet Union.

In sum, the Soviet threat was mediated through the CPD's construal of the future: through projections of what the Soviet threat would mean for the character of the global future and for America's status and role vis-à-vis that future. In this way the CPD discourse served as an anticipatory regime that mediated the present through projections of the future and the future through construals of the present. It was a regime according to which "the future arrives already formed in the present, as if the emergency has already happened" (Adams et al. 2009: 249). Just as the original Cold War had served to "discipline the ambiguity of global life" in the wake of World War II (Campbell 1998: 16), the CPD's threat campaign sought to discipline a "world in flux" in the era of detente (Tyroler 1984: 3).

The CPD's construal of the Soviet threat, and the temporal devices and maneuvers underlying that construal, did not originate in its re-securitization campaign. As my analysis demonstrates, a rhetorical blueprint was provided in NSC 68 for how to render present and future is such a way that portrayed the Soviet Union as a dynamic, determined, and threatening Other that, if left unchecked, would be empowered to determine the evolution of global society. The CPD's re-securitization project didn't rest solely on re-establishing the Soviet Union as America's radical Other, however. It also involved reasserting the fundamentally exceptional identity of the American Self through a public performance of the nation's geopolitical standing, mission, and responsibilities. By telling America's grand story, President Reagan recalled the nation's special destiny and divinely sanctioned mission. This story, in turn, underscored the legitimacy of a foreign policy strategy focused on maintaining the nation's global preeminence and, thereby, ensuring that the United States, not the Soviet Union, would be the global power that "build[s] the future."

In my final analytic chapter, I switch my focus from the reignition of the Cold War in the early 1980s to its ending in the late 1980s and early 1990s and examine how the nation's identity and geopolitical purpose were construed in the absence of an apparent Radical Other.

[132]   *The Great Nation of Futurity*

CHAPTER 6

From the American Century to the End of History

An American Future of Democratic Peace

INTRODUCTION

This chapter examines the construal and legitimation of the nation's identity and geopolitical role at a moment when its status as the world's lone superpower was not challenged or threatened by a clear global competitor: the ending of the Cold War in the late 1980s and early 1990s. My data comprises statements on foreign policy made by the George H. W. Bush and Bill Clinton administrations, both of which oversaw the ending of the Cold War and the inception of the post–Cold War era. The Bush administration ran from 1989 to 1993; the Clinton administration ran from 1993 to 2001. Although American national identity was not construed in these statements in relationship to a radical Other, both presidents' foreign policy discourse evoked two Self/Other contrasts in their representation of the national Self: Active/Passive American Self and American Self/Periphery Other. As in the preceding chapters, I examine how these Self/Other contrasts are created through and draw on space-time contrasts.

I carry out my analysis through the lens of the American jeremiad (hereafter "jeremiad"), which, as noted in Chapter 2, has served as a potent genre through which American national identity and geopolitical purpose have been formulated and sustained. I understand the jeremiad to be a rhetorical vehicle of both identification and action: it projects a particular conception of the nation's identity as a means for compelling action. That is, the jeremiad

---

The Great Nation of Futurity. Patricia L. Dunmire, Oxford University Press. © Oxford University Press 2023.
DOI: 10.1093/oso/9780197658222.003.0006

combines the existential modality of *is* with the obligational modality of *must*: since America is X, it must do Y. My analysis identifies the linguistic and rhetorical means by which American national identity and the post–Cold War security environment were construed through the jeremiad to warrant the need for a foreign policy approach aimed at shaping the geopolitical future. It is my contention that foreign policy discourse in the early years of the post–Cold War era drew on key elements of the jeremiad in order to legitimize an activist foreign policy posture and, in so doing, reaffirmed and sustained the nation's identity as "the great nation of futurity."

In what follows, I discuss the impact the ending of the Cold War had on the discourse of American national identity. I then provide a rationale for examining post–Cold War foreign policy discourse in terms of the jeremiad and overview the three key themes—chosen-ness, declension, prophecy—which frame my analysis. My analysis takes each of these themes in turn and examines how they are realized and function in the foreign policy discourse of the George H. W. Bush and Bill Clinton administrations.

AMERICAN NATIONAL IDENTITY AND THE ENDING OF THE COLD WAR

The ending of the Cold War is a relevant moment for studying American national identity because, despite its apparent victory over the Soviet Union, politicians and pundits raised questions and concerns about the role the United States would play in a geopolitical environment absent a Soviet Union. Moreover, the ending of the Cold War was claimed to represent a unique moment not only in the history of the United States but also in the history of mankind, which would have repercussions for the nation's approach to foreign policy. According to Francis Fukuyama (1989), the fall of the Berlin Wall and the breakup of the Soviet Union signaled not just "the passing of a particular period of postwar history" but "the end of history" itself and, thus, the "universalization of liberal democracy as the final form of human government" (1).[1] America had been selected, so the thinking went, by "the logic of historical development" as the world's lone superpower and its system of free market democratic capitalism as the only viable economic and political system (Smith 2012: 207). At the close of the 20th century the American present seemed to be the moment when the nation had moved from "promise to fulfillment" (Bercovitch 2012: 93).

If history had indeed come to an end, Fukuyama (1989) argued, there would no longer be a viable political-economic system that could challenge democratic capitalism; rather, the global environment would become a "universal homogenous state" defined by the "Common Marketization of world politics" (7, 9, 16). As the preeminent liberal democracy, this Cold War

[134] *The Great Nation of Futurity*

"victory" represented the triumph and vindication of American values and way of life: the *American Way* had proven to be *The* way. Moreover, given the dominant Cold War conception of the Soviet Union as an existential threat to the United States, as well as to the West, the demise of this radical Other and the ending of the Cold War on favorable terms could have led, at least in theory, to an easing of the nation's interventionist role in global affairs (Layne 2006: 13; Bacevich 2002: 71).

As a moment of geopolitical change, the ending of the Cold War, nevertheless, brought to the fore questions about the nation's geopolitical identity and purpose, as well as claims about the threats and challenges the nation would face in the new era. That is, politicians and pundits asked whether the United States would reap the benefits of its Cold War victory by extending its political-economic system globally or turn inward, thereby giving reign of the future to the post–Cold War Other, namely, the forces of "chaos" and "anarchy." The George H. W. Bush administration, for example, invoked the isolationist tendency of the 1920s as a warning for the current moment, insisting that such a posture "had near disastrous consequences then" and that a similar posture "would be even more disastrous now" (USNSC 1991: 2). Similarly, the Clinton administration doubled down on the nation's global leadership by rejecting a turn "inward" and a retreat from "the challenge of the moment" in favor a foreign policy that "reach[es] out" and "exerts [American] leadership abroad" (USNSC 1995: 2). Consequently, calls for a retreat from the world stage were answered by the insistence that the United States make the most of its unipolar status by confronting the geopolitical "challenges" and seizing the "opportunities" facing it in the new era.

THE AMERICAN JEREMIAD: CHOSEN-NESS, DECLENSION, PROPHECY

As a consequential geopolitical turning point, the inception of the post–Cold War era was ripe for the jeremiad ritual.[2] That is, such moments of change, decision, and uncertainty have been identified as moments in which politicians and pundits employ the jeremiad for political ends (Jones and Rowland 2005). Ritter (1980), for example, identifies the invocation of a "historical juncture" in presidential nomination speeches as a commonplace that evinces the jeremiad (162). Johannesen (1986) demonstrates how depictions of a society as being "on the verge" act as the impetus for jeremiadic calls for decision and action (84). The transition from the Cold War to the post–Cold War era represented such a pivotal point, as it was consistently rendered as a unique historical moment that raised concerns about the nation's geopolitical role and the purpose of its foreign policy. The jeremiad is designed to address such moments, as its "ritual import" derives from combining "anxiety" with "direction and purpose" (Bercovitch 2012: 24). Doing so enables the jeremiad to "sustain process by imposing control, and to justify control by presenting a certain form of process as the only road to the future kingdom" (Bercovitch 2012: 24). As noted earlier, the jeremiad manifests through three central themes: chosen-ness, declension, and prophecy, which I discuss in turn.

Chosen-ness is grounded in the premise that America and its people have been singled out to undertake the divinely sanctioned mission of shaping a progressive future. Bercovitch (2012) explains that from its earliest conception, America has been characterized as comprising "a peculiar people" who have not only been "called but *chosen* . . . as instruments of a sacred and historical design . . . to prepare 'the way for the future, glorious times'" (7–8, 99; emphasis added). Much more than a geographical place, America is a "culture on an errand" that bears the imprint of a "grand providential design" (Bercovitch 2012: 23, 109). The purpose of the jeremiad is to leverage this identity in order to "direct an imperiled people of God toward the fulfillment of their destiny" (Bercovitch 2012: 9). Moreover, the jeremiad's "progressive figural outlook" casts the success of the errand as the ultimate realization of providential design (Bercovitch 2012: 143–144). It is through the ritual of the jeremiad that "*This* [American] way of life" is rendered as "futurity itself" (Bercovitch 2012: xx; emphasis in original). Within the theme of chosen-ness, the Self/Other trope juxtaposes an American Self charged with the mission of shaping the post–Cold War world with an Other of "turmoil and development" that both threatens and necessitates that mission.

Throughout the nation's history, the jeremiad has served as a "disciplinary instrument," as a "tool of popular control" to ensure "compliance with the . . . political and religious ordinances" (Rodgers 2018: 83). It has done so, in part, through a ritualistic lament of national decline. That is, the theme of *declension* involves a lament that the nation is neglecting its mission and founding principles and a warning of the calamity that will ensue if this decline is not remedied (Jendrysik 2002; Johannensen 1986; Ritter 1980). This feature of the jeremiad reminds the nation of its providentially sanctioned errand while, at the same time, raising the possibility that it will fail to complete the errand. In the Puritan jeremiad, for example, this lament reminded the community of the "acute sense of the conditionality of God's promises" and that, "having been elected by God as his own," there would be no respite from his "judging gaze" (Rodgers 2018: 55–56, 42). Should they fail in their mission "[God] would choose another, better people," and New Englanders would be, as John Winthrop warned, "'made a story and a byword throughout the world'" (as quoted in Rodgers 2018: 56). As we'll see below, the post–Cold war lament of declension invokes the shape-the-future trope that juxtaposes two American Selves: a Self that accepts its post–Cold War mission and a Self that abandons that mission and, thereby, its opportunity—indeed, its responsibility—to shape the post–Cold War future.

[136] *The Great Nation of Futurity*

The generic theme of *prophecy* involves a call for the nation to recommit to its unique responsibilities and a prophetic assurance that it will successfully fulfill its mission. That is, the jeremiad "offers a prophetic vision of an ideal future, of the good things to come" while conditioning that future on a recommitment to foundational responsibilities and principles (Johannensen 1986: 158). This prophetic theme answers the question "When is our errand to be fulfilled?" (Bercovitch 2012: 11). The rhetorical and material import of this question derives from its warning that the nation's mission remains unfulfilled yet prophesizes that it will be. In this way, the jeremiad's prophetic dimension joins the space-time of the "not yet" with that of the "will be" in order to provide assurances of the ultimate success of the nation's errand. The Self/Other trope is realized in the prophecy theme through a rhetoric of promise and threat that identifies the American Self as the embodiment and agent of the promise of the post–Cold War era and the Other as an amorphous array of threats that place that promise at risk.

THE POST–COLD WAR JEREMIAD

The data set for this chapter comprises statements on foreign policy made in presidential speeches archived at *The American Presidency Project* (Woolley and Peters 2010) and by relevant administration officials (i.e., national security advisor), as well as the national security strategy documents of each administration. I examined speeches that had a clear foreign policy focus as well as statements on foreign policy incorporated into speeches with a domestic focus (e.g., inaugural and State of the Union addresses). I coded these statements in terms of the themes of chosen-ness, declension, and prophecy that are central to the American jeremiad. In brief, chosen-ness manifests in statements that claim a unique role for the United States (e.g., a nation with a high moral purpose; the indispensable nation). The theme of declension is realized through conditional statements (if/then) and statements that position the nation at a crucial moment (e.g., turning point; a moment of choice and decision). Finally, statements realizing the theme of prophecy project particular visions of the post–Cold War future, typically in terms of the promises and threat that lie ahead (e.g., big changes and the promises they hold; a place of peril). I take each theme in turn in the following analysis.

Chosen-Ness: Democratic Peace as Geopolitical Errand

While the demise of the Soviet Union and the repudiation of Soviet-style communism affirmed for many the global primacy of the United States and its political-economic system, these developments also resulted in a "threat blank" for the nation's foreign policy (van Voorst 1990; Dunmire 2009).

AN AMERICAN FUTURE OF DEMOCRATIC PEACE [137]

Without a Soviet Union to portray as America's enemy, the nation, seemingly, no longer had a radical Other against which it could distinguish itself, legitimate is geopolitical purpose, and craft its foreign policy. Rather, according to the 1992 *National Military Strategy of the United States*, the "real threat we now face is the threat of the unknown, the uncertain" (Bacevich 2021: 93). Although it was seen as undeniably promising, the post–Cold War future was also marked by a sense of uncertainty concerning the nature of the geopolitical future and the nation's role with respect to it.

Lest the nation be "mesmerized by uncertainty" in the wake of the Cold War, the Bush and Clinton administrations provided assurances that the United States continued to be exceptional nation on an errand and mapped out the terrain and purpose of that errand (Dr. Martin L. King, as quoted in Murphy and Jasinski 2009: 112). As can be seen in Table 6.1, through a lexis of hope, dream, promise, and foresight the administrations, taken together, reassert America's exceptionalist identity and its special meaning and responsibility to the global future. As the "indispensable nation," the American Self embodies the "enduring dream" of "people everywhere," "an idea which has become the ideal for billions," and the "last, best hope on earth." Because it "sees further . . . into the future" than other nations, America is obliged to serve "a higher moral purpose" of "lead[ing] the world . . . toward a brighter promise of a better day." Indeed, America must realize its "eternal promise"

Table 6.1. THE MEANING AND RESPONSIBILITY OF AMERICA

Bush administration	Clinton administration
• "has meaning beyond what we see" (1989, January 20)	• "eternal promise" (1995, January 24)
• "high moral purpose" (1989, January 20)	• "more than a place . . . an idea that has become the ideal for billions" (1995, November 27)
• "historic responsibility . . . to advance peace and democracy" (1989, May 31)	• "the indispensable nation . . . and for all the people of the world" (1996, October 22)
• "the enduring dream [that is] alive in the minds of people everywhere" (1990, January 31)	• "profound responsibility to build a new era of peace" (1998, January 29)
• "purpose higher than ourselves, a shining purpose" (1991, January 29)	• "indispensable nation [that] sees further than other countries into the future" (Albright 1998, February 19)
• "lead the world away from . . . dark chaos . . . toward a brighter promise of a better day" (1991, January 29)	• "the solemn responsibility to shape a more peaceful, democratic world" (1999, February 26)
• "a rising nation, the once and future miracle that is still . . . the hope of the world" (1992, January 28)	• "aspiring nations of the world trust us" (Powell 1993, September 30)
• "last, best hope on earth" (1992, April 9)	

---

[138]   *The Great Nation of Futurity*

by assuming its "historic responsibility . . . to advance peace and democracy" around the globe.

The story of America as an exceptional nation on an errand was adorned in the early years of the post–Cold War era in the "verbal vestments" (Bakhtin 1986: 88) of "democratic peace." Rooted in Kant's (1991) conception of "perpetual peace," democratic peace theory holds that democracies typically do not wage war against each other and, thus, are inherently peaceful.[3] The more democracy expands globally, so the thinking goes, the better the chances for a global peace. Having defeated the Soviet Union's "design" of imposing its "absolute authority over the rest of the world," the test now facing the nation would be its ability to secure "the peace of the world" by expanding "the perimeter of democratic government and free market capitalism to the ends of the earth" (May 1993: 25; Smith 2012: 207).

According to Hobson and Kurki (2012) America's global democratizing project became one of the "defining characteristics of the post–Cold War international order," as a world organized in terms of market-based democracy became "the consensus end point being worked toward"(1). Ish-Shalom (2013) similarly explains that as a term and concept, democratic peace "truly came of age" in the post–Cold War era (51). The prevalence of the democratic peace concept in foreign policy discourse was partially due to its coherence with the nation's collective identity as an exceptional nation seeking global peace and freedom (Ish-Shalom 2013: 69). As such, it lent the post-Cold War project definitional rigor and provided a remedy for the identity crisis pundits claimed was facing the nation after the demise of the Soviet Union (Smith 2012: 204; Ish-Shalom 2013: 70).

After initially searching for a concise conceptualization of post–Cold War foreign policy, the Bush administration seized upon democratic peace theory early in 1992, characterizing the post–Cold War era as a moment for exploring the "new frontier" created by the demise of the Soviet Union:

1. Americans have always responded best when a *new frontier* beckoned. And I believe the *next frontier* for us, and for *the generation that follows*, is to secure a democratic peace in Europe and the former U.S.S.R. that *will ensure a lasting peace for the United States*. The democratic peace *must be* founded on the twin pillars of political and economic freedom. The success of reform . . . *will be* the single best guarantee of our security, our prosperity, and our values. (Bush 1992, April 9)

This vision was reiterated several days later by Secretary of State James Baker:

2. [W]hat I would call a "zone of peace and prosperity" . . . has opened *new horizons* for so many nations in Europe and Asia and, not the least, for the

United States . . . in the post–Cold War era, we face a . . . summons to leadership . . . it is about winning a peace . . . for the whole world. (Baker 1992, April 21)

As can be seen in these excerpts, America's "new frontier" is designated in geographical terms, "Europe and the former U.S.S.R.," "nations in Europe and Asia," and "the whole world." Although the "new frontier" phrase functions as a spatial designation, it also bears future meaning. That is, a declaration of a "*new* frontier" has projective force as it simultaneously functions as a call to action and a symbol of the nation's prospects and potential.

As Bercovitch (2012) explains, the Puritans transformed the frontier from being a restrictive border separating different peoples to being a "mythical threshold . . . the outskirts of the advancing kingdom of God" (163–164). According to this conception, the very existence of the frontier served as a call to the nation's citizens to expand across the continent (Bercovitch 2012: 164). After the Revolutionary War, a distinctly American conception of the frontier replaced the European conception: it no longer represented "history and restriction" but, rather, "prophecy and unlimited prospects" (Bercovitch 2012: 164). By the close of the 19th century the frontier had been wholly transformed from a geographical place into a "mythic space" and "set of symbols" that have served to explain America's historical purpose (Slotkin 1992: 61). Its categories have been metaphorically extended to account for various moments in the nation's foreign policy history, while the very concept of frontier has been reconstituted "in terms appropriate to the modern era" (Slotkin 1992: 53–54). It has served, in sum, as "a moving stage for the quintessentially American drama of destined progress" (Bercovitch 2012: 164).

The stage for the post–Cold War phase of America's progress drama lay well beyond the nation's physical territory, in the metaphorically "unsettled" and "uninhabited"[4] spaces of the "Europe and the former Soviet Union." This designation of America's new frontier situates these spaces within the temporal domain of the *yet to be*, thereby rendering them as not fully developed members of the modern global community. Both Europe and the former Soviet Union were, of course, settled and inhabited in the early 1990s. Yet, according to the space-time underlying the American mission of extending the democratic peace they were not settled or inhabited *in the right way*: they remained places that had yet to realize their ultimate fulfillment; a particular future still awaited them. Indeed, as President Clinton declares, "The great opportunity the Russian people have is to define themselves in terms of the future, not the past" (Clinton 1996, October 22). Thus, to "win" the post–Cold War democratic peace, the United States would have to embark on an "errand into the wilderness" (Miller 1956) of sorts: it would have to work to reform the economic and political structures of nations outside the "zone of peace and

[140]   *The Great Nation of Futurity*

prosperity" and integrate them into a global system of free market capitalism and liberal democracy.

President Clinton was clear about the nation's post–Cold War future and its responsibility in bringing that future to fruition, declaring that "The promise of our future lies in the world. . . . Because of our unique position, America must lead with confidence in our strengths and with a clear vision of what we seek to avoid and what we seek to advance" (1999, February 26). The future that America must "advance" is a future grounded in a democratic peace:

3. [T]o the extent *that democracy and market economies hold sway in other nations,* our nation will be more secure, prosperous, and influential, while the broader *world will be more humane and peaceful.* (Lake 1993, September 21)[5]
4. In a new era of peril and opportunity our overriding purpose must be to *expand and strengthen the world's community of market-based democracies.* (Clinton 1993, September 27)
5. [T]he *habits of democracy are the habits of peace.* . . . Democracies rarely wage war on one another. (Clinton 1993, September 27)
6. To build a more peaceful 21st century world . . . we're renewing alliances that *extend the areas where wars don't happen.* (Clinton 1999, February 26)
7. The United States has the opportunity . . . and the solemn responsibility *to shape a more peaceful, prosperous democratic world.* (Clinton 1999, February 26)

Implicit within these calls for a global democratic peace is a geopolitical space-time that orients and structures the nation's foreign policy in the absence of the Soviet Other. The post–Cold War world would be defined by a Self/Other contrast rooted in a temporal assessment of which nations have developed into modern liberal, market-based democracies and which have not yet achieved this state of political-economic development. Returning to Fukuyama (1989), the post–Cold War geopolitical environment was to be understood in temporal terms, as comprising advanced nations that were "post-historical" and nations "still caught in the grip of history" (17, 14). Within this scheme, the "end of history" did not mean the end of an active geopolitical posture for the United States, as work to shape the future of global society still remained. The task facing "societies . . . at the vanguard of civilization" in the post–Cold War era, Fukuyama (1989) insisted, would be to "implement liberalism more fully" by ameliorating the gap between societies that "have already emerged on the other side of history" and those still "very much mired in history" (3, 17, 14).

The temporality of post–Cold War foreign policy discourse coheres with its spatiality, specifically the use of the concept of "zones" for configuring the geopolitical environment. This space-time embeds temporal contrasts reminiscent of those prescribed at the onset of the Cold War. Specifically, the post–Cold War "real world order" was rendered in terms of "zones of peace, wealth, and democracy" and "zones of turmoil, war, and development" (Singer and Wildvansky 1993). In brief, the zones of peace hold "most of the power in the world" and comprise modern, future-oriented states that subscribe to "democracy, market economies, and ethical and social values" (Singer and Wildvansky 1993: 3, 11). The zones of turmoil comprise traditional, past-oriented nations that are riddled with violence and turbulence and have difficulty developing politically and economically (Singer and Wildvansky 1999: 6–7).

Table 6.2 provides a summary of all the terms used by each administration to characterize these divergent zones. Not surprisingly, the zone discourse employs a moral lexis to value positively the zones of peace, wealth, and democracy and value negatively the zones of turmoil, war, and development. The former are "peaceful," "stable," "prosperous" societies that "cooperate" with each other, follow "the rule of law," respect "human rights," and are "progressively minded." They are spaces of "dignity," "hope," and "promise" in which "the forces of democracy" have taken hold. The zones of turmoil are "troubled" spaces marked by "turbulence," "radicalism," and "explosive division." They are home to "repressive" and "violent extremism," "militant nationalism," and the

Table 6.2. CONFIGURATION OF POST-COLD WAR WORLD

	Zones of peace, wealth, and democracy	Zones of turmoil, war, and development
Bush	peaceful; stable; cooperative; commonality/sharedness; independent and integrated; prosperous; democratic; market economies; free; rule of law; human rights; communal; progressive	turmoil; destructive forces; threatening; radicalism; dislocations and dangers; turbulence; upheavals; troubled; volatile; need; security problems; isolated; statist: unstable; crisis-prone; conflict: looking for guidance, needing help; authoritarian; forces of fragmentation that threaten order, peace, and stability; ethnic and aggressive nationalistic tensions; explosive; division
Clinton	dignity and hope; promise; open; free; secure; forces of democracy	troubling uncertainties; clear threats; wrenching; repressive; violent extremism, militant nationalism, and ethnic religious strife; enemies of democracy and free markets; outlaw states and ethnic conflict; defiant forces of nationalism

[142]   *The Great Nation of Futurity*

"enemies of freedom of democracy." Finally, they comprise societies "looking for guidance" and "needing help."

As hinted in the Bush and Clinton administrations' calls for a global democratic peace, the zone configuration assumes a prominent place in both administrations' official national security strategies. This configuration, as can be seen in Table 6.3, identifies the primary threat of the new era, explains how that threat should be addressed, and outlines the role of the United States in ensuring the future of the post–Cold War world order.

The geopolitical errand of extending the democratic peace can be understood as representing the contemporary "rededication" of American foreign policy to the nation's "divine cause" (Bercovitch 2012: xiii). This foreign policy project, in turn, sustained the conviction that the nation was an instrument of historical design. Like the modernization theorists before them, the Bush and Clinton administrations positioned the United States as the nation best suited to lead "people around the world" to a "more democratic and peaceful future." The rededication of the nation's energy and focus was important because, as we'll see below, the nation's Cold War victory raised the specter of a retreat from the world stage.

Table 6.3. ZONE STATEMENTS

	Post–Cold War threat	Threat response	U.S. geopolitical role
Bush	"As we provide American leadership to extend the 'zone of peace' and enhance the forces of integration . . . we must also provide . . . leadership to inhibit *forces of fragmentation that threaten order, peace, and stability.*" (USNSC 1993: 6)	"It is in our national interest to *help the democratic community of nations continue to grow* while ensuring stability." (USNSC 1993: 6)	"*We must lead* because we cannot otherwise hope to achieve a more democratic and peaceful future in a world still rife with turmoil and conflict." (USNSC 1993: 2)
Clinton	"A common purpose—to secure and strengthen the gains of democracy and free markets while turning back *their enemies.*" (USNSC 1998: iii)	"All of America's strategic interests are served by *enlarging the community of democratic and free market nations.*" (USNSC 1995: 22)	"*Our nation's . . . responsibility* is to sustain its [leadership] role by harnessing the forces of integration for the benefit of our own people and people around the world." (USNSC 1998: iii)

Declension: Liminality and Conditionality

In designating securing a democratic peace as the nation's post–Cold War errand, President Bush was careful to situate his call within the broader context of the nation's historical development. By reminding the nation that "Americans have always responded best when a new frontier beckoned," the president, as explained earlier, drew upon the "myth of the frontier." In so doing, he positioned the nation in a liminal moment, as "poised" between "the cultural ideal and its disastrous alternative" (Bercovitch 2012: 137). Moreover, he coded the nation's geopolitical status within a conditional modality: the nation could stay true to its ideal Self and continue on with its global errand, or it could repress that Self, fail to fulfill its responsibilities, and, ultimately, abandon its geopolitical role.

As explained in the previous section, the concept of the frontier signifies the possibility for and site of a progressive future. In Slotkin's (1985) words, it serves as the site of a "grand tournament between representatives of a dying past and the progressive future," with the stakes of this tournament being "the power to shape a progressive future" (9). Because of the importance of an "empty" frontier to the development of the nation's institutions and character, the "passing of the frontier" is understood as portending a national crisis (Slotkin 1992: 30). With no space to move into, the nation would be in stasis, which, as Campbell (1998) argues, could mean the decline, even demise, of the state (12). Such a crisis can be forestalled or prevented by declaring the opening of a new frontier. In this way, the invocation of the frontier myth serves as a "vehicle of the jeremiad: to create anxiety, to denounce backsliders, to reinforce social values, and (summarily) to define the American consensus" (Bercovitch 2012: 164).

By declaring a new frontier for American foreign policy, President Bush forestalled the closing of the 21st-century figural frontier by construing the end of the Cold War era not as the end of history but as the inception of the next "season" of "national probation" (Bercovitch 2012: 119). By proffering a democratic peace as the post–Cold War errand, the President issued a challenge: Cold War victory aside, the nation must decide whether it will stay true to its exceptional Self and continue on with it global mission or whether it will abandon that Self by determining that Americans "have no special role, no special place" and, thus, "can turn away from the world" (Bush 1992, January 28). He, in effect, juxtaposes two American Selves: an active Self that embraces "the world of possibilities" (Slotkin 1985: 45) and a passive Self that allows those possibilities to slip away.

The theme of liminality points to the post–Cold War variation on the jeremiadic lament of declension, which typically concerns either the present state of moral decline of American society (Jendrysik 2002; Johannesen 1986; Murphy 1990) or the failure of contemporary society to live up to the promise

[144] *The Great Nation of Futurity*

of its founding principles for all citizens (Harrell 2011; Howard-Pitney 2005; Murphy and Jasinski 2009). Although such claims of *present* declension occur in post–Cold War rhetoric, I have identified statements, such as those below, that project *future* declension to be a key feature of the post–Cold War jeremiad:

8. I believe global change is inexorable and can work to our advantage *or to our disadvantage, depending on what we do.* (Clinton 1992, August 13)
9. [T]he U.S. has an opportunity to mold an international system more compatible with the values we have held for two centuries. *But we may be letting that chance pass through our fingers.* (Scowcroft 1993, July 2)[6]
10. *We can let this moment slip away.* Or we can mobilize our nation in order to enlarge democracy, enlarge markets, and enlarge our future. (Lake 1993, September 21)

Each of these statements situates America and its capacity to impact the global future in a liminal space, as straddling the present moment of success and a future moment of possible failure. That is, they voice concerns regarding whether the nation is willing to ensure that global change "works to our advantage," to "mold the international system," and to "enlarge democracy . . . markets . . . and our future" or whether it will "let this moment slip away." From a geopolitical perspective, the nation's "present" at the end of the 20th century was a moment of ascension rather than declension: the United States was the world's lone superpower and had unprecedented military, economic, and political power. At issue, then, was not whether the nation had strayed from its founding principles but whether it would spread those principles until they were "everywhere triumphant." Consequently, in addition to representing the site of great national promise, the post–Cold war future was also rendered as the site of possible national decline, as both administrations warned that the nation might neglect it responsibility to the global future. Laments of future declension are articulated through three temporal tropes: pivotal moment, unrealized errand, and shape the future. I take each in turn.

The liminality of the nation's current geopolitical status is construed through statements, presented in Table 6.4, that situate the nation temporally at a "pivotal" moment in a space-time between present and future, as "poised at that figural nick of time" between present and future, as "on the brink of some momentous decision" (Bercovitch 2012: 147).

Despite its Cold War victory, situating the United States at a pivotal moment renders the current moment as yet another test of the nation's resolve to fulfill its global errand—another moment that will define the nation and during which the nation's course will be charted and, possibly, its purpose renewed. These statements invoke both the alternative-future and

AN AMERICAN FUTURE OF DEMOCRATIC PEACE [145]

Table 6.4. PIVOTAL MOMENT STATEMENTS

Bush administration	Clinton administration
• "[W]e stand today at *a unique and extraordinary moment*." (Bush 1990, September 11)	• "[O]ur nation's policies toward the world stand at *an historic crossroads*." (Lake 1993, September 21)
• "[W]e stand at *a defining hour*." (Bush 1991, January 29)	• "[N]ations . . . *must decide whether* they are prepared to rise to *the occasions history presents them*." (Clinton 1993, February 17)
• "[N]ow we are facing *another defining hour for America* and the world." (Bush 1991, January 29)	• "Now that era is upon us. It is *a moment of unparalleled opportunity*." (Lake 1993, September 21)
• "[W]ith the passing of the cold war . . . we stand at *history's hinge point*." (Bush 1992, April 9)	• "This pivotal moment" (Clinton 1996, August 5)
• "*this defining moment*" (Bush 1992, April 9)	• "[N]ow we must rise to *the decisive moment*, to make a nation and a world better than any we have ever known." (Clinton 1997, February 4)
• "[T]oday we have reached *a turning point*." (Bush 1992, April 9)	• "[N]ow we stand at *another moment of choice and decision*, another moment to be foresighted." (Clinton 1997, February 4)

shape-the-future tropes to signify that the nation's mission, rather than being realized, has yet to be fully accomplished. That is, they implicate the two alternative futures that inhere in contrasting American Selves: a future defined by an America that embraces its "extraordinary moment" and decides to "rise to the occasion history presents" and a future defined by an America that fails "to be farsighted."

The pivotal-moment statements cohere with statements expressing concern about the status of the nation's errand. That is, despite unequivocal assertions of "the triumph of the West, of the Western idea" (Fukuyama 1989: 1), a simmering anxiety emerged in the late 1980s and early 1990s over whether the nation would continue on with its errand. Within the jeremiad, such anxiety serves to "excite and fortify expectations" (Bercovitch 2012: 146). As with jeremiads past, "no sooner [is] peace declared" than politicians and policymakers "resum[e] their lament" about the nation's future prospects (Bercovitch 2012: 118–119).

As can be seen in the following excerpts, the post–Cold War jeremiad embeds a space-time that juxtaposes the triumphant present with a future of uncertainty and struggle. Rhetorically, this space-time signifies that although the nation was successful in the Cold War, its work is not yet done; America "must" remain a "culture on an errand."

[146]   *The Great Nation of Futurity*

11. But with the passing of the cold war, a new order *has yet to take its place*. . . . We *have defeated* imperial communism. *We've not yet* won the victory for democracy, though. This democratic peace *will not be* easily won . . . democracy and economic freedom *will be* years in the building. America *must*, therefore, resolve that our commitment be equally firm and *lasting* . . . a new order *has yet to take its place*. (Bush 1992, April 9)
12. Democracy and market economics *are ascendant* in this new era, but they *are not everywhere triumphant*. There remain vast areas in Asia, Africa, the Middle East and elsewhere where democracy and market economics *are at best new arrivals*. . . . Thus we *have arrived* at neither the end of history nor the clash of civilizations, but a moment of immense democratic and entrepreneurial *opportunity*. We *must* not waste it. (Lake 1993, September 21)

Temporally, these statements signal the fulfilled-yet-unfulfilled status of America's geopolitical errand. Through the perfective aspect, Bush characterizes the present as both a moment in which the nation has won a battle in the war for global democracy ("have defeated imperial communism") and a moment in which the war for that global future continues ("have not yet won"). He projects the future of this battle for a "new order" that "has yet to take its place" as a long and difficult one and, thus, as requiring "firm and lasting" American resolve. In the transition from the second to the third sentences, we see the president derive the obligational "must be" from this projection of future "reality."

The statement from President Clinton's national security advisor, Anthony Lake, regarding the current state of "democracy and free market economics" echoes Bush's but also specifies the terrain on which the nation's commitment will be enacted. Moreover, he indexes the space-time construal from the post–World War II moment by designating particular spaces as past, spaces in which American political and economic systems "are not . . . triumphant" and are "at best new arrivals." The present moment, then, is not "the end of history," Lake avers, but, rather, a moment of "opportunity." It is this moment of opportunity to develop "vast areas" around the globe, not recent accomplishments, that must be the nation's focus. In sum, both administrations perform a jeremiad lament by insisting that the Cold War battle "just past . . . did not resolve the crisis" facing the nation; the "great season of our national probation had just begun," as the errand was yet to be fully realized (Bercovitch 2012: 119).

Assurances that the United States will succeed in its errand of extending the democratic peace assume that the nation has committed to fulfilling its geopolitical obligations. That is, both administrations, as did their forebears in the wake of World War II (see Chapter 3), draw on the shape-the-future trope to characterize both the nation's exceptional status and its geopolitical responsibility:

13. We are Americans. We are the nation that believes in the future. We are *the nation that can shape the future.* (Bush 1991, January 29)
14. We have a once-in-a-century opportunity to *shape the course of history and to define a new age* of peace. (Baker 1992, April 21)
15. We also must set our sights on a more distant horizon. Through . . . the power of our example, America has *a unique ability to shape a world* of greater security and prosperity, peace, and freedom. (Clinton 1996, October 22)
16. man the frontiers of freedom abroad. . . . But more than just maintaining the peace, we now have a chance *to shape the future, to build a world* more secure, more prosperous than any we have ever known . . . or could . . . even have dreamed of. (Clinton 1998, January 29)

At the same time, however, both presidents raise the possibility that the nation could cast off its exceptional identity and neglect its global obligations. They do so by contrasting two temporal Selves for the United States: a nation that assumes a passive stance "toward an approaching future over which [it has] little control" versus an active, intentional Self "striding toward" a future it believes it "can control and design" (Mische 2009: 701). In the absence of the nation's Cold War Other, the Bush and Clinton administrations conjure a passive Self against that assumes an active role regarding the global future:

17. Either we answer the summons to leadership or we do not. Either *we take hold of history or history will take hold of us.* (Baker 1992, April 21)
18. The choice for America is this: we can either win this peace through *a deliberate policy . . . to shape our times,* or we can stand aside and drift . . . while *times shape us.* (Baker 1992, April 21)
19. History is calling our nation to decide anew whether *we will lead or defer* . . . whether *we will shape a new era or instead be shaped by it.* (Clinton 1992, April 1: 425)
20. Now in the new century, we'll have a remarkable opportunity *to shape a future* more peaceful than the past, but only if we stand strong against the enemies of peace. (Clinton 1998, December 16)
21. Will America *stay engaged* in the new post–Cold War world it has helped create? Or will we instead heed those who would . . . *restrict our nation's unique ability to shape the world's future and our own*? (Lake 1996, May 3)

The "promise" of the new era will be realized if the United States chooses to actively "shape" a progressive future by "tak[ing] hold of history" while the "threats" of the new era will come to fruition if the nation assumes the passive position of letting "times shape us." As such, if the nation is to remain ascendant, it must decide anew to "shape a new era" lest it "be shaped by it." Should the nation abdicate this responsibility, the prospects for both it and global society will be greatly diminished, as the "enemies of peace" will most assuredly triumph over a future "more peaceful than the past." By situating the United States at the temporal intersection of the promise of continued ascendance and the threat of future declension, the post–Cold War jeremiad turns this conditional moment into a "mode of socialization" by challenging the nation to recommit itself to its mission of designing a progressive future for global society.

Prophecy: Revitalizing the Errand

The post–Cold War lament of declension was not just a rhetorical performance of anxiety concerning the possible abandonment of the nation's geopolitical errand; it also functioned dialogically to create a rhetorical space for a response that would both exploit and assuage that anxiety. That is, having raised the possibility of the nation neglecting its exceptional Self, both the Bush and Clinton administrations were careful to issue calls for a recommitment to the nation's errand and provide assurances of its ultimate success. Through the jeremiad's prophetic dimension they joined the *not yet* with the *will be* in order to ensure a new era of global engagement. While this discourse exalts in the nation's glorious past, it exalts, even more so, in anticipation of what lies ahead for the nation and, thus, for the world (Bercovitch 2012: 146). This anticipatory inclination of the American character rejects the "Old World ideal of stasis" in favor of a "New World vision of the future" that propels the nation forward by showing its people how they can "act in history" (Bercovitch 2012: 23).

By "joining lament and celebration" (Bercovitch 2012: 11) in this way, the post–Cold War jeremiad exploits a missionary zeal for global improvement by trumpeting its merits while simultaneously warning of the obstacles and dangers standing in the way. It does so through the ritualistic juxtaposing of promise and threat that serves as a rhetorical vehicle for engaging the "restless 'progressivist' energies required for the success of the venture" (Bercovitch 2012: 23). That is, post–Cold War foreign policy discourse further affirms the need for a geopolitically engaged and assertive American Self by proffering a host of vague Others that, although not posing the type of threat attributed to the Soviet Union, are deemed as threats to America's vision of the geopolitical future. The rhetoric of promise projects a vision of the future that will result from the nation's errand of extending the democratic peace. The rhetoric of threat comprises projections of "a range of dangers that might occupy the place of the old" (Campbell 1998: 7) and, thereby, provides the post–Cold War Other that opposes the American future, and, concomitantly, underscores the need for American global leadership. This rhetoric is at once energizing and visionary: it urges the nation to push through the uncertainty and challenges of the post–Cold War moment while also offering a vision that provides "assurance about the future during a troubled period of transition" (Bercovitch 2012: 23, 80). As I'll demonstrate below, both administrations were careful to laud the promise that the nation's Cold War victory foretold while also warning of an array of "threats," "challenges," and "dangers" that lay ahead.

In the early months of the post–Cold War era, President Bush asserts that, freed from the threats of global communism, the prospects for global democratic capitalism seem quite clear. In his first State of the Union Address, the president claims a clarity of vision about the post–Cold War future, proclaiming that the "right path" to this "unclouded future" (Bercovitch 2012: 146) is fully apparent:

22. There are times when the future seems thick as a fog; you sit and wait, hoping the mists will lift and reveal the right path. But this is a time when the future seems a door you can walk right through into a room called tomorrow. (Bush 1989, January 20)

In subsequent statements, the Bush administration tempers assurances of future promise with warnings of future threats:

23. I mean to speak tonight of big changes and the promises they hold, and of some big problems. . . . We gather . . . at a dramatic and deeply promising time in our history and the history of man on Earth. . . . There are still threats. But the long, drawn out dread is over. . . . But even in the midst of celebration, we must keep caution . . . the world is still a dangerous place. (Bush 1992, January 28)
24. The failure of the democratic experiment could bring a dark future, a return to authoritarianism or a descent into anarchy . . . the outcome would threaten our peace, prosperity, and security for years to come. But we should focus not on the dangers of failure but on the dividends of success. (Bush 1992, April 9)
25. We are building something . . . that mankind has never seen before—the first truly, completely democratic hemisphere in the world. . . . There are dangers on the way to the future we seek . . . democracy remains fragile, and it remains threatened by . . . ever-present temptations to seek a different, supposedly more efficient, anti-democratic course. (Baker 1992, April 13)

In statement 23, we see President Bush align change with both promise and threat as he urges the nation to celebrate its geopolitical victory over communism while cautioning that in the "midst of celebration" the nation must understand that this victory is not total—"There are still some threats" and "the world is still a dangerous place." He counters this warning by announcing that "the long drawn out dread [of the Cold War] is over." Furthermore, he aligns

[150]   *The Great Nation of Futurity*

"the history of man on Earth" with "our history" by declaring the universality of the promises entailed in the "big changes" brought about by the ending of the Cold War. That is, implied in this universalizing of the post–Cold War promise is a logic that holds that if America's future is promising, then so is the future of the global community. In excerpt 24, the president advocates for the nation's continued participation in the "democratic experiment" by projecting an image of an alternative future that "could" result if that experiment fails, "a dark future, a return to authoritarianism or a descent into anarchy," and the consequences that future "would" have for the nation's "peace, prosperity, and security." Although the president wants the American people to be aware of this possible future, he doesn't want it to be the object of their focus as he advises that they "should focus" not on "the dangers of failure" but on the "dividends of success." Finally, in excerpt 25, Secretary of State Baker lauds the present state of the nation's democratic experiment in Central and South America, noting that the United States is currently involved in "building" a future "that mankind has never seen before." This future is under threat, however, by the "ever present temptations" of an alternative "anti-democratic course" to this future.

As both a candidate and president, Clinton similarly deploys the threat/ promise rhetoric to characterize the inception of the new era:

26. [E]ven as the American Dream is inspiring people around the world. . . . We face . . . great foreign policy challenges. . . . The collapse of communism does not mean the end of danger. A new set to threats . . . will force us . . . to keep our guard up. (Clinton 1991, December 12)
27. We [Americans] stand blessed as the inheritors of a new world. It is a world of hope and opportunity. . . . It is a cause for rejoicing. . . . But this new world we have helped create . . . remains a place of peril. (Clinton 1992, August 13)
28. This is a promising moment . . . of course there are still dangers in the world. (Clinton 1994, January 24)
29. For all the promise of our time, we are not free from peril . . . forces of destruction live on. (Clinton 1996, August 5)
30. We live in a time of tremendous promise for our nation in the world . . . even as we welcome this hopeful moment we all acknowledge that . . . challenges persist. (Clinton 1998, January 29)

Like President Bush, Clinton sees in the nation's Cold War victory "a world of hope and opportunity," "a promising moment," "a time of tremendous promise for our nation in the world." Indeed, as the "blessed . . . inheritors of a new world," the nation has "cause for rejoicing." Yet, despite the triumph of democratic capitalism over authoritarian communism, the nation must continue to pursue its geopolitical errand: it must "keep [its] guard up" against "a new set of threats," "dangers in the world," "forces of destruction," and "challenges."

AN AMERICAN FUTURE OF DEMOCRATIC PEACE [151]

In both the Bush and Clinton administrations' promise/threat discourse, we see the persistence of the American Self working relentlessly on behalf of the global community for a future of freedom and democracy. The construal of the post–Cold War Other, however, exemplifies the shape-shifting nature of this rhetorical trope as the Cold War Other of authoritarian communism is replaced with a variety of post–Cold War Others: a "return to authoritarianism," a "descent into anarchy," "temptations" of an "anti-democratic course," "a set of new threats," "dangers on the way to the future," and "forces of destruction." Furthermore, in their assessment of the post–Cold War security environment, both administrations construe the nation's Other in temporal terms by drawing on the concept of change and the journey and building metaphors: the promise entailed in the American-dominated present is threatened by a possible "*return* to authoritarianism," a "*descent* into anarchy," "dangers *on the way to* the future," an "anti-democratic *course*," and "forces of *destruction*."

The post–Cold War jeremiad's threat/promise trope also manifests in a lexis of opportunity, challenge, and danger that both administrations use to characterize the post–Cold War future and the nation's place in it. For example, both use this lexis in their national security strategy documents to construe the new security environment:

31. Shaping a security strategy for a new era will require an understanding of the extraordinary trends at work today—an accurate sense of the *opportunities* that history has put forth before us and a sober appreciation of the *dangers* that remain. (USNSC 1991: 1)

32. It is a new era that holds *great opportunities*—but also *great dangers*. (USNSC 1993: preface)[7]

33. Never has American leadership been more essential—to navigate the shoals of the world's *new dangers* and to capitalize on its *opportunities*. (USNSC 1995: i)

34. The security environment in which we live is dynamic and uncertain, replete with a *host of threats and challenges* that have the potential to grow more deadly, but also offering *unprecedented opportunities* to avert those threats and advance our interests. (USNSC 1998: 1)

For both presidents, this configuration of the security environment demands American leadership:

35. There is a new world of challenges and opportunities before us and there's a need for *leadership that only America can provide*. (Bush, 1990, January 31)

36. The end of the Cold War and collapse of the Soviet empire pose an unprecedented opportunity to make our future more prosperous and secure . . . *America must lead* the world we have worked so hard to make. . . .

[152] *The Great Nation of Futurity*

If we don't take the lead, *no one else can, and no one else will*. (Clinton 1992, April 1)

During the Bush administration, the threats and promises, opportunities and challenges of the new era were brought into full relief by Iraq's incursion into Kuwait. The administration, in turn, construed the conflict as a warning of the "perils" of the nation's "high enterprise" (Bercovitch 2012: 4). In the following statements we see a conception of post–Cold War space-time according to which a violation of the spatial domain represents a violation of the temporal domain:

37. The present aggression in the Gulf is a menace not only to one region's security but to *the entire world's vision of our future*. It threatens to turn *the dream* of a new international order into *a grim nightmare* of anarchy in which the law of the jungle supplants the law of nations. (Bush 1990, October 1)
38. A year after the joyous *dawn of freedom's light* in Eastern Europe, *a dark evil* has descended in another part of the world. (Bush 1991, January 9)
39. If we do not follow the dictates of our inner moral compass . . . [Saddam Hussein's] lawlessness will threaten the peace and democracy of *the emerging world order we now see*: this *long dreamed of vision* we've all worked toward for so long. (Bush 1991, January 9)
40. What's at stake is more than one small country; it's a big idea: a *new world order*, where diverse nations are drawn together in common cause to achieve *the universal aspirations of mankind*: peace and security, freedom, the rule of law. (Bush 1991, January 29)

President Bush transforms the conflict from a regional dispute over territory and borders into an attack on America's vision of the geopolitical future: "the long dreamed of vision" of "a new world order" that will "achieve the universal aspirations of mankind." In so doing, he resituates the "present aggression" from the physical space of Kuwait to the temporal space of the future, thereby redefining it as an attack on "the entire world's vision of the future." Moreover, similar to President Truman's transformation of the local events in Greece and Turkey into a harbinger of the post–World War II future, President Bush renders this regional conflict as a portent of the post–Cold War future should the nation not commit to its global errand. If America fails to act, the consequences of the "present aggression" will extend far beyond Kuwait and the Persian Gulf region: it could lead to a future in which "the dream of a new international order" is replaced by "a grim nightmare of anarchy." Should it act, however, the nation will "chart the future of the world for the next 100 years" (Bush 1991, January 16). In this way, President Bush uses the conflict to "revitalize the errand" by "fetching good out of evil" (Bormann 1977: 131). In

AN AMERICAN FUTURE OF DEMOCRATIC PEACE [153]

honoring its "obligation—to stop ruthless aggression," the nation, along with those who ally with it, "step forward with a new sense of purpose, a new sense of possibilities" (Bush 1991, January 9; Bush 1990, October 1).

President Clinton distills the threat/promise and opportunity/challenge tropes into the concept of "two powerful tendencies" at work in the new era: forces of "integration" that are "fueling a welcome explosion of entrepreneurship and political liberalization" and forces of "resurgent aspirations of ethnic and religious groups" that threaten the power of international and state institutions (1993, September 27). Given this climate, President Clinton exhorts the nation to "redeem the promise of America in the 21st Century" (1997, January 20). "Shuttling between sacred past and sacred future" (Bercovitch 2012: 148), the president insists that the nation's "journey" will be "guided" and "sustain[ed]" by "the ancient vision of a promised land" and by "the promise of America . . . born in the 18th century" and "extended and preserved in the 19th century, when our Nation spread across the continent" (1997, January 20). And while the nation's geographical frontier has long been closed, the president reassures the nation that this territorial limitation will not constrain the promise the future holds: "The promise we sought in a *new land* we will find again in a land of *new promise* . . . our land of *new promise*" (1997, January 20; emphasis added). Yet he cautions the nation to not let "our progress . . . mask the peril that remains" (1997, February 4).

CONCLUSION

The ending of the Cold War was deemed by politicians and policymakers to raise crucial questions about the role the nation would play in the post–Cold War era and how that role would be legitimated in the absence of a Soviet Union. As did the Cold War discourse that preceded it, the foreign policy discourse initiating the post–Cold War era embeds a space-time that situates America in a privileged position and grants it a special role vis-à-vis the global future. Examining the Bush and Clinton administrations' foreign policy discourse through three key themes of the jeremiad—chosen-ness, declension, and prophecy—enabled me to demonstrate the means by which each reasserted and reaffirmed the nation's claim of exceptionalism and positioned the United States vis-à-vis the geopolitical future.

The concept of chosen-ness was realized through the post–Cold War mission of "extending the democratic peace" and declarations that the United States was uniquely qualified to undertake that mission. My analysis demonstrates that it embeds a geopolitical space-time that called for the United States to take an activist role in shaping the post–Cold War future. This space-time situated certain "zones" in the temporal domain of "yet-to-be" and construed that temporal status as both a challenge to and opportunity for the

United States. America, concomitantly, was rendered as exemplifying the future that awaits the peoples comprising these zones and as uniquely capable of leading them to it.

Through the rhetoric of potential declension, both administrations warned of the contingent nature of the American Self, of the possibility that the nation would fail to embrace its exceptionalist identity and role and, thus, neglect its responsibility for the post–Cold War future. This warning was articulated through three temporal tropes: pivotal moment, unrealized errand, and the shape the future. Taken together, they juxtaposed the present moment of American triumph with a future of uncertainty and possible complacency, highlighted the unfinished status of the nation's geopolitical errand, and challenged the nation to stay true to its fundamental identity and purpose.

Finally, through the prophetic dimension of the jeremiad, the Bush and Clinton administrations grounded their calls for the nation to accept its post–Cold War mission in assurances that, despite the "threats" that lay ahead, the nation would succeed in extending the democratic peace. This rhetoric drew on Self/Other contrasts that identified the United States as the unchallenged vanguard of the post–Cold War future, whose mission was both necessitated and threatened by a range of amorphous Others.

By juxtaposing visions of a progressive global future with those of its "catastrophic alternative" (Bercovitch 2012: 150), the post–Cold War jeremiad channeled the nation's energy and attention away from its Cold War victory and toward a new era of global engagement and intervention. The jeremiad, a genre that has been "cited, imitated, and followed" throughout the nation's history and has provided the "leading ideas" for conceptualizing and legitimating America's place and purpose in the world, provided a template for the geopolitical role the United States should assume in the wake of the demise of the Soviet Union (Bakhtin 1986: 88). Moreover, the genre incorporated that role into a historical rhetorical ritual that has been central to the constitution of American identity and purpose, a ritual whereby the nation is identified in temporal terms as an "unfolding prophecy" that manifests "the climax of history and the pattern of things to come" (Bercovitch 2012: xiii, 143–144).

CHAPTER 7
The Future of American Exceptionalism

SUMMARY OF ANALYSIS

The central concern of this book has been to identify the ways the future figured conceptually, manifested linguistically, and functioned rhetorically in conceptions of American national identity and geopolitical purpose within Cold War foreign policy discourse. I addressed this issue through a critical discourse analysis of texts generated at moments when the nation's geopolitical role was a central focus of politicians and policymakers. The discursive construal of the nation's postwar role drew upon and, thereby, perpetuated the identification of America as the exceptional nation destined to lead the world. It was this distinctive identity and the geopolitical mission it entailed that its advocates insisted positioned the United States as best qualified to remedy the "unfinished and endangered nature of the world" (Campbell 1998: 61). Moreover, it was this identity and purpose that were claimed to be under constant threat during the Cold War.

My argument, however, is not merely that exceptionalist appeals were a central feature of Cold War foreign policy discourse. As noted in Chapter 1, the persistence of the rhetoric of exceptionalism in construals of American national identity has been established by a plethora of scholarship. In terms of the Cold War specifically, Lagerfeld (2020) notes that while it has a long history, American exceptionalism was "reborn" in the aftermath of World War II as the nation's leaders sought to position the United States as the necessary counterforce to the rise and influence of Soviet communism (95). In a 1952 editorial in the *Partisan Review*, Phillips and Rahv characterized this role in terms of the unique value American-style democracy held for the global community: "The democratic values which America either embodies or promises . . . are necessary conditions for civilization and represent the

The Great Nation of Futurity. Patricia L. Dunmire, Oxford University Press. © Oxford University Press 2023.
DOI: 10.1093/oso/9780197658222.003.0007

only immediate alternative as long as Russian totalitarianism threatens world domination" (as quoted in Lagerfeld 2020: 95).

Rather, the current volume contributes to discussions of American exceptionalism by demonstrating that to understand the full force of exceptionalist claims, such as those made by Phillips and Rahv and examined in this book, we must understand their temporal dimension—the way America's self-proclaimed identity as the exceptional nation positions it with respect to the global future and implicates an American claim on that future. As Andersson and Rindzeviciute (2015) explain, the future was a prominent focus of Cold War "political imaginaries" concerned with how the postwar world would evolve and the strategies the United States would deploy in its efforts to shape that evolution (14). My analysis likewise demonstrates that the global future was a key discursive and ideological construct of Cold War foreign policy discourse.

I go beyond merely corroborating Andersson and Rindzeviciute's argument, however, by demonstrating that a key rhetorical strategy within this discourse was to claim the future as the special province of the United States and ground that claim in a temporal construal of American national identity. That is, I show how Cold War political imaginaries manifested linguistically and functioned rhetorically to authorize a privileged position for the United States vis-à-vis the postwar global future. This discursive process involved a host of space-time construals and Self/Other contrasts that articulated and disarticulated particular global actors and constituencies with and from the temporal domain of future.

The American/periphery dyad was rooted in a space-time scheme according to which "modern man" is positively valued and rendered as the "living exemplar" of democracy and, thus, as uniquely qualified to demonstrate the values, principles, and benefits of democracy to others (Doty 1996: 155, 139). The periphery, on the other hand, is identified as comprising "the emerging people" who have been "outpaced and left behind" but who, nevertheless, have "democratic potential" that "modern man" must bring to fruition (Doty 1996: 131–132; Hansen 2006: 25). Within the modern/traditional spatiotemporal scheme, the urgency of this mission stems from the fact that the "underdeveloped" status of the periphery poses a "grave menace to the future" of the nations at the center of the global system, the United States in particular (Doty 1996: 111).

In this way, the periphery served as a key Other against which American identity and purpose were constructed and legitimated in the texts examined herein. This use of the periphery was seen at the inception of the Cold War era as well as in its enactment and at its conclusion: the "underdeveloped areas/countries" of the Truman Doctrine and modernization theory and the "zones" of the post–Cold War era. At the onset of the Cold War and its enactment, a lexis of aspiration and promise served to align the future of the periphery with the United States and to render that future as the legitimate province of the nation's Cold War policy. America was not just identified as further along the timescale of past, present, and future relative to the periphery; it was also rendered as embodying the future toward which the development of the periphery was to be oriented. Moreover, the alternative-futures trope was used to project the catastrophic futures that would result if the periphery developed along lines antithetical to American geopolitical interests. At the conclusion of the Cold War we saw the use of a new formulation of the periphery—"zones of turmoil, war, and development"—to fill the threat blank left by the demise of the Soviet Union and, thereby, to help legitimize a continued activist role for the United States in the post–Cold War era, a role focused on shaping the post–Cold War global future.

The American Self/Soviet Union dyad was rooted in a space-time that situated the two superpowers as coeval and, thus, as offering alternative paths to the postwar future. According to this scheme, the Soviet threat was construed in temporal terms, as stemming from its offering an alternative future for the periphery that challenged American claims on the future of the newly decolonized societies. At the formulation, enactment, and reassertion of the Cold War, the American and Soviet futures were discursively represented in such a way as to affirm America's claimed role vis-à-vis the global future. That is, through an "evangelism of fear" (Campbell 1998: 61) the foreign policy discourse examined in the previous chapters construed the Cold War environment to necessitate and sanction the creation of the postwar global environment grounded in an American vision of the future. This discourse involved projecting and juxtaposing alternative American and Soviet futures and evaluating the authenticity of each superpower's claim on the future.

Both of these discursive moves were initiated by President Truman's projection of the "two ways of life" that lay ahead for the global community in the wake of World War II. He deployed a moral lexis that rendered Their way of life as leading to a future of fear, terror, and domination and Ours as leading to a future of freedom, liberty, and democracy. He also juxtaposed the claims each made on the future of the "underdeveloped areas," insisting that while American claims were rooted in the genuine desires and wants of the people of the periphery, the Soviet claim was exploitative and offered only "false promises." Truman's discursive strategies redounded in subsequent Cold War foreign policy discourse. Modernization theorists drew upon the alternative-futures trope to evaluate the American future positively and to evaluate the Soviet future negatively. A rhetoric of commonality and authenticity was used to underwrite the American claim on the future of the periphery and, by implication, to delegitimize the Soviet claim. Ultimately, the American future was transformed into the natural, inevitable future of global society through linguistic and rhetorical devices that objectified and universalized the modernization process and, thereby,

[158] *The Great Nation of Futurity*

removed it from the geopolitical context of the Cold War and American foreign policy.

While it served as the nation's radical Other at the height of the Cold War, the Soviet Union was deemed to be its less-than-radical Other during the period of detente. The Committee on the Present Danger (CDP), however, discursively resuscitated the radical relation of difference between the United States and Soviet Union by imbuing the future with present-ness. That is, the CPD projected a catastrophic Soviet future and rendered it as imminent, though not necessarily inevitable. Through aspectual markers, the CPD represented the Soviet Union as making rapid progress toward its alleged goal of world domination and the United States as enabling that progress. It used this projection of the future to call for an aggressive military posture for the United States and, more broadly, for the nation to reclaim the geopolitical future from the Soviets. The CPD's project was rooted in earlier Cold War articulations of the Soviet threat and was legitimated by the mythopoetic performance of Ronald Reagan. By retelling the "grand story of America" Reagan put the nation back on its true course and reclaimed its geopolitical identity and mission as the "great nation of futurity."

At both the inception and close of the Cold War we saw the use of a Self/Other construct that pitted an active American Self against a passive Self in arguments concerning the role the nation should play on the world stage. This construct was rooted in the shape-the-future trope that posed the question of whether the United States would embrace its privileged role vis-à-vis the future or whether it would cede that role to some threatening Other, be it the Soviet Union or the forces of chaos and anarchy. In the wake of World War II, the "future pattern" of global relations was deemed by President Truman to depend upon the decisions and actions of the United States, on whether it would decide to serve as the "powerhouse" of Western democratic ideals or remain their mere "sanctuary." This construal of America's geopolitical role introduced a temporal conception of national security that prioritized shaping the global future as a key means of ensuring the nation's security and prosperity. At the inception of the post–Cold War era, both the Bush and Clinton administrations drew on the shape-the-future trope to raise the specter of America neglecting its role regarding the future and, thereby, warranting an interventionist geopolitical posture. That is, both emphasized that the ending of the Cold War did not mean the end of America's geopolitical mission. On the contrary, if it was to lead the world to a "progressive future," the United States would have to continue to embrace and act on its "solemn responsibility" of shaping the post–Cold War global future. At stake was whether this future would be a future of a global democratic peace or a future shaped and dominated by the "enemies of peace."

Throughout the documents examined herein the issue of who America is, what it stands for, and the geopolitical role it plays was mediated through the temporal domain of the future. Futurity, in addition to serving as a projective space and rhetorical resource, was rendered as an essential aspect of the nation's identity and purpose. As I've demonstrated, a key litmus test of whether the nation was or would remain an exceptional nation centered on whether it would accept its identity as "the great nation of futurity" and act accordingly. Would it continue to serve as an example of how democratic societies should function? As the exemplar of what a democratically minded people could become? As the living manifestation of other people's aspirations and desires? As we've seen, this test served to distinguish America from various external, foreign Others that were deemed to threaten the American way of life and its claim on the global future. Indeed, as Bacevich (2021) notes, Secretary of State Albright's claim that America "sees further" into the future than other nations epitomizes the "lingua franca of American statecraft" (6).

This discourse is not, however, limited to Cold War foreign policy discourse and its discursive practice of construing relations of identity and difference. As more recent events demonstrate, such interrogations of American national identity can arise within domestic contexts in which what the nation is and what it represents for others are the focus of a national conversation. I'm referring here to the ruminations of politicians and opinion leaders over the nation's claim of exceptionalism prompted by President Trump, namely, by his election in 2016, his response to the 2020 presidential election results, and his supporters' attack on the U.S. Capitol on January 6, 2021.

In what follows, I demonstrate that the analytic lens and precepts used to examine Cold War foreign policy discourse can also be used to examine this contemporary discourse of national self-reflection and, moreover, that this reflexive discourse further reveals the important role that futurity plays in conceptions of American exceptionalism. As such, I conclude my study by considering how America's temporal identity has figured in articulations of exceptionalism made in the context of Trump's election, his rejection of the 2020 presidential election results, and the attack on the U.S. Capitol. My hope is to demonstrate further that temporality, generally, and futurity, specifically, are part and parcel of the discourse of American national identity and purpose.

REFLECTIONS ON AMERICAN EXCEPTIONALISM IN THE AGE OF TRUMP

From the moment of Trump's election in 2016 through to the events of January 6, 2021, concerns and questions have been raised about the nation's current and future status as the exceptional nation. The United States, and the world, have been witness to events most believed "can't happen here": the rejection of the outcome of the 2020 presidential election by the sitting president and many members of the Republican party, the former president's failure to support the peaceful transfer of power, and an attack on the U.S. Capitol during which symbols of white supremacy were openly displayed by people claiming to be there to "Save America." Symbols and ideas once thought to be part of the darkest moments in the nation's past, or merely fringe views of its present, were resurrected in a purported effort to "Keep America Great" by keeping Donald Trump in the presidency. Moreover, this unprecedented display also raised concerns about what the attack might presage for the future of American democracy and the nation's claim of exceptionalism. Politicians and pundits have deemed this exceptional moment a national identity crisis, a crisis over what America means for both its own citizens and for people around the world.

As reactions to it make clear, the Capitol insurrection, which *Washington Post* columnist Michael Gerson (2021) described as "a post-apocalyptic vision of chaos and national humiliation," was not a future anticipated by adherents to American exceptionalism. It did not fit with the narrative of progress that characterizes the United States as "the leading player in a divinely guided history of liberty, leading the world to redemption by modeling and spreading any number of national values" (Van Engen 2020: 285). In the immediate aftermath of the attack, pundits and politicians insisted that Trump supporters' ransacking of the Capitol did not reflect the nation's true Self. House Minority Leader Kevin McCarthy, Representative Liz Cheney, former Homeland Security Advisor Tom Bossert, former President Jimmy Carter, and President-elect Joe Biden insisted, respectively, that "what we saw last night was not the American Way," "This is what America is not," "It's un-American," "this is a national tragedy and is not who we are as a nation," and "The scenes of chaos do not reflect a true America. Do not represent who we are" (Baker 2021; LeBlanc 2021).

On the contrary, Ishaan Tharoor (2021), foreign affairs columnist for the *Washington Post*, noted that commentators and politicians characterized these scenes through language typically used to talk about the nation's, and democracy's, Other: "the rage of crowds" was likened to "the instability of war zones in the Middle East," Trump was said to have displayed "the venality of tin-pot despots in banana republics" in his incitement of the crowd, and the chaos inside the Capitol was described as "third-world style anti-American anarchy." ABC News' Chief Global Affairs Correspondent Martha Raddatz (2021) was incredulous that what was happening at the Capitol was happening in America: "It is so horrible to know, we are in America where this is happening . . . I'm not in Baghdad. I'm not in Kabul. I'm not in a dangerous situation overseas. We are in America." Republican Representative Mike Gallagher (2021) declared, "We are witnessing absolute banana republic crap in the United States right now." Republican Senator Marco Rubio (2021) insisted that "There is nothing patriotic about what is occurring on Capitol Hill. This is 3rd world style anti-American anarchy." According to former President George W. Bush, the attack on the Capitol is "how election results are disputed in a banana republic . . . not our democratic republic" (Leblanc 2021). Also deemed unimaginable was the use of terms once foreign to the discourse of American democracy to describe the events of January 6: "Coup. Insurrection. Sedition" (Baker 2021). Indeed, according to Peter Baker (2021) of the *New York Times*, the attack rendered America in 2021 as its Other, as a nation led by "a defeated leader trying to hang onto power as if America were just another authoritarian nation." "The scene in Washington," he insisted, represented an event that "would have once been unimaginable" within the American context.

What had been imagined by those committed to the exceptional nature of the nation's identity and purpose was a future in which anyone regardless of race, ethnicity, gender, or class "can become anything" (Noonan 2017), including president of the United States. Enter Barack Obama and the declaration and celebration of "post-racial" America. The brutality of slavery and its legacy of racism were now declared to be officially, and finally, relegated to the past. "Hope" and "change," it seemed, had won the day. America's progress narrative was also understood to anticipate a future in which a woman would become president. Nearly a hundred years after American women won the right to vote, Hillary Clinton appeared poised to win the presidency.

Enter Donald Trump. Rather than a female president and, thereby, further confirmation that the nation continued its progress toward "a more perfect union," an older, white male who held demonstrably racist, xenophobic, and misogynistic views was now the nation's leader—and the leader of the world's most powerful and prominent democracy. As *New York Times* columnist Charles Blow (2020) put it, in electing Trump "America," blinded by its belief in inevitable, unceasing national progress, "did the unthinkable, shocking itself and the world." In return, Trump "delivered a generational retreat into darkness" and a "reality that . . . women, minorities, and immigrants hoped was an artifact of former times" (Blow 2020). It is a reality, according to Finan O'Toole (2020: 6) of the *New York Review of Books*, in which "the unquestionable right of being white and male was restored."

With "what had once been unimaginable" becoming reality, attention turned to figuring out how Trump fit into the exceptionalist narrative: Is his presidency a mere detour on the journey to "a more perfect union," the exception that proves the rule? Or does it represent a crack in the foundation of the exceptionalist ideology? For some, the Trump phenomenon does not threaten the viability of American exceptionalism because its "brand of politics [has] no future" and, thus, represents "a merely temporary departure . . . from the true course of American history" (O'Toole 2020: 6).[1] In this view, President Trump, like presidents before him who held racist views, represents only "a stutter step in which the country took a small step back among great strides forward" (Blow 2020).[2] According to William Galston of the *Wall Street Journal* (2020), however, Trump "has crystallized a fundamental shift in America's view of

[162] *The Great Nation of Futurity*

the future," a shift in which "hope gave way to fear, confidence to doubt." In "Can the West Still Lead?" *Wall Street Journal* essayist Yaroslav Trofimov (2020) similarly notes that whereas "3–4 years ago" citizens of the West "were convinced we were going to have golden ages and that everybody would be brought inside the big tent," the aftermath of the 2020 election has signaled the possibility of the "end of the West."

Much of this anxiety about the nation's claim to being an exceptional nation and the geopolitical role it could play with Trump at the helm is rooted in Trump's own rejection of the exceptionalist mantle. At the inception of his bid for the presidency in 2015 candidate Trump famously declared that the "American dream is dead" (Trump 2015). When asked during the campaign to "define American Exceptionalism" and to say whether it "still exists," Trump responded "I never liked the term . . . I don't want to say that we are exceptional" (Byrnes 2016). As such, it's not surprising that the concepts of " 'exceptionalism,' the American 'idea,' or the American political 'tradition' never worked their way into his [2016] campaign speeches" (Rodgers 2018: 285; Van Engen 2020: 282).[3] When the rhetoric of exceptionalism, specifically the phrase "city on a hill," did appear during the 2016 campaign, it took shape in criticisms of Trump launched by Republicans running against him (Van Engen 2020: 283). Indeed, Van Engen (2020) argues that an efficient way to locate criticism of Trump during the campaign was to search for the "city on a hill" phrase (284).

Daniel Sargent (2018), formerly of the Hoover Institute and writing in the journal *Foreign Policy*, explains that in place of American exceptionalism Trump offered "America First" and, thereby, characterized America not as special and superior to friends and allies but as their mere "equivalent" (2). Trump's jettisoning of exceptionalism as the core of the nation's identity, he argues, represents a "radical repudiation of long-standing, even foundational commitments," a rejection of the idea of "distinctive American virtue," and a "disavowal of American righteousness." Similarly, *New York Times* columnist David Brooks (2019) argues that "Trump's vision of what it means to be American contradicts the traditional American idea in every particular." One key aspect of Trump's vision, expressed most prominently through the "Make American Great Again" slogan, Brooks (2019) explains, is its past orientation—its valuing of nostalgia over futurity. For Trump, being American means being nostalgic and believing that "America's values were better during some golden past" (Brooks 2019). Such a vision, Brooks insists, is an affront to the "real America": a nation that is "future-oriented and universal."

The nation's exceptionalism derives from the fact that "it is the only nation on earth that defines itself in terms of its future, not its past"; the nation is exceptional because it was "launched with a dream" (Brooks 2019). From the moment of its founding, the nation's "citizens saw themselves in a project that would have implications for all of mankind" (Brooks 2019). The nation's enduring project has been to "leap into the future, to give life meaning and shape by extending opportunity and dignity to all races and nations" (Brooks 2019). As such, America has been "understood to be the land of futurity, the vanguard that would lead all mankind to a dignified and democratic future" (Brooks 2019). Under Trump's leadership, rather than serving as the "great nation of futurity," America has become its opposite: "a harbinger of darker days to come" (Tharoor 2021).

Brooks' characterization of the nation's unique temporal identity is echoed by other journalists. As Andrew Michta of the *Wall Street Journal* (2020) put it, "despite its problems" what sets the "American Ideal" apart is that it has "offered something no other culture could, namely the chance to reinvent and renew one's life, advance one's position, and create a better future." Similarly, Michta's colleague and speechwriter for President Reagan, Peggy Noonan (2020), explains that "what distinguished America from Old Europe" was its dynamism, which "bred hope," offered "so many paths" to citizens and migrants, and created an "aspirational culture."

It is this temporal conception of the nation's identity and global mission that politicians and pundits have identified as threatened by both Trump's election in 2016 and his contest of the 2020 results and as assaulted by his supporters' attack on the Capitol. By favoring equivalency over exceptionalism, the former president is said to have abandoned the nation's historical role of exemplifying the type of society other nations and peoples should strive for and, thus, the type of future that awaits all the world's people. The desecration of the Capitol—the site and symbol of American democracy—has been interpreted as not just a physical attack on the nation's democratic process but as an attack on the world's "beacon" of democracy. It was an attack that many have characterized as undermining the nation's capacity to serve as a source of inspiration to others and as a champion of their aspirations. That is, pre-Trump the thinking was, in the words of Walter Russell Mead (2020), "if boobs like us can make democracy work, then there's a chance for people to make it work everywhere." By calling into question the strength of American democracy, the insurrection called into question the future viability of democracy itself, and thus, the chance of self-governance taking root everywhere. If "such things" like the Capitol attack "can happen here," *New York Times* columnist and Nobel Prize winner Paul Krugman (2020) averred, "they can happen anywhere."

The American soul searching in the aftermath of the insurrection was preceded by similar reflective reactions to Trump's refusal to accept defeat, which, according to Trofimov (2020), ignited an "existential crisis" for the world's leading democracy. This refusal, according to Mead (2020), poses a challenge to the possibility of the United Sates—"the world's biggest billboard"—continuing in its geopolitical role as an "example to the world." Because "nothing that happens here stays here," Mead (2020) insists that "the success or failure

[164]   *The Great Nation of Futurity*

of the U.S. experiment in self-governance continues to matter to . . . billions of people." As still the world's "most arresting figure," the failure of American democracy, he warns, would mean that its "promise for the rest of the world," its "power to electrify the world," would be "blighted and diminished for generations" (Mead 2020).

Moreover, by contesting the election results, Trump drew unprecedented attention to Congress's certification of the electoral college vote on January 6, a process that heretofore was viewed as a mere formality. On this occasion, however, Senator Charles Schumer saw fit to "appeal to the American ideal" to convey to his colleagues the gravity of the moment for both the 2020 presidential election and the future of democracy (Tharoor 2021). He cautioned that "the eyes of the world are on this chamber, questioning whether America is still the shining example of democracy, the shining city on the hill" (Tharoor 2021). The significance of the moment, he continued, rested on "what message" the certification proceedings "will send . . . to the fledgling democracies, who . . . mirror our laws and traditions, in the hopes that they, too, can build a government ruled by the consent of the governed" (Tharoor 2021).

Lest some see the Capitol attack as an aberrant moment of chaos that was ultimately quelled, Ann Applebaum (2021) of the *Atlantic* insists that it is a lesson that "Trump and His Mob Taught the World about America," a lesson owing to the fact that, throughout its history, the nation's "most important weapon" has been "the power of example." The American example was particularly potent in the wake of World War II, a moment when, Applebaum (2021) explains, Western European nations "chose to become democracies because they aspired to resemble their liberators." Likewise, in 1989 it inspired nations of Eastern Europe, as well as "a variety of countries in Asia, Africa, and South America" since, "to join the great, prosperous, freedom-loving, American-lead democratic alliance" because "they wanted to be like us" and saw a path to freedom and justice by "imitating us" (Applebaum 2021).

In light of its historical role as an exemplar for others, Applebaum argues that "Americans are not the ones who will suffer most" the loss of the American example; "the true cost will be borne by those residents of Moscow, Beijing, Tehran, Caracas, Riyadh, and Minsk . . . the would-be democrats who . . . want . . . to enjoy the things Americans take for granted" (Applebaum 2021). Senator Mitt Romney similarly lamented what the attack would mean to "people . . . in China and Russia and Afghanistan, and Iraq and [in] other places who yearn for freedom and who look to this building and these shores as a place of hope" (*Washington Post* 2021, January 7). Because of January 6, these aspirants of democracy "will have one less source of hope" as "the power of America's example will be dimmer than it once was" (Applebaum 2021). For Applebaum (2021), Trump's post-election antics and the Capitol attack "badly damaged" the power of the American example and, thereby, "the validity of democracy itself."

For Sargent (2018) Trump's "positing of equivalence and deriding exceptionalism" harks back to Cold War warnings that an American loss was a Soviet gain. If the nation "fail[s] to correct [its] present course," Sargent (2018) warns, it risks enabling Russia, still "the dark mirror to American ideals" and the "antonym to the avowed US values," to become "a plausible model for America's, and the West's, own future." If the nation continues on the course laid out by Trumpism what could have been "just a wrong turn" in the nation's foreign policy "could prove a turning point for the United States" (Sargent 2018). Although avoiding direct reference to the Cold War, Krugman (2020) also warns that after 70 years the nation is now at risk of abdicating its "special role in the world, a role no one has ever played before." He further cautions that although America would continue to be a model to others, it would be a negative model as "others may emulate America's bad habits." Consequently, without America's positive example to order and guide it, the world would "become a more dangerous, less fair place" (Krugman 2020). According to the *Wall Street Journal's* Anders Fogh Rasmussen (2020), this future has already arrived. Despite proclamations that the demise of the Soviet Union brought about "the end of history" and the accompanying conviction that "the continued advancement of freedom was inevitable," an alternative future has come to fruition, a future brought about by the loss of America's global leadership: "freedom has retreated as America has retreated from its place as the global leader" (Rasmussen 2020).

When considered through the lens offered by the framework and analyses presented in the preceding chapters, this contemporary discourse of national self-reflection and existential anxiety can be read as embedding assumptions about America's temporal identity and its self-proclaimed role regarding the future. It is a discourse grounded in a narrative of progress that renders particular futures as imaginable and as part of the American project and others as unimaginable, as more fitting to earlier times and less enlightened societies, societies the United States has historically viewed as "unable to govern themselves," the "unsophisticated," and "simple minded" (Pecanha 2021). It is a discourse that universalizes the American way of life and claims the future as Ours. It is a discourse that insists that if America is to remain exceptional, or reclaim its exceptionalism, it must assume a privileged position vis-à-vis the global future. Finally, it is a discourse that reveals a deep-seated conception of America's exceptionalist identity: that it represents the "great nation of futurity" and, thus, is authorized to serve as a model and exemplar of how others ought to live.

It's important to bear in mind, however, that the ubiquity and certitude of this discourse of American exceptionalism is not an indication of an underlying truth or reality. Nor do the space-times embedded within and projected through it represent natural spatiotemporalities. Rather, this discourse of America-as-future must be understood as an "unquestioned, sedimented

[166] *The Great Nation of Futurity*

or 'common sense' discourse of the future" (Goode and Godhe 2017: 112), a discourse that exerts its power by privileging certain futures and the interests those futures serve. What would be truly exceptional, it seems to me, would be a conception of American national identity that, rather than laying claim to the future of others, recognizes the inherent right of people to claim their own future, a future that serves Their interests rather than Ours.

NOTES

PREFACE

1. My concluding chapter presents an informal analysis of some of the discourse generated in response to Trump's election, his contest of the 2020 election results, and the attack on the U.S. Capitol on January 6, 2021.

CHAPTER 1

1. I provide a full explication of and rationale for my data set later in this chapter.
2. The following review of futures studies scholarship is an update of that presented in Dunmire 2011.
3. Andersson's (2019) intellectual history maps out "the complex activity called *futurism, futurology, futures studies, prognostics,* or, quite simply, *futures research*" (2).
4. For analyses of the future orientation of policy discourse see Fairclough (2003), Graham (2001, 2002, 2017), Lemke (1995), Muntigl (2000).
5. Historians of the future focus on past "horizons of expectation," that is, on how historical subjects imagined the future (Engerman 2012: 1402).
6. According to Dalby (1990) foreign policy in the post–World War II era "has been intimately entangled with defense policy under the overall rubric of 'national security'" (43). Yergin (1977) similarly explains "national security" as the concept uniting military affairs and foreign policy (194). Campbell (1998) characterizes "national security policy" as the late modern form of foreign policy (70).
7. I do not necessarily subscribe to the idea that the United States is a genuinely exceptional nation, radically unique and superior to other nations. However, the purpose of this project is not to engage in the argument concerning whether the mantle of exceptionalism is an accurate characterization of the nation's history, ideals, or practices. Rather, my concern is to demonstrate the temporal logic embedded within the discourse of American exceptionalism and how that logic has been used rhetorically in foreign policy discourse to conceptualize and rationalize the nation's geopolitical role and practice.

   The scholarly literature on American exceptionalism, some of which is discussed in this and the following chapter, is quite extensive. It examines the historical development of the conceptualization of America as an exceptional nation and the domains of American life that are purported to be exceptional (e.g., politics, art, social structure, economics; see Edwards and Weiss 2011). Scholarship also addresses the issue of whether America is or has been exceptional is some empirically measurable way. Those arguing in the affirmative include Deneen (2012), Kammen (1993), Lipset (1997), Restad (2012, 2015), and Shafer (1991). Those critical of the idea that the nation has been demonstrably exceptional, as well as the idea that exceptionalism could be measured empirically, include Adas (2001), Bell (1975), Lepgold and McKeown (1995), Smith (2012), Tyrell (1991), and Wilson (1998). For reviews and syntheses of empirical research on American exceptionalism see Lipset (1997), Shafer (1999), and Wilson (1998). See Hodgson (2009: 11–13) and Ceasar (2012: 4–11) for discussions of the different ways American exceptionalism has been conceptualized. For an overview of historiographic work on American exceptionalism see Adas (2001).

8. Fairclough also grounds his approach to space-time in the work Bourdieu (1977) and Giddens (1991).

9. The examples included in this explication, as well as those provided in Table 1.2, represent only a portion of the linguistic and rhetorical features identified and examined in the analytic chapters.

10. My use of "center" and "periphery" is grounded in a construal of the global environment anchored in the central-peripheral orientation metaphor that has served as an important interpretative scheme in foreign policy discourse (Chilton 1996: 132; Lakoff and Johnson 1980: 14). In brief, the metaphor structures the world in terms of the relationships between states that occupy the "center" of the geopolitical world and those that reside outside that center, in the "periphery." In the context of the Cold War, this relationship was one in which the central powers sought the loyalties and resources of the periphery (Leffler 1992: 10–12).

11. CDA work on legitimation is grounded in the work of Berger and Luckmann (1966), Habermas (1976), and Weber (1964).

12. A bibliography for the documents examined in each chapter is presented in the Appendix.

13. Leffler (1992) dates the inception of the Cold War to early 1946 when the nation's leaders began viewing the Soviet Union as an enemy (100). Interestingly, the previous year the consensus view was that the postwar geopolitical environment would be created through American–Soviet collaboration. According to a Brookings Institute report issued in March 1945, American international experts imagined the postwar era—"The Age [of] the Big Two"—as an age of "intimate and continuous collaboration" whereby leaders of the United States and Russia would collaborate in shaping the future of global society (Dunn et al. 1945). Although not optimistic about the likelihood of a "permanent peace," advocates of American–Soviet collaboration did champion "the prospect for a lasting peace, a peace which will last long enough so that the statesmen of the next generation will have an opportunity to make it last still longer" (Dunn et al. 1945).

CHAPTER 2

1. For the quotation in the chapter title, see Lapham (2011: 14).

2. This phrasing, which I discuss later in the chapter, comes from Robert Rantoul, Thomas Paine, and John Adams, respectively.

3. In fact, Rodgers' (2018) study of the origins and life of Winthrop's text and the iconic phrase "as a city on a hill" complicates the assertion that "exceptionalism" is attributable to the Puritans' arrival in New England in the early 1630s (also see Van Engen 2020). He argues that concepts that were to become key aspects of American national identity—exceptionalism, mission, chosen people—were not, in fact, present in Winthrop's text. Moreover, although Winthrop's message was one of "hope," Rogers demonstrates that the themes of "doubt and caution" were equally prominent as "conditionality, not assurance, governed" the New England settlement (30, 57).

[170]   *Notes*

4. America, of course, was not a "virgin" land, as it had been peopled for millennia. Moreover, the new nation did not, in fact, arise out of nowhere. As Hodgson (2009) puts it, the nation "did not emerge . . . by a kind of geopolitical virgin birth," nor did it exist in its early years in a totally disconnected, isolated position vis-à-vis the rest of the world (20). Rather, its founding ideals and principles were very much rooted in European Enlightenment thinking, and it was "always part of the Atlantic and oceanic world" (16–20; also see Molho and Wood 1998).

CHAPTER 3

1. NSC 68 is reproduced in full in May (1993), which is the source I used to access the document.
2. Luce's essay was published in February 1941, roughly 10 months before the Japanese attack on Pearl Harbor.
3. President Eisenhower made the first explicit reference to "dominoes" in a press conference concerning Indochina on April 7, 1954.
4. Dean Acheson was Secretary of State for the Truman administration and played a central role in shaping the nation's Cold War strategy, including the formation of the Truman Doctrine.
5. Portions of the following analysis were originally presented in Dunmire (2014).
6. The Long Telegram, an earlier document which helped shape the nation's Cold War approach, provided a "psychological/ideological" analysis of Soviet policy; it gave scant attention to United States interests and military capabilities and did not offer recommendations for military objectives and priorities (Leffler 1992: 108–109). NSC 68 mapped out a series of military options which would enable the nation to maintain its "preponderant position in the international system" (Leffler 1992: 314).
7. Its assessment of Soviet capabilities and intentions, however, rendered the Soviet threat identified three years earlier in National Security Council Resolution 20/4 (NSC 20/4) as "more immediate than previously estimated" (May 1993: 76). NSC 68 explained that "The growing intensity of the conflict which has been imposed upon us" requires a new document which outlines a strategy for addressing the "intensifying struggle" the nation faces with the Soviet Union. See Chapter 5 for an analysis of how the Soviet threat was construed within NSC 20/4.
8. See Chilton (1996: 219) for an alternative analysis.
9. Nathanson (1988) provides an extended discussion of this point and documents the lack of a Soviet threat to the United States.

CHAPTER 4

1. The phrase "modernizing the Other" came from Edwin Martin, Assistant Secretary of State for the Kennedy administration (as quoted in Latham 2000: 95).
2. For an extended account of the institutional and intellectual history of modernization theory see Gilman (2003) and Ekbladh (2010). For analyses of its application see Connelly (2008), Cullather (2010), Latham (2000), and Pearce (2001). Like its critics (Escobar 1995; Frank 1966; Gilman 2003; Tipps 1973), I understand MT's statements about the "underdeveloped areas" and its people not as reflections of some empirical reality but as politically motivated and interested representations grounded in an elitist and ethnocentric worldview. As Tipps (1973) puts it, MT's claims about indigenous societies, which have no "empirical referents," neglect "indigenous aspects of social structure and culture" as well as indigenous "struggles for political and economic autonomy" (220, 212). By insisting on

Notes [171]

a universal development scheme, MT denied that the so-called underdeveloped societies operate according to their own "autonomous cultural-logic," that "different cultural orders have . . . their own historical practice," and that there is no single or simple "human course" according to which all societies develop (Sahlins 1985: vii, 34). It was a scheme that "relegated to the past" the idiosyncracies of the so-called underdeveloped areas and oriented them to a future grounded in the American way (Dalby 2008: 427). The supposed scientific approach of MT, then, didn't serve as a means for gaining knowledge about the Third World but, rather, for advancing American national interests, in particular the Cold War strategy (Tipps 1973: 210). Thus, like Gilman (2003), the following analysis doesn't seek to explain "the real of the third world"; rather, it examines the linguistic nature and rhetorical function of the spatiotemporal representations embedded within and disseminated through MT.

3. Staley was a Stanford University economist centrally involved in the Kennedy administration's Vietnam policy. Ekbladh (2010) explains that Staley's conception of the postwar global environment and his argument that securing a liberal global order required modernizing the postcolonial societies "framed early Cold War understandings of the development issue" (111). In *The Future of Underdeveloped Countries* Staley presented his argument that securing a liberal global order against a totalitarian threat in the postwar era would require a program for modernizing the "underdeveloped countries" (Ekbladh 2010: 111).

Millikan and Rostow's *A Proposal* helped justify aid programs by insisting that advancing free trade in a way that protected both U.S. security and global stability would require the nation's leaders to undertake "an enlarged global initiative . . . in support of development" (Gilman 2003: 175). The authors claimed their work provided policymakers with a "rational design and coherent purpose" for the nation's Third World policy that was grounded in a scientific approach (Gilman 2003: 179).

Finally, Lerner's contribution to transforming MT into policy came at the theoretical level. His "classic" work *The Passing of Traditional Society* "embodied the spirit of modernization as completely as any other work" (Gilman 2003: 171; Ekbladh 2010: 173). A "pioneer" in the new "policy sciences," Lerner was the first to provide an explicit and systematic theory of the modernization process, which held that modernization comprised wholly positive and distinct intrinsic qualities that came together as a "consistent whole" (Pearce 2001: 3; Gilman 2003: 5).

4. The president's statement about aiding the development of decolonized societies took shape as policy in the Point Four Program, so named because it was the fourth point in his 1949 inaugural address, which committed the United States to providing economic and technical assistance to the "underdeveloped areas." The Truman administration envisioned the program as having the dual function of providing material support to the Third World and countering the Communist ideal with an "idealized portrait of the United States and its scientific capacity" (Gilman 2003: 71). It was through the Point Four Program that engagement with the development issues of the postcolonial nations became official U.S. policy (Gilman 2003: 71). According to Gilman (2003) the program contained the "ideological core of modernization theory" (71).

CHAPTER 5

1. All of the Committee's papers are compiled in *Alerting America: The Papers of the Committee on THE PRESENT DANGER*, edited by Charles Tyroler. This volume is

[172] *Notes*

the source of the data examined in the first part of the analysis presented in this chapter.

2. Eugene Rostow was Walter Rostow's brother.

3. Although the CPD declares that the possibility of winning a nuclear war was "unthinkable," it does appear that policymakers did, in fact, think about it. May (1993) suggests that Paul Nitze, a leading member of the CPD, viewed nuclear war as survivable and winnable, explaining that "Nitze carried away the lesson [from the bombing of Hiroshima] that nuclear weapons did not necessarily mean no victor or loser in a future war" (4). In his 1983 article "Periods of Peril" Robert H. Johnson explains that the United States, along with the Soviet Union, "has engaged in planning for the fighting and winning of a nuclear war" (956). Based on new archival research, Podvig (2008) insists that the Soviets, in fact, did not plan, nor did they have the capability to fight and win a nuclear war (138).

4. In the American context, and particularly the rhetoric of Ronald Reagan, the strategy of mythopoesis echoes the genre of the American jeremiad. In the following chapter I use the jeremiad to analyze the post–Cold War rhetoric of presidents George H. W. Bush and Bill Clinton.

5. Chilton (1996) explains that "schemas" are grounded in bodily experience and serve as the "pre-conceptual basis of conceptual organization and linguistic organization" (49). He identifies four "image schemas" that serve as the source domains for metaphorically conceptualizing the practices of international relations, defense, and security: CONTAINER, PATH (with JOURNEY being a particular type of PATH), FORCE, and LINK (50–55).

6. Although made famous by Donald Trump, the phrase "make America great again" as a presidential campaign slogan originated with Ronald Reagan.

CHAPTER 6

1. See Fukuyama (1992) for the author's subsequent reconsideration of this view.

2. While the following explication relies heavily on Bercovitch's influential book on the American jeremiad, my identification of these themes is also grounded in the following studies of the nature and function of the jeremiad in political rhetoric: Bormann (1977), Jendrysik (2002), Johannesen (1986), Jones and Rowland (2005), J. M. Murphy (1990), A. R. Murphy (2009), Ritter (1980), and Schlatter (1969).

3. The literature concerning the details and validity of the democratic peace thesis is quite extensive. See Ish-Shalom (2013) and Brown et al. (1996) for synopses of the debates and additional sources on the democratic peace thesis. Also, see Dunmire (2013) for a discussion comparing Kant's (1991) conception of perpetual peace to the conception of democratic peace.

4. I ground this interpretation in the *Oxford English Dictionary*'s definition of frontier.

5. Anthony Lake was President Clinton's national security advisor.

6. Brent Scowcroft served as President Bush's national security advisor. This statement is from a speech he delivered after President Clinton took office.

7. The Bush administration released its final National Security Strategy on January 1, 1993; President Clinton took office on January 20, 1993.

CHAPTER 7

1. O'Toole is referring here to statements made by Joe Biden and Senator Jeff Flake. In his speech accepting the Democratic nomination, Biden (2020) likened the

Notes [173]

Trump presidency to a "season of darkness," while Flake declared Trumpism "a dead end . . . a demographic cul-de-sac" (O'Toole 2020: 6).

2. Blow identifies Andrew Johnson and Richard Nixon as presidents with racist views.

3. President Trump did, however, opportunistically embrace the concept of exceptionalism in his 2020 nomination acceptance speech as a cudgel in his effort to fend off a Biden victory (Trump 2020). America, he proclaimed, is "the torch that enlightens the whole world," "the most free, just, and exceptional nation on earth," "the greatest and most exceptional nation in the history of the world," "the most exciting and incredible adventure in human history." It is a country that "is blessed by God and has a special purpose in this world," "a nation of pilgrims, pioneers, adventurers, explorers and trailblazers who refuse to be . . . held back," a nation "where nothing is impossible." It is a nation "united" by "an unshakeable confidence in [its] destiny." America, he declared, is without peers as "there is no one like us on earth."

Rather than seeing it as fundamental to the nation's history, however, Trump rendered exceptionalism as one of *his* accomplishments and declared it to be under threat in the "most important election in the history of this country" (Trump 2020). That is, while explaining in the 2015 interview that he didn't like the idea of claiming that America is exceptional, he did state that he'd "liked to make us exceptional. And I'd like to talk later instead of now. We may have a chance in the not-too-distant future" to be exceptional (Byrnes 2016). This accomplishment was under threat in 2020, as Trump warned his supporters that "everything we have achieved is now in danger." This danger, he explained, derives from the possibility that the electorate could choose the wrong vision for the nation's future: a vision that will "allow a socialist agenda to demolish our cherished destiny" rather than a vision that will "save the American dream" (Trump 2020).

In mapping out these two alternative futures, Trump conjures an alternative America Self against which he seeks to defend the nation, a Self embodied by Joe Biden. According to Trump, Biden is a threat to the nation's exceptional Self and its future because he represents a "backward view" and is a politician who "has spent his entire career on the wrong side of history" (Trump 2020). Trump, in contrast, represents the true American Self that will "rescue American liberty" and enable "Americans [to] build their future" rather than "tear down our past." He embodies the American Self that will show the world that "for America there is a dream."

[174] *Notes*

APPENDIX: DATA BIBLIOGRAPHY

CHAPTER 3

Acheson, D. 1950, January 12. "Crisis in Asia—an Examination of U.S. Policy. Speech Delivered at the National Press Club, New York." *Department of State Bulletin XXII* (551): 111–118.

Acheson, D. 1950, March 16. "Tensions between the United States and the Soviet Union. Speech Delivered at the University of California at Berkeley." *Department of State Bulletin XXII* (560): 473–478.

Acheson, D. 1950, November 30. "The Strategy for Freedom." *Vital Speeches of the Day XVII* (5): 130–133.

Luce, H. 1999/1941. "The American Century." *Diplomatic History 23* (2): 159–171.

May, E., ed. 1993. *American Cold War Strategy: Interpreting NSC 68.* Boston: Bedford/St. Martins.

Truman, H. S. 1947, March 6. "Address on Foreign Economic Policy, Delivered at Baylor University." Gerhard Peters and John T. Woolley, *The American Presidency Project.* http://www.presidency.ucsb.edu/ws/?pid=12842.

Truman, H. S. 1947, March 12. "Special Message to the Congress on Greece and Turkey: The Truman Doctrine." Gerhard Peters and John T. Woolley, *The American Presidency Project.* http://www.presidency.ucsb.edu/ws/?pid=12846.

Truman, H. S. 1949, January 20. "Inaugural Address." Gerhard Peters and John T. Woolley, *The American Presidency Project* https://www.presidency.ucsb.edu/node/229929.

Truman, H. S. 1950, October 17. "Address in San Francisco at the War Memorial Opera House." Gerhard Peters and John T. Woolley, *The American Presidency Project.* http://www.presidency.ucsb.edu/ws/?pid=13644.

Truman, H. S. 1951. "Annual Message to the Congress on the State of the Union." Gerhard Peters and John T. Woolley, *The American Presidency Project.* https://www.presidency.ucsb.edu/node/231403.

Truman, H. S. 1953, January 7. "Annual Message to the Congress on the State of the Union." Gerhard Peters and John T. Woolley, *The American Presidency Project.* https://www.presidency.ucsb.edu/node/231314.

Truman, H. S. 1953, January 15. "The President's Farewell Address to the American People." Gerhard Peters and John T. Woolley, *The American Presidency Project.* https://www.presidency.ucsb.edu/node/231372.

CHAPTER 4

Lerner, D. 1958. *The Passing of Traditional Society: Modernizing the Middle East*. Glencoe, IL: The Free Press.

Millikan, M. F., and Rostow, W. 1957. *A Proposal: Key to an Effective Foreign Policy*. New York: Harper & Brothers.

Staley, E. 1961. *The Future of Underdeveloped Countries*. London: Council on Foreign Relations.

CHAPTER 5

May, E., ed. 1993. *American Cold War Strategy: Interpreting NSC 68*. Boston: Bedford/St. Martins.

Reagan, R. 1976, March 31. "To Restore America, Ronald Reagan's Campaign Address." https://www.reaganlibrary.gov/archives/speech/restore-america.

Reagan, R. 1980, July 17. "Address Accepting the Presidential Nomination at the Republican National Convention in Detroit." Gerhard Peters and John T. Woolley, *The American Presidency Project*. https://www.presidency.ucsb.edu/node/251302.

Reagan, R. 1980, August 18. "Address to the Veterans of Foreign Wars Convention in Chicago." Gerhard Peters and John T. Woolley, *The American Presidency Project*. https://www.presidency.ucsb.edu/node/285595.

Reagan, R. 1980, October 19. "A Strategy for Peace in the '80s." Gerhard Peters and John T. Woolley, *The American Presidency Project*. https://www.presidency.ucsb.edu/node/285592.

Reagan, R. 1980, November 3. Election Eve Address: "A Vision for America." Gerhard Peters and John T. Woolley, *The American Presidency Project*. https://www.presidency.ucsb.edu/node/285591.

Reagan, R. 1981, January 20. "Inaugural Address." Gerhard Peters and John T. Woolley, *The American Presidency Project*. https://www.presidency.ucsb.edu/node/246336.

Reagan, R. 1982, January 26. "Address Before a Joint Session of the Congress Reporting on the State of the Union." Gerhard Peters and John T. Woolley, *The American Presidency Project*. https://www.presidency.ucsb.edu/node/245636.

Reagan, R. 1982, June 8. "Address to Members of the British Parliament." Online https://www.reaganlibrary.gov/research/speeches/60882a.

Reagan, R. 1982, November 29. "Remarks at the Annual Convention of the National League of Cities in Los Angeles, California." Gerhard Peters and John T. Woolley, *The American Presidency Project*. https://www.presidency.ucsb.edu/node/245802.

Reagan, R. 1983, January 25. "Address Before a Joint Session of the Congress on the State of the Union." Gerhard Peters and John T. Woolley, *The American Presidency Project* https://www.presidency.ucsb.edu/node/263103.

Reagan, R. 1983, February 22. "Remarks at the Annual Washington Conference of the American Legion." Gerhard Peters and John T. Woolley, *The American Presidency Project*. https://www.presidency.ucsb.edu/node/262549.

Reagan, R. 1983, March 3. "Remarks at the Annual Convention of the National Association of Evangelicals in Orlando." Accessed August 13, 2018. https://www.reaganlibrary.gov/research/speeches/30883b.

Reagan, R. 1983, October 27. "Address to the Nation on Events in Lebanon and Grenada." Gerhard Peters and John T. Woolley, *The American Presidency Project*. https://www.presidency.ucsb.edu/node/261953.

Reagan, R. 1984, January 25. "Address Before a Joint Session of the Congress on the State of the Union." Gerhard Peters and John T. Woolley, *The American Presidency Project*. https://www.presidency.ucsb.edu/node/261634.

Tyroler, C., ed. 1984. *Alerting America: The Papers of the Committee on THE PRESENT DANGER*. Washington, DC: Pergamon-Brassey.

CHAPTER 6
G. H. W. Bush Administration

Baker, J. 1992, April 13. "Address Before the Organization of American States." *United States Department of State Dispatch* 3 (16): 309.

Baker, J. 1992, April 21. "Address Before the Chicago Council on Foreign Relations, Chicago." *United States Department of State Dispatch* 3 (17): 321.

Bush, G. H. W. 1989, January 20. "Inaugural Address." Gerhard Peters and John T. Woolley, *The American Presidency Project*. https://www.presidency.ucsb.edu/node/247448.

Bush, G. H. W. 1989, May 31. "Remarks to the Citizens in Mainz, Federal Republic of Germany." Gerhard Peters and John T. Woolley, *The American Presidency Project*. https://www.presidency.ucsb.edu/node/262786.

Bush, G. H. W. 1990, January 31. "Address Before a Joint Session of the Congress on the State of the Union." Gerhard Peters and John T. Woolley, *The American Presidency Project*. https://www.presidency.ucsb.edu/node/263819.

Bush, G. H. W. 1990, August 2. "Remarks at the Aspen Institute Symposium in Aspen, Colorado." Gerhard Peters and John T. Woolley, *The American Presidency Project*. https://www.presidency.ucsb.edu/node/264984.

Bush, G. H. W. 1990, September 11. "Address Before a Joint Session of the Congress on the Persian Gulf Crisis and the Federal Budget Deficit." Gerhard Peters and John T. Woolley, *The American Presidency Project*. https://www.presidency.ucsb.edu/node/264415.

Bush, G. H. W. 1990, October 1. "Address Before the 45th Session of the United Nations General Assembly in New York, New York." Gerhard Peters and John T. Woolley, *The American Presidency Project*. https://www.presidency.ucsb.edu/node/264816.

Bush, G. H. W. 1991, January 9. "Open Letter to College Students on the Persian Gulf Crisis." Gerhard Peters and John T. Woolley, *The American Presidency Project*. https://www.presidency.ucsb.edu/node/265658.

Bush, George. 1991, January 16. "Address to the Nation Announcing Allied Military Action in the Persian Gulf." Gerhard Peters and John T. Woolley, *The American Presidency Project*. https://www.presidency.ucsb.edu/node/265756.

Bush, G. H. W. 1991, January 29. "Address Before a Joint Session of the Congress on the State of the Union." Gerhard Peters and John T. Woolley, *The American Presidency Project*. https://www.presidency.ucsb.edu/node/265956.

Bush, G. H. W. 1992, January 28. "Address Before a Joint Session of the Congress on the State of the Union." Gerhard Peters and John T. Woolley, *The American Presidency Project*. https://www.presidency.ucsb.edu/node/266921.

Bush, G. H. W. 1992, April 9. "Remarks to the American Society of Newspaper Editors." Gerhard Peters and John T. Woolley, *The American Presidency Project*. https://www.presidency.ucsb.edu/node/266587.

United States National Security Council. (1991). *National Security Strategy of the United States*. Available at https://history.defense.gov/Portals/70/Documents/nss/nss1991.pdf?ver=3sIpLiQwmknO-RplyPeAHw%3d%3d.

Appendix [177]

United States National Security Council. (1993). *National Security Strategy of the United States*. Available at https://history.defense.gov/Portals/70/Documents/nss/nss1993.pdf?ver=Dulx2wRKDaQ-ZrswRPRX9g%3d%3d.

Clinton Administration

Albright, M. 1998, February 19. Interview on NBC "The Today Show" with Matt Lauer. https://1997-2001.state.gov/statements/1998/980219a.html.

Clinton, W. J. 1991, December 12. "A New Covenant for American Security. Remarks to Students at Georgetown University." https://thetechnocratictyranny.com/PDFS/1991_Clinton_New_Covenant_Security.pdf.

Clinton, W. J. 1992, April 1. "Strategy for Foreign Policy: Assistance to Russia. Speech Delivered to the Foreign Policy Association." *Vital Speeches of the Day 58* (14): 421–425.

Clinton, W. J. 1992, August 13. "Remarks of Governor Bill Clinton at the Los Angeles World Affairs Council." http://www.ibiblio.org/pub/academic/political-science/speeches/clinton.dir/c63.txtp.

Clinton, W. J. 1993, February 17. "Address Before a Joint Session of Congress on Administration Goals." Gerhard Peters and John T. Woolley, *The American Presidency Project*. https://www.presidency.ucsb.edu/node/218852.

Clinton, W. J. 1993, September 27. "Remarks to the 48th Session of the United Nations General Assembly in New York City." Gerhard Peters and John T. Woolley, *The American Presidency Project*. https://www.presidency.ucsb.edu/node/217952.

Clinton, W. J. 1994, October 10. "Address to the Nation on Iraq." Gerhard Peters and John T. Woolley, *The American Presidency Project*. https://www.presidency.ucsb.edu/node/218493.

Clinton, W. J. 1995, January 24. "Address Before a Joint Session of the Congress on the State of the Union." Gerhard Peters and John T. Woolley, *The American Presidency Project*. https://www.presidency.ucsb.edu/node/221902.

Clinton, W. J. 1995, November 27. "Address to the Nation on Implementation of the Peace Agreement in Bosnia-Herzegovia." Gerhard Peters and John T. Woolley, *The American Presidency Project*. http://www.presidency.ucsb.edu/ws/index.php?pid=50808#axzz1wqFgNofS.

Clinton, W. J. 1996, August 5. "Remarks on International Security Issues at George Washington University." Gerhard Peters and John T. Woolley, *The American Presidency Project*. https://www.presidency.ucsb.edu/node/223382.

Clinton, W. J. 1996, October 22. "Remarks to the Community in Detroit." Gerhard Peters and John T. Woolley, *The American Presidency Project*. https://www.presidency.ucsb.edu/node/222157.

Clinton, W. J. 1997, January 20. "Inaugural Address." Gerhard Peters and John T. Woolley, *The American Presidency Project*. https://www.presidency.ucsb.edu/node/224843.

Clinton, W. J. 1997, February 4. "Address Before a Joint Session of the Congress on the State of the Union." Gerhard Peters and John T. Woolley, *The American Presidency Project*. https://www.presidency.ucsb.edu/node/223396.

Clinton, W. J. 1998, January 29. "Remarks at the National Defense University." Gerhard Peters and John T. Woolley, *The American Presidency Project*. https://www.presidency.ucsb.edu/node/224369.

Clinton, W. J. 1998, December 16. Address to the Nation Announcing Military Strikes on Iraq. Gerhard Peters and John T. Woolley, *The American Presidency Project*. https://www.presidency.ucsb.edu/node/225749.

[178] *Appendix*

Clinton, W. J. 1999, February 26. "Remarks on United States Foreign Policy in San Francisco." Gerhard Peters and John T. Woolley, *The American Presidency Project*. https://www.presidency.ucsb.edu/node/228940.

Clinton, W. J. 2000, January 27. "Address Before a Joint Session of the Congress on the State of the Union." Online by Gerhard Peters and John T. Woolley, *The American Presidency Project*. https://www.presidency.ucsb.edu/node/227524.

Lake, Anthony 1993, September 21. *From Containment to Enlargement*. Johns Hopkins University School of Advanced International Studies, Washington, DC. http://academic.brooklyn.cuny.edu/history/johnson/lake.htm.

Lake, Anthony. 1996, May 3. "A Second American Century." https://www.washingtonpost.com/archive/opinions/1996/05/03/a-second-american-century/4e48d110-614d-4e46-84f3-fab3918a9cc4/.

Powell, Colin. 1993, September 30. "Military Retirement Celebration Address." Available at https://www.americanrhetoric.com/speeches/colinpowellmilitaryretirementspeech.htm.

Scowcroft, Brent. 1993, July 2. "Who Can Harness History? Only the U.S." www.nytimes.com/1993/07/02/opinion/who-can-harness-history-only-the-us.html.

United States National Security Council. 1995. *A National Security Strategy of Engagement and Enlargement*. Available at https://history.defense.gov/Portals/70/Documents/nss/nss1995.pdf?ver=pzgo9pkDsWmIQqTYTC6O-Q%3d%3d.

United States National Security Council. (1998). *A National Security Strategy for a New Century*. Available https://history.defense.gov/Portals/70/Documents/nss/nss1998.pdf?ver=zl1p-sJtgDvXOM01YVnfqA%3d%3d.

REFERENCES

Adam, Barbara. 1995. *Timewatch: The Social Analysis of Time*. Cambridge: Polity Press.

Adams, John. 1765. *Diary 10, 24 January—21 February 1765, August 1765 [electronic edition]. Adams Family Papers: An Electronic Archive*. Massachusetts Historical Society. http://www.masshist.org/digitaladams/.

Adams, Vincanne, Murphy, Michelle, and Clarke, Aadele. 2009. "Anticipation: Technoscience, Life, Affect, Temporality." *Subjectivity 28*: 246–265.

Adas, Michael. 2001. "From Settler Colony to Global Hegemon: Integrating the Exceptionalist Narrative of the American Experience into World History." *American Historical Review 106* (5): 1692–1720.

Aiezza, Maria C. 2015. "'We May Face the Risks . . . Risks That Could Adversely Affect Our Face': A Corpus-Assisted Discourse Analysis of Modality Markers in CSR Reports." *Studies in Communication Sciences 15*: 68–76.

Alqvist, Toni, and Rhisiart, Martin. 2015. "Emerging Pathways for Critical Futures Research: Changing Contexts and Impacts of Social Theory." *Futures 71*: 91–104.

Anderson, Benedict. 1983. *Imagined Communities: Reflections on the Origin and Spread of Nationalism*. London: Verso.

Anderson, Fred. 2005. *French and Indian: The War That Made America*. New York: Penguin.

Andersson, Jenny. 2006. "Choosing Futures: Alva Myrdal and the Construction of Swedish Futures Studies, 1967–1972." *International Review of Social History 51*: 277–295.

Andersson, Jenny. 2012. "The Great Future Debate and the Struggle for the World." *American Historical Review 117* (5): 1411–1430.

Andersson, Jenny. 2019. *The Future of the World: Futurology, Futurists, and the Struggle for the Post-Cold War Imagination*. Oxford: Oxford University Press.

Andersson, Jenny, and Rindzeviciute, Egle. 2015. "Introduction: Toward a New History of the Future." In *The Struggle for the Long Term in Transnational Science and Politics: Forging the Future*, Jennifer Andersson and Egle Rindzeviciute (eds.), 1–15. London: Routledge.

Appadurai, Arjun. 2013. *The Future as Cultural Fact*. London: Verso.

Applebaum, Anne. 2021, January 7. "What Trump and His Mob Taught the World About America." *The Atlantic*. Available at https://www.theatlantic.com/ideas/archive/2021/01/what-trump-and-his-mob-taught-world-about-america/617579/.

Aradau, Claudia, and Blanke, Tobias. 2017. "Politics of Prediction: Security and the Time/Space of Governmentality in the Age of Big Data." *European Journal of Social Theory 20* (3): 373–391.

Ashley, Richard. 1987. "Foreign Policy as Political Performance." *International Studies Association Notes 13*: 51–55.

Bacevich, Andrew. 2002. *American Empire: The Realities and Consequences of U.S. Diplomacy*. Cambridge: Harvard University Press.

Bacevich, Andrew. 2021. *After the Apocalypse: America's Role in a World Transformed*. New York: Metropolitan Books.

Baker, Peter. 2021, January 6. "A Mob and the Breach of Democracy: The Violent End of the Trump Era." *New York Times*. Available at https://www.nytimes.com/2021/01/06/us/politics/trump-congress.html.

Bakhtin, Mikhail M. 1981. *The Dialogical Imagination: Four Essays*. Edited by Michael Holquist; translated by Caryl Emerson and Michael Holquist. Austin: University of Texas Press.

Bakhtin, Mikhail M. 1986. *Speech Genres and Other Late Essays*. Edited by Caryl Emerson and Michael Hoquist; translated by Vern W. McGee. Austin: University of Texas Press.

Balzacq, Thierry, ed. 2011. *Securitization Theory: How Security Problems Emerge and Dissolve*. London: Taylor & Francis.

Bell, Daniel. 1975, Fall. "The End of American Exceptionalism." *The Public Interest 41*: 193–224.

Bell, Daniel. 1989. "American Exceptionalism Revisited: The Role of Civil Society." Available at https://www.nationalaffairs.com/public_interest/detail/american-exceptionalism-revisited-the-role-of-civil-society.

Bercovitch, Sacvan. 2012. *The American Jeremiad*. Madison: University of Wisconsin Press.

Berger, Peter, and Luckmann, Thomas. 1966. *The Social Construction of Reality*. Hardmondsworth: Penguin.

Bergs, Alexander. 2010. "Expressions of Futurity in Contemporary English: A Construction Grammar Perspective." *English Language and Linguistics 14* (2): 217–238.

Biden, Joseph. 2020, August 8. "Nomination Acceptance Speech." *Democratic National Convention*. Available at https://www.cnn.com/2020/08/20/politics/biden-dnc-speech-transcript/index.html.

Blow, Charles. 2020, October 29. "America Shocked Itself and the World." *New York Times*. Available at https://www.nytimes.com/2020/10/29/opinion/trump-american-politics.html.

Bondi, Marina. 2016. "The Future in Reports." *Pragmatics & Society 7* (1): 57–81.

Bormann, Ernest. G. 1977. "Fetching Good out of Evil: A Rhetorical Use of Calamity." *Quarterly Journal of Speech 63*: 130–139.

Bourdieu, Pierre. 1977. *Outline of a Theory of Practice*. Cambridge: Cambridge University Press.

Bourdieu, Pierre, Waquant, Locic, and Farage, Sanar. 1994. "Rethinking the State: Genesis and Structure of the Bureaucratic Field." *Sociological Theory 12* (1): 1–18.

Brands, Henry W. 1998. *What America Owes the World: The Struggle for the Soul of Foreign Policy*. Cambridge: Cambridge University Press.

Brooks, David. 2019, July 18. "Donald Trump Hates America." *New York Times*. Available at https://www.nytimes.com/2019/07/18/opinion/trump-america-election.html.

Brown, Michael E., Lynn-Jones, Sean. M., and Miller, Steven E., eds. 1996. *Debating the Democratic Peace: An International Studies Reader*. Cambridge, MA: MIT Press.

Burrow, John. 2009. *History of Histories: Epics, Chronicles, and Inquiries from Herodotus and Thucydides to the Twentieth Century*. New York: Vintage.

Bush, George W. 2002, October 7. "President Bush Outlines Iraqi Threat." www.whitehouse.gov/news/releases/2002/10/20021007-8.html.

Bussey, Marcus. 2007. "The Public Clock: Temporal Ordering and Policy." *Futures* 39: 53–64.

Buzan, Barry. 1997. "Rethinking Security After the Cold War." *Cooperation and Conflict* 32 (1): 5–28.

Buzan, Barry, and Wæver, Ole. 2003. *Regions and Powers: The Structure of International Security*. Oxford: Oxford University Press.

Buzan, Barry, Wæver, Ole, and de Wilde, Jaap. 1998. *Security: A New Framework for Analysis*. Boulder: Lynne Rienner Publishing.

Byrnes, Jesse. 2016, June 7. "Trump on American Exceptionalism: 'I Never Liked the Term.'" *The Hill*. Available at https://thehill.com/blogs/blog-briefing-room/news/282449-trump-on-american-exceptionalism-i-never-liked-the-term.

Campbell, David. 1998. *Writing Security: United States Foreign Policy and the Politics of Identity* (2nd ed.). Minneapolis: University of Minnesota Press.

Cap, Piotr. 2010. "Axiological Aspects of Proximation." *Journal of Pragmatics* 42: 392–407.

C.A.S.E. Collective. 2006. "Critical Approaches to Security in Europe: A Networked Manifesto." *Security Dialogue* 37 (4): 443–487.

Cavelty, Myriam D., and Mauer, Victor, eds. 2010. *The Routledge Handbook of Security Studies*. London: Routledge.

Ceasar, James W. 2012. "The Origins and Character of American Exceptionalism." *American Political Thought: A Journal of Ideas, Institutions, and Culture* 1: 3–27.

Charteris-Black, Jonathan. 2004. *Corpus Approaches to Critical Metaphor Analysis*. London: Palgrave.

Charteris-Black, Jonathan. 2011. *Politicians and Rhetoric: The Persuasive Power of Metaphor*. New York: Palgrave MacMillan.

Chilton, Paul. 1988. *Critical Discourse Moments and Critical Discourse Analysis: Toward a Methodology*. Working Paper No. 7, First International Conference on Discourse, Peace, Security, and International Society. Available at https://escholarship.org/uc/item/5383t78x.

Chilton, Paul. 1996. *Security Metaphors: Cold War Discourse from Containment to Common House*. New York: Peter Lang.

Chilton, Paul. 2004. *Analyzing Political Discourse: Theory and Practice*. London: Routledge.

Commager, Henry S. 1974. *The Defeat of America: Presidential Power and the National Character*. New York: Simon Schuster.

Committee on Foreign Affairs. 1949. *Point Four Program: Background and Program*. Washington, DC: U.S. Government Printing Office.

Comrie, Bernard. 1976. *Aspect*. Cambridge: Cambridge University Press.

Connelly, Matthew. 2008. *Fatal Misconceptions: The Struggle to Control World Population*. Cambridge, MA: Belknap Press.

Connelly, Matthew, Fay, Matt, Ferrini, Giulia, Kaufman, Micki, Leonard, Will, Monsky, Harrison, Musto, Ryan, Paine, Tauton, Standish, Nicholas, and Walker, Lydia. 2012. "'General, I Have Fought Just as Many Nuclear Wars as You Have': Forecasts, Future Scenarios, and the Politics of Armageddon." *American Historical Review* 117 (5): 1431–1440.

Connolly, William. E. 1991. *Identity/Difference: Democratic Negotiations of Political Paradox*. Minneapolis: University of Minnesota Press.

References [183]

Connor, Stuart. 2017. "An Examination of Independent Fiscal Councils and Their Orientation to the Future and Policy Making." *European Journal of Futures Research* 5 (19): 1–8.

Cruz, Consuelo. 2000. "Identity and Persuasion: How Nations Remember Their Past and Make Their Futures." *World Politics* 52 (3): 275–312.

Cullather, Nick. 2010. *The Hungry World: America's Cold War Battle Against Poverty in Asia*. Cambridge, MA: Harvard University Press.

Dalby, Simon. 1988. "Geopolitical Discourse: The Soviet Union as Other." *Alternatives* XIII: 415–422.

Dalby, Simon. 1990. *Creating the Second Cold War: The Discourse of Politics*. London: Pinter.

Dalby, Simon. 2008. "Imperialism, Domination, Culture: The Continued Relevance of Critical Geopolitics." *Geopolitics* 13: 413–436.

Davies, Merryl W. 1999. "Other Futures Studies: A Bibliographic Essay." In *Rescuing All Our Futures: The Future of Futures Studies*, Ziauddin Sardar (ed.), 234–249. Westport, CT: Praeger.

Debray, Regis. 1973. *Prison Writings*. New York: Vintage Books.

de Jouvenal, Bernard. 1965. *The Art of Conjecture*. New York: Basic Books.

Democratic Review. 1840. "Thomas's American Reminiscences." *The United States Magazine and Democratic Review* VIII: 226–252.

Democratic Review. 1842. "Lucian and His Age." *The United States Magazine and Democratic Review* XI: 225–246.

Deneen, Patrick J. 2012. "Cities of Man on a Hill." *American Political Thought: A Journal of Ideas, Institutions, and Culture* 1: 29–51.

de Saint-Georges, Ingrid. 2013. "Anticipatory Discourse." In *The Encyclopedia of Applied Linguistics*, Carol A. Chapelle (ed.), 1–7. Hoboken, NJ: Wiley & Sons.

Dolbeare, Kenneth M., and Dolbeare, Patricia. 1976. *American Ideologies: The Competing Political Beliefs of the 1970s* (3rd ed.). Chicago: Rand McNally College Publishing.

Doty, Roxanne L. 1996. *Imperial Encounters: The Politics of Representation in North-South Relations*. Minneapolis: University of Minnesota Press.

Dunmire, Patricia L. 2005. "Preempting the Future: Rhetoric and Ideology of the Future in Political Discourse." *Discourse & Society* 16 (4): 481–513.

Dunmire, Patricia L. 2008. "The Rhetoric of Temporality: The Future as Linguistic Construct and Rhetorical Resource." In *Rhetoric in Detail*, Barbara Johnstone and Christopher Eisenhart (eds.), 81–112. Amsterdam: John Benjamins Publishing.

Dunmire, Patricia L. 2009. "'9/11 Changed Everything': An Intertextual Analysis of the Bush Doctrine." *Discourse & Society* 20 (2): 195–222.

Dunmire, Patricia L. 2011. *Projecting the Future Through Political Discourse: The Case of the Bush Doctrine*. Amsterdam: John Benjamins.

Dunmire, Patricia L. 2013. "'New World Coming': Narratives of the Future in U.S. Post–Cold War National Security Discourse." In *The Discourse of War and Peace*, Adam Hodges (ed.), 23–46. Oxford: Oxford University Press.

Dunmire, Patricia L. 2014. "'American Ways of Organizing the World': Designing the Global Future Through U.S. National Security Strategy." In *Contemporary Critical Discourse Studies*, Christopher Hart and Piotr Cap (eds.), 321–347. London: Bloomsbury.

Dunn, Frederick S., Earle, Edward M., Fox, William T. R., Kirk, Grayson L., Rowe, David N., Sprout, Harold, and Wolders, Arnold. 1945, March 8. *A Security Policy for PostWar America*. Washington, DC: Brookings Institution.

Edelman, Murray. 1971. *Politics as Symbolic Action: Mass Arousal and Quiescence*. Chicago: Markham.

Edelman, Murray. 1988. *Constructing the Political Spectacle*. Chicago: University of Chicago Press.

Edwards, Jason, and Weiss, David, eds. 2011. *The Rhetoric of American Exceptionalism: Critical Essays*. Jefferson, NC: McFarland & Co.

Ekbladh, David. 2010. *The Great American Mission: Modernization and the Construction of an American World Order*. Princeton, NJ: Princeton University Press.

Emerson, Ralph W. 1844. "Young American." Available at www.emersoncentral.com/youngam.htm.

Engelhardt, Tom. 2010. *The American Way of War: How Bush's Wars Became Obama's*. Chicago: Haymarket Books.

Engerman, David C. 2012. "Introduction: Histories of the Future and the Futures of History." *American Historical Review* 117 (5): 1402–1410.

Escobar, Arturo. 1995. *Encountering Development: The Making and Unmaking of the Third World*. Princeton, NJ: Princeton University Press.

Evered, Roger. 1983. "Who's Talking About the Future? An Analysis of the U.S. Presidents." *Technological Forecasting and Social Change* 24: 61–77.

Fabian, Johannes. 1983. *Time and the Other: How Anthropology Makes Its Object*. New York: Columbia University Press.

Fairclough, Norman. 1989. *Language and Power*. London: Longman.

Fairclough, Norman. 1995. *Critical Discourse Analysis: The Critical Study of Language*. London: Longman.

Fairclough, Norman. 2003. *Analysing Discourse: Textual Analysis for Social Research*. London: Routledge.

Fairclough, Norman. 2004. "Critical Discourse Analysis in Researching Language in New Capitalism: Overdetermination, Transdisciplinarity, and Textual Analysis." In *Systemic Functional Linguistics and Critical Discourse Analysis: Studies in Social Change*, Lynne Young and Claire Harrison (eds.), 103–122. London: Continuum.

Fleischman, Suzanne. 1982. *The Future in Thought and Language*. Cambridge: Cambridge University Press.

Fousek, John. 2000. *To Lead the Free World: American Nationalism and the Cultural Roots of the Cold War*. Chapel Hill: The University of North Carolina Press.

Frank, Andre G. 1966, September. "The Development of Underdevelopment." *Monthly Review* 18 (4): 17–30.

Fraser, Julius T. 1975. *Of Time, Passion, and Knowledge* (2nd ed.). Princeton, NJ: Princeton University Press.

Fukuyama, Francis. 1989. "The End of History?" *National Interest* 16: 1–18.

Fukuyama, Francis. 1992. *The End of History and the Last Man*. New York: Avon Books.

Gaddis, John L. 2005. *Strategies of Containment: A Critical Appraisal of American National Security Policy During the Cold War*. Oxford: Oxford University Press.

Gallagher, Mike. 2021, January 6. We are witnessing absolute banana republic crap in the United States Capitol right now. Twitter. twitter.com/repgallagher/status/1346912246291603465.

Galston, William. A. 2020, November 13. "Trump Remade His Party and the World." https://www.wsj.com/articles/trump-remade-his-party-and-the-world-11605294269.

Galtung, Johan, and Jungk, Robert. 1969. "Postscript: A Warning and a Hope." In *Mankind 2000*, Robert Jungk and Johan Galtung (eds.), 368. Universitets forlaget and London: Allen and Unwin.

Gerson, Michael. 2021, January 7. "Trump's Evangelicals Were Complicit in the Desecration of Our Democracy." https://www.washingtonpost.com/opinions/

trumps-evangelicals-were-complicit-in-the-desecration-of-our-democracy/ 2021/01/07/69a51402-5110-11eb-83e3-322644d82356_story.html.

Giddens, Anthony. 1991. *Modernity and Self Identity*. Cambridge: Polity Press.

Giddens, Anthony. 1994. "Living in a Post-Traditional World." In *Reflexive Modernization: Politics, Tradition, and Aesthetics in the Modern Social Order*, Ulrich Beck, Anthony Giddens, and Scott Lash (eds.), 56–109. Cambridge: Polity Press.

Gilman, Nils. 2003. *Mandarins of the Future: Modernization Theory in Cold War America*. Baltimore, MD: John Hopkins.

Gilpin, William. 1974/1873. *Mission of the North American People, Geographical, Social, and Political*. Philadelphia: Lippincott & Co.

Glasbey, Sheila R., Barnden, John, Lee, Mark, and Wallington, Alan. 2002. "Temporal Metaphors in Discourse." Available at https://www.researchgate.net/publicat ion/249716515_Temporal_Metaphors_in_Discourse.

Godhe, Michael, and Goode, Luke. 2018. "Critical Future Studies—A Thematic Introduction." *Culture Unbound 10* (2): 151–162.

Goode, Luke, and Godhe, Michael. 2017. "Beyond Capitalist Realism—Why We Need Critical Future Studies." *Culture Unbound 9*: 108–129.

Graham, Phil. 2001. "Space: Irrealis Objects in Technology Policy and Their Role in a New Political Economy." *Discourse & Society 12* (6): 761–788.

Graham, Phil. 2002. "Predication and Propagation: A Method for Analyzing Evaluative Meanings in Technology Policy." *Text 22* (2): 227–268.

Graham, Phil. 2019. "Negative Discourse Analysis and Utopias of the Political." *Journal of Language and Politics 18* (3): 1–23.

Graham, Phil, Keenan, Thomas, and Dowd, Anne-Marie. 2004. "A Call to Arms at the End of History: A Discourse-Historical Analysis of George W. Bush's Declaration of War on Terror." *Discourse and Society 15* (2–3): 199–221.

Graham, Phil, and Luke, Allan. 2003. "Militarizing the Body Politic: New Media as a Weapon of Mass Instruction." *Body and Society 9* (4): 149–168.

Gregory, Derek. 2004. *The Colonial Present: Afghanistan, Palestine, Iraq*. Malden, MA: Blackwell Publishing.

Grosz, Elizabeth. 1999. "Becoming: An Introduction." In *Becomings: Explorations in Time, Memory, and Futures*, Elizabeth Grosz (ed.), 17–39. Ithaca: Cornell University Press.

Habermas, Jurgen. 1976. *Legitimation Crisis*. London: Heinemann.

Hall, Stuart. 1992. "The West and the Rest." In *The Formations of Modernity: Understanding Modern Societies*, Bram Gieben and Stuart Hall (eds.), 184–227. New York: Wiley.

Hall, Stuart. 1996. "Introduction: Who Needs Identity?" In *Questions of Cultural Identity*, Stuart Hall and Paul Du Gay (eds.), 1–17. London: Sage.

Halliday, Fred. 1983. *The Making of the Second Cold War*. London: Verso.

Halliday, Michael. 1994. *Introduction to Functional Grammar* (2nd ed.). London: Arnold.

Hannell, Linnea. 2018. "Anticipatory Discourse in Prenatal Education." *Discourse & Communication 12* (1): 3–19.

Hansen, Lene. 2006. *Security as Practice: Discourse Analysis and the Bosnian War*. New York: Routledge.

Harrell, William, Jr. 2011. *The Origins of the African American Jeremiad: The Rhetorical Strategies of Protest and Activism 1760–1861*. Jefferson, NC: McFarland & Co.

Harvey, David. 1996. *Justice, Nature and the Geography of Difference*. Oxford: Blackwell.

Heller, Agnes. 1999. *A Theory of Modernity*. London: Blackwell.

Herring, George. 2008a. *The American Century and Beyond: U.S. Foreign Relations, 1893–2014*. Oxford: Oxford University Press.

Herring, George. 2008b. *From Colony to Superpower: U.S. Foreign Relations Since 1776*. Oxford: Oxford University Press.

Hobson, Christopher, and Kurki, Milja, eds. 2012. *The Conceptual Politics of Democracy Promotion*. London: Routledge.

Hodges, Adam. 2015. "Intertextuality in Discourse." In *The Handbook of Discourse Analysis*, Deborah Tannen, Heidi Hamilton, and Deborah Schriffin (eds.), 42–60. New York: Wiley Blackwell.

Hodgson, Godfrey. 2009. *The Myth of American Exceptionalism*. New Haven, CT: Yale University Press.

Hostetler, Michael J. 2011. "Henry Cabot Lodge and the Rhetorical Trajectory." In *The Rhetoric of American Exceptionalism: Critical Essays*, Jason A. Edwards and David Weiss (eds.), 118–131. Jefferson, NC: McFarland & Company.

Howard-Pitney, David. 2005. *The African American Jeremiad: Calls for Justice in America*. Philadelphia: Temple University Press.

Hunt, Michael. 1987. *Ideology and U.S. Foreign Policy*. New Haven, CT: Yale University Press.

Huntington, Samuel. 1968. *Political Ordering in Changing Societies*. New Haven, CT: Yale University Press.

Inayatullah, Sohail. 1996. "What Futurists Think: Stories, Methods and Visions of the Future." *Futures 28* (6/7): 509–517.

Inayatullah, Sohail. 1999. "Reorienting Futures Studies." *In Rescuing All Our Futures*, Ziauddin Sadar (ed.), 49–60. Westport, CT: Praeger.

Ish-Shalom, Piki. 2013. *Democratic Peace: A Political Biography*. Ann Arbor: University of Michigan Press.

James, Deborah. 1982. "Past Tense and the Hypothetical: A Cross-Linguistic Study." *Studies in Language 3*: 375–403.

Jancenelle, Vivien, Storrud-Barnes, Susan, and Iaquinto, Anthony. 2019. "Making Investors Feel Good During Earnings Conference Calls: The Effect of Warm Glow Rhetoric." *The Journal of General Management 44* (2): 63–72.

Jaworski, Adam, and Fitzgerald, Richard. 2008. "'This Poll Hasn't Happened Yet': Temporal Play in Election Predictions." *Discourse and Communication 2* (1): 5–27.

Jaworski, Adam, Fitzgerald, Richard, and Morris, Deborah. 2003. "Certainty and Speculation in News Reporting of the Future: The Execution of Timothy McVeigh." *Discourse Studies 5* (1): 33–49.

Jefferson, Thomas. 1801a, March 4. "Inaugural Address." Gerhard Peters and John T. Woolley, *The American Presidency Project*. https://www.presidency.ucsb.edu/node/201948.

Jefferson, Thomas. 1801b, March 6. "Letter to John Dickinson." Available at http://www.let.rug.nl/usa/presidents/thomas-jefferson/letters-of-thomas-jefferson/jefl136.php.

Jendrysik, Mark S. 2002. "The Modern Jeremiad: Bloom, Bennett, and Bork on American Decline." *Journal of Popular Culture 36* (2): 361–383.

Johannesen, Richard L. 1986. "Ronald Reagan's Economic Jeremiad." *Central States Speech Journal 37* (2): 79–89.

Johnson, Robert H. 1983. "Periods of Peril: The Window of Vulnerability and Other Myths." *Foreign Affairs 61* (4): 950–970.

Jones, John, and Rowland, Robert. 2005. "A Covenant-Affirming Jeremiad: The Post-Presidential Ideological Appeals of Ronald Wilson Reagan." *Communication Studies 56* (2): 157–174.

Judge, Edward H., and Langdon, John W., eds. 1999. *The Cold War: A History Through Documents*. Upper Saddle River, NJ: Prentice Hall.

Junker, Kirk W. 1999. "How the Future Is Cloned: Rethinking Future Studies." In *Rescuing All Our Futures*, Ziauddin Sadar (ed.), 19–35. Westport, CT: Praeger.

Kagan, Robert. 2006. *Dangerous Nation: America's Place in the World from Its Earliest Days to the Dawn of the Twentieth Century*. New York: Knopf.

Kammen, Michael. 1993. "The Problem of American Exceptionalism: A Reconsideration." *American Quarterly* 45 (1): 1–43.

Kant, Immanuel. 1991. "Perpetual Peace." In *Kant: Political Writings*, Hans S. Reiss (ed.), 93–130. Cambridge: Cambridge University Press.

Koteyko, Nelya, and Ryazanova-Clarke, Lara. 2009. "The Path and Building Metaphors in the Speeches of Vladimir Putin: Back to the Future?" *Slovonica* 15 (2): 112–127.

Kraus, Keith, and Williams, Michael, eds. 1997. *Critical Security Studies: Concepts and Cases*. Minneapolis: University of Minnesota Press.

Kress, Gunther. 1995. "The Social Production of Language: History and Structures of Domination." In *Discourse in Society: Systemic Functional Perspectives*, Peter H. Fries and Michael Gregory (eds.), 115–140. Norwood, NJ: Ablex.

Krugman, Paul. 2020, November 16. "Why the 2020 Election Makes It Hard to Be Optimistic About the Future." www.nytimes.com/2020/11/16/opinion/coronavirus-climate.html?action=click&module=Opinion&pgtype=Homepage.

Lagerfeld, Steve. 2020. "America, the Exceptional?" *Hedgehog Review* 22 (3): 92–101.

Lakoff, George, and Johnson, Mark. 1980. *Metaphors We Live By*. Chicago: University of Chicago Press.

Lakoff, George, Espenson, Jane, and Schwartz, Alan. 1991. "Master Metaphor List." Available at http://araw.mede.uic.edu/~alansz/metaphor/METAPHORLIST.pdf.

Lapham, Lewis. H. 1992. "Who and What Is America?" *Harper's Magazine* 284 (1700): 43–49.

Lapham, Lewis. H. 2011. "Kingdom Come." *Lapham's Quarterly* 4 (4): 12–19.

Latham, M. E. 2000. *Modernization as Ideology: American Social Science and "Nation Building" in the Kennedy Era*. Chapel Hill: University of North Carolina Press.

Layne, Christopher. 2006. *The Peace of Illusions: American Grand Strategy from 1940 to the Present*. Ithaca, NY: Cornell University Press.

Leblanc, Paul. 2021, January 7. "The Four Living Former Presidents Deride US Capitol Breach in Pointed Statements." www.cnn.com/2021/01/06/politics/george-w-bush-capitol-breach/index.html.

Leffler, Melvyn P. 1992. *A Preponderance of Power: National Security, the Truman Administration, and the Cold War*. Stanford, CA: Stanford University Press.

Lemke, Jay. 1995. *Textual Politics: Discourse and Social Dynamics*. London: Taylor and Francis.

Lepgold, Joseph, and McKeown, Timothy. 1995. "Is American Foreign Policy Exceptional? An Empirical Analysis." *Academy of Political Science* 110 (3): 369–384.

Lipset, Seymour. M. 1997. *American Exceptionalism: A Double-Edged Sword*. New York: Norton.

Loye, David. 1978. *The Knowledge of the Future: A Psychology of Forecasting and Prophecy*. New York: John Wiley and Sons.

Madsen, Deborah. 1998. *American Exceptionalism*. Jackson: University of Mississippi Press.

Martin-Rojo, Luisa, and van Dijk, Teun A. 1997. "'There Was a Problem, and It Was Solved': Legitimating the Expulsion of 'Illegal' Migrants in Spanish Parliamentary Discourse." *Discourse and Society* 8 (4): 523–566.

McCartney, Paul. T. 2004. "American Nationalism and U.S. Foreign Policy from September 11 to the Iraq War." *Political Science Quarterly* 119 (3): 399–423.

McCartney, Paul. T. 2006. *Power and Progress: American National Identity, the War of 1898, and the Rise of American Imperialism*. Baton Rouge: Louisiana State University.

McCrisken, Trevor B. 2003. *American Exceptionalism and the Legacy of Vietnam: U.S. Foreign Policy Since 1974*. Basingstoke, UK: Palgrave.

McEvoy-Levy, Siobhan. 2001. *American Exceptionalism and U. S. Foreign Policy*. Basingstoke, UK: Palgrave.

McKeever, Robert J. 1989. "American Myths and the Impact of the Vietnam War: Revisionism in Foreign Policy and Popular Cinema." In *Vietnam Images: War and Representation*. Jeffrey Walsh and James Aulich (eds.), 43–56. Basingstoke, UK: MacMillan.

Mead, Walter R. 2020, November 3. "The World Still Watches America." *Wall Street Journal* https://www.wsj.com/articles/the-world-still-watches-america-11604360015.

Michta, Andrew A. 2020, October 26. "The American Experiment Is on Life Support." *Wall Street Journal*. https://www.wsj.com/articles/the-american-experiment-is-on-life-support-11603728139.

Miller, Perry. 1956. *Errand into the Wilderness*. New York: Harper Torchbooks.

Mische, Ann. 2009. "Projects and Possibilities: Researching Futures in Action." *Sociological Forum* 24 (3): 694–704.

Mohlo, Anthony, and Wood, Gordon S. 1998. "Introduction." In *Imagined Histories: American Historians Interpret the Past*, Anthony Mohlo and Gordon S. Wood (eds.), 3–20. Princeton, NJ: Princeton University Press.

Monroe, James. 1824. "Eighth Annual Message." Gerhard Peters and John T. Woolley, *The American Presidency Project*. https://www.presidency.ucsb.edu/node/205780.

Muntigl, Peter. 2000. "Dilemmas of Individualism and Social Necessity." In *European Union Discourses on Un/employment: An Interdisciplinary Approach to Employment Policy-making and Organizational Change*, Peter Muntigl, Gilbert Weiss, and Ruth Wodak (eds.), 145–183. Amsterdam: John Benjamins Publishing.

Murphy, Andrew R. 2009. *Prodigal Nation: Moral Decline and Divine Punishment from New England to 9/11*. Oxford: Oxford University Press.

Murphy, John M. 1990. "'A Time of Shame and Sorrow': Robert F. Kennedy and the American Jeremiad." *Quarterly Journal of Speech* 76 (4): 401–414.

Murphy, John M., and Jasinski, James. 2009. "Time, Space and Generic Reconstitution: Martin Luther King's 'A Time to Break Silence' as Radical Jeremiad." In *Public Address and Moral Judgement: Critical Studies in Ethical Tensions*, Sean J. Parry-Giles and Trevor Parry-Giles (eds.), 97–125. East Lansing: Michigan State University Press.

Nandy, Ashis. 1999. "Futures and Dissent." *In Rescuing All Our Futures*, Ziauddin Sardar (ed.), 227–233. Westport, CT: Praeger.

Nash Smith, Henry. 1950. *Virgin Land: The American West as Symbol and Myth*. Cambridge, MA: Harvard University Press.

Nathanson, Charles E. 1988. "The Social Construction of the Soviet Threat: A Study in the Politics of Representation." *Alternatives XIII*: 443–483.

Nayak, Meghana. 2006. "Orientalism and 'Saving' U.S. State Identity After 9/11." *International Feminist Journal of Politics* 8 (1): 42–61.

Neumann, Rico, and Coe, Kevin. 2011. "The Rhetoric in the Modern Presidency." In *The Rhetoric of American Exceptionalism: Critical Essays*, Jason A. Edwards and David Weiss (eds.), 11–30. Jefferson, NC: McFarland &Company.

Noonan, Peggy. 2017, April 6. "What's Become of the American Dream?" *Wall Street Journal.* https://www.wsj.com/articles/whats-become-of-the-american-dream-1491521229.

Nunez, Raphael E., and Sweetser, Eve. 2006. "With the Future Behind Them: Convergent Evidence from Aymara Language and Gesture in Cross-Linguistic Comparison of Spatial Construals of Time." *Cognitive Science 30*: 401–450.

Obama, Barack. 2009, December 1. "Remarks by the President in Address to the Nation on the Way Forward in Afghanistan and Pakistan." West Point Military Academy. Available at https://obamawhitehouse.archives.gov/the-press-office/remarks-president-address-nation-way-forward-afghanistan-and-pakistan.

Oddo, John. 2011. "War Legitimation Discourse: Representing 'Us' and 'Them' in Four U.S. Presidential Addresses." *Discourse & Society 22* (3): 287–314.

Oddo, John. 2014. "Variation and Continuity in Intertextual Rhetoric." *Journal of Language and Politics 13* (3): 512–537.

Onuf, Peter S. 2000. *Jefferson's Empire: The Language of American Nationhood.* Charlottesville: University of Virginia Press.

O'Sullivan, John. 1839. "The Great Nation of Futurity." *The United States Magazine and Democratic Review 6* (23): 426–430.

O'Sullivan, John. 1845. "Annexation." *The United States Magazine and Democratic Review 17* (1): 5–10.

O'Toole, Fintan. 2020. "Democracy's Afterlife." *New York Review of Books LXVII* (19): 4–9.

O'Tuathail, Gearoid. 1996. *Critical Geopolitics.* Minneapolis: Minnesota University Press.

Paine, Thomas. 1997/1776. *Common Sense.* Mineola, NY: Dover Publications.

Palmer, Frank. 2001. *Mood and Modality.* Cambridge: Cambridge University Press.

Pearce, Kimber C. 2001. *Rostow, Kennedy, and the Rhetoric of Foreign Aid.* East Lansing: Michigan State University Press.

Pencanha, Sergio. 2021, January 7. "The End of American Exceptionalism." https://www.washingtonpost.com/opinions/2021/01/07/end-american-exceptionalism/?arc404=true&_=ddid-1-1610049060&itid=lk_inline_manual_19.

Pfaff, William. 2010. *The Irony of Manifest Destiny.* New York: Walker and Company.

Podvig, Pavel. 2008. "The Window of Vulnerability That Wasn't: Soviet Military Buildup in the 1970s—A Research Note." *International Security 33*: 118–138.

Polak, Fred. 1973. *The Image of the Future.* Amsterdam: Elsevier Scientific Publishing.

Pratt, Julius W. 1927. "The Origin of 'Manifest Destiny.'" *American Historical Review 32* (4): 795–798.

Raddatz, Martha. 2021, January 6. "It is so horrible to know, we are in America where this is happening, on Capitol Hill. I'm not in Baghdad. I'm not in Kabul. I'm not in a dangerous situation overseas." Twitter. twitter.com/gma/status/1346936089920102401.

Rasmussen, Anders F. 2020, December 15. "A New Way to Lead the Free World." *Wall Street Journal.* https://www.wsj.com/articles/a-new-way-to-lead-the-free-world-11608053780.

Rasmussen, Mikkel V. 2002. "'A Parallel Globalization of Terror': 9/11, Security and Globalization." *Cooperation and Conflict: Journal of the Nordic International Studies Association 37* (3): 323–349.

Restad, Hilde E. 2012. "Old Paradigms in History Die Hard in Political Science: United States Foreign Policy and American Exceptionalism." *American Political Thought: A Journal of Ideas, Institutions, and Culture 1*: 53–76.

Restad, Hilde E. 2015. *American Exceptionalism: An Idea That Made a Nation and Remade the World*. New York: Routledge.

Ritter, Kurt W. 1980. "American Political Rhetoric and the Jeremiad Tradition: Presidential Nomination Acceptance Addresses, 1960–1976." *Central States Speech Journal 31* (3): 152–171.

Rodgers, Daniel T. 1998. "Exceptionalism." In *Imagined Histories: American Historians Interpret the Past*, A. Mohlo and G. S. Wood (eds.), 21–41, Princeton, NJ: Princeton University Press.

Rodgers, Daniel T. 2004. "American Exceptionalism Revisited." *Raritan 24*: 21–47.

Rodgers, Daniel T. 2018. *As a City on a Hill: The Story of America's Most Famous Sermon*. Princeton, NJ: Princeton University Press.

Rostow, Walter. 1971. *Stages of Economic Growth: A Non-Communist Manifesto* (2nd ed.). Cambridge: Cambridge University Press.

Rubio, Marco. 2021, January 6. "There is nothing patriotic about what is occurring on Capitol Hill. This is 3rd world style anti-American anarchy." Twitter. twitter.com/marcorubio/status/1346909901478522880.

Sahlins, Marshall. 1985. *Islands of History*. Chicago: University of Chicago Press.

Said, Edward. 1978. *Orientalism*. New York: Vintage Books.

Salkie, Raphael. 2010. "*Will*: Tense or Modal or Both?" *English Language and Linguistics 14* (2): 187–215.

Sanders, Jerry W. 1983. *Peddlers of Crisis: The Committee on the Present Danger and the Politics of Containment*. Boston: South End Press.

Sanford, Charles L. 1974. *Manifest Destiny and the Imperialism Question*. New York: John Wiley & Sons.

Sardar, Ziauddin 1993. "Colonizing the Future: the 'Other' Dimension of Futures Studies." *Futures 25* (2): 179–187.

Sardar, Ziauddin, ed. 1999. "The Problem of Future Studies." In *Rescuing All Our Futures: The Future of Futures Studies*, Ziauddin Sardar (ed.), 9–18. Westport, CT: Praeger Publishing.

Sargent, Daniel. 2018, July 23. "RIP American Exceptionalism, 1776–2018." *Foreign Policy*. Available: https://foreignpolicy.com/2018/07/23/rip-american-excepti onalism-1776-2018/.

Schlatter, Richard 1962. "The Puritan Strain." In *The Reconstruction of American History*, John Higham (ed.), 25–45. Westport, CT: Greenwood Publishing.

Schlesinger, Arthur, Jr. 1977. "America: Experiment or Destiny?" *The American Historical Review 82* (3): 505–522.

Schneider, Susanne. 2006. "Future Time Reference in English and Italian: A Typologically Guided Comparative Study." Available at https://123dok.org/document/4yro1m8y-future-reference-english-italian-typologically-guided-comparative-study.html.

Scollon, Suzanne, and Scollon, Ron. 2000. "The Construction of Agency and Action in Anticipatory Discourse: Positioning Ourselves Against Neo-Liberalism." Paper presented at the III Conference for Sociocultural Research, Sao Paulo, July 16–20.

Shafer, Byron E. 1991. *Is America Different? A New Look at American Exceptionalism*. Oxford: Clarendon Press.

Shafer, Byron E. 1999. "American Exceptionalism." *Annual Review of Political Science 2*: 445–463.

Shapiro, Michael, ed. 1988. "The Constitution of the Central American Other: The Case of 'Guatemala.'" In *The Politics of Representation*, 89–191. Madison: University of Wisconsin Press.

Silver, Peter. 2008. *Our Savage Neighbors: How Indian War Transformed Early America*. New York: Norton & Co.

Singer, Max, and Wildavsky, Aaron. 1993. *The Real World Order: Zones of Peace / Zones of Turmoil*. Chatham, NJ: Chatham House Publishers.

Slotkin, Richard. 1985. *The Fatal Environment: The Myth of the Frontier in the Age of Industrialization, 1800–1890*. Norman: University of Oklahoma Press.

Slotkin, Richard. 1992. *Gunfighter Nation: The Myth of the Frontier in Twentieth-Century America*. New York: Antheneum.

Smith, Tony. 2012. "From 'Fortunate Vagueness' to 'Democratic Globalism': American Democracy Promotion as Imperialism." In *Conceptual Politics of Democracy Promotion*, Christopher Hobson and Milja Kurki (eds.), 201–214. London: Routledge.

Stephanson, Anders. 1995. *Manifest Destiny: American Expansionism and the Empire of Right*. New York: Hill and Wang.

Stritzel, Holger. 2007. "Towards a Theory of Securitization: Copenhagen and Beyond." *European Journal of International Relations* 13 (3): 357–383.

Tarnas, Richard. 1993. *The Passion of the Western Mind: Understanding the Ideas That Have Shaped Our World View*. New York: Ballantine Publishing.

Tavory, Iddo, and Eliasoph, Nina. 2013. "Coordinating Futures: Toward a Theory of Anticipation." *American Journal of Sociology* 118 (4): 908–942.

Tharoor, Ishaan. 2021, January 7. "The End of the Road for American Exceptionalism." *Washington Post*. https://www.washingtonpost.com/world/2021/01/07/ameri can-exceptionalism-end-capitol-mob/.

Thompson, Geoff. 2004. *Introducing Functional Grammar*. London: Arnold.

Tipps, Dean C. 1973. "Modernization Theory and the Comparative Study of Societies: A Critical Perspective." *Comparative Studies in Society and History* 15 (2): 199–226.

Trofimov, Yaroslav. 2020, November 7. "Can the West Still Lead?" *Wall Street Journal*. https://www.wsj.com/articles/can-the-west-still-lead-11604678307.

Trump, Donald. J. 2015, June 16. "Full Transcript: Trump Announces Presidential Bid." https://www.washingtonpost.com/news/post-politics/wp/2015/06/16/ full-text-donald-trump-announces-a-presidential-bid/.

Trump, Donald. J. 2020, August 8. "Full Transcript: President Trump's Republican National Convention Speech." https://www.nytimes.com/2020/08/28/us/polit ics/trump-rnc-speech-transcript.html.

Turner, Frederick J. 1920. "The Significance of the Frontier in American History." Paper read at the meeting of the American Historical Association in Chicago, July 12, 1893. Available at xroads.virginia.edu/~hyper/turner/chapter1.html.

Tyrell, Ian. 1991. "American Exceptionalism in an Age of International History." *The American Historical Review* 96 (4): 1031–1055.

Udayakumar, S. P. 1999. "Futures Studies and Future Facilitators." In *Rescuing All Our Futures*, Ziauddin Sardar (ed.), 98–116. Westport, CT: Praeger.

Ultan, Russell. 1978. "The Nature of Future Tenses." In *Universals in Human Language, IV: Word Structure*, Joseph H. Greenberg (ed.), 83–124. Stanford, CA: Stanford University Press.

United States National Security Council. 2002. *The National Security Strategy of the United States of America*. Available at https://2009-2017.state.gov/documents/ organization/63562.pdf.

United States National Security Council. 2010. *National Security Strategy*. Available at https://obamawhitehouse.archives.gov/sites/default/files/rss_viewer/nationa l_security_strategy.pdf.

van Dijk, Teun. A. 1993. *Elite Discourse and Racism*. Newbury Park, CA: Sage.

van Dijk, Teun. A. 1998. *Ideology: A Multidisciplinary Approach*. London: Sage.

van Dijk, Teun. A. 2008. *Discourse and Context: A Sociocognitive Approach*. Cambridge: Cambridge University Press.

van Dijk, Teun. A. 2009. *Society and Discourse: How Social Contexts Influence Text and Talk*. Cambridge: Cambridge University Press.

Van Engen, Abram C. 2020. *City on a Hill: A History of American Exceptionalism*. New Haven, CT: Yale University Press.

van Leeuwen, Theo. 2008. *Discourse and Practice: New Tools or Critical Discourse Analysis*. Oxford: Oxford University Press.

van Munster, Rens. 2004. "The War on Terror: When the Exception Becomes the Rule." *International Journal for the Semiotics of Law 17*: 141–153.

van Voorst. Bruce. 1990, May 5. "Sticking to His Guns: Cheney Chops the Pentagon Budget but Refuses to Reshape It." *Time Magazine 135* (19). http://content.time.com/time/subscriber/article/0,33009,970051,00.html.

Wæver, Ole. 1995. "Securitization and Desecuritization." In *On Security*, Ronnie Lipschultz (ed.), 46–86. New York: Columbia University Press.

Wæver, Ole. 1996. "European Security Identities." *Journal of Common Market Studies 4* (1): 103–132.

Wæver, Ole. 2002. "Identity, Communities and Foreign Policy: Discourse Analysis as Foreign Policy Theory." In *European Integration and National Identity: The Challenge of the Nordic States*, Lene Hansen and Ole Wæver (eds.), 20–49. London: Routledge.

Washington, George. 1789, April 30. "Inaugural Address." Gerhard Peters and John T. Woolley, *The American Presidency Project*. https://www.presidency.ucsb.edu/node/200393.

Washington, George. 1796. "Farewell Address." Available at https://www.govinfo.gov/content/pkg/GPO-CDOC-106sdoc21/pdf/GPO-CDOC-106sdoc21.pdf.

Washington Post. 2021, January 7. Opinion: To Heal America, We Must Repudiate Not Just Trump but His Politics of Demonization. https://www.washingtonpost.com/opinions/to-heal-america-we-must-repudiate-not-just-trump-but-also-his-politics-of-demonization/2021/01/07/8f6a7388-5117-11eb-b96e-0e54447b23a1_story.html.

Weber, Max. 1964. *The Theory of Social and Economic Organization*. New York: Free Press.

Weinberg, Albert. 1958. *Manifest Destiny: A Study of Nationalist Expansionism in American History*. Baltimore, MD: John Hopkins Press.

Wekker, Herman C. 1976. *The Expression of Future Time in Contemporary British English: An Investigation into the Syntax and Semantics of Five Verbal Constructions Expressing Futurity*. Amsterdam: North-Holland Publishing.

Wells, Herbert G. 1985. "The Discovery of the Future." *Futures Research Quarterly* Summer: 56–73.

Wells, Herbert. G. 1987. "Wanted: Professors of Foresight!" *Futures Research Quarterly* Spring: 89–91.

Westad, Odd A. 2007. *The Global Cold War*. Cambridge: Cambridge University Press.

Whitcomb, Roger S. 1998. *The American Approach to Foreign Affairs: An Uncertain Tradition*. Westport, CT: Praeger.

Whitman, Walt. 1871. "Democratic Vistas." Accessed June 21, 2019. http://xroads.virginia.edu/~Hyper/Whitman/vistas/vistas.html.

Wilson, Graham K. 1998. *Only in America? The Politics of the United States in Comparative Perspective*. Chatham, NJ: Chatham House.

Winthrop, John. 1630. "A Model of Christian Charity." Available at https://www.wint hropsociety.com/_files/ugd/9a2d3b_4d9f243ce4b34c0fad7f4f41df29d992. pdf?index=true.

Wodak, Ruth, de Cillia, Rudolph, Reisigl, Martin, and Liebhart, Karin. 1999. *The Discursive Construction of National Identity*. Edinburgh: Edinburgh University Press.

Wodak, Ruth, and Meyer, Michael, eds. 2001. *Methods of Critical Discourse Analysis*. London: Sage.

Wolfe, Alan. 1983. Foreword to *Peddlers of Crisis: The Committee on the Present Danger and the Politics of Containment*, by J. W. Sanders. Boston: South End Press.

Wood, Gordon S. 2002. *The American Revolution: A History*. New York: Modern Library

Woolley, John T., and Peters, Gerard. 2010. *The American Presidency Project*. http://www.presidency.ucsb.edu/index.php.

Yergin, Daniel. 1977. *Shattered Peace: The Origins of the Cold War*. New York: Penguin.

Young, Lynne, and Harrison, Claire. 2004. *Systemic Functional Linguistics and Critical Discourse Analysis*. London: Continuum.

INDEX

For the benefit of digital users, indexed terms that span two pages (e.g., 52–53) may, on occasion, appear on only one of those pages.

Note: Tables are indicated by *t* following the page number

absolute power, 71–72, 119
active/passive American Self dyad, 51–52, 133, 144, 148–49, 159
Adams, John, 33–34
Adams, John Quincy, 38
Albright, Madeline, 48
"The American Century" (Luce), 24, 52, 53–58
American exceptionalism
  American national identity and, 26–27, 31
  Cold War and, 15–27, 156–60
  Committee on the Present Danger and, 108
  Discourse of, 12–15
  foreign policy and, 12–15
  futurity and, 12–15, 31–45
  identity of, 26–27
  laws of history, 41–45
  legitimation and, 21–23, 45–49
  New World Order, 35, 41–45
  Reagan, Ronald and, 123–31, 126*t*, 128*t*
  separate and different, 38–41
  special nation, special destiny belief, 32–38, 43
  summary of, 49–50
  summary of analysis, 156–60
  Trump, Donald and, 160–67
American global leadership, 2, 59, 77, 135, 149–50, 166

American jeremiad, 23, 29, 36, 133–34, 135–37
American national identity
  American exceptionalism and, 26–27, 31
  American jeremiad and, 133–34, 135–37
  chosen-ness in, 137–43
  critical futures perspective, ix, 1–5
  declension in, 137, 144–49
  futurity and foreign policy discourse, x, 8–10
  introduction to, 28, 133–34
  legitimation through, 123–31
  liminality in, 144–45, 146*t*
  overview of, 27–30
  post-Cold War jeremiad, 137–43, 138*t*, 142*t*, 143*t*, 149–50
  prophecy and, 137, 149–54
  space-time and, 18
  as spatiotemporal practice, 10–12
  spatiotemporal practice and, 10–12
  temporality of, 2–3
American Revolution, 47, 140
American Self/periphery Other, 133, 157–58
American Self/Soviet Union dyad, 158
American-Soviet tensions. *See*
  Cold War foreign policy;
  Committee on the Present Danger;
  Soviet Union

American utopia, 48
America Revolution, 34–35
anticipatory regime, 2, 6, 118
anticipatory security practice, 6
Applebaum, Ann, 165
Arendt, Hannah, 49
Asia, 66
atomic capability of US, 121
authoritarianism, 75, 150–51, 152

backwards people, 81
Baker, James, 139–40, 150–51
Baker, Peter, 161–62
Baldwin, Hanson, 15
Biden, Joe, 161
Blow, Charles, 162
Bossert, Tom, 161
Breese, Sydney, 44
Brooks, David, 163–64
Brownson, Orestes, 35–36
Bush, George H. W., 26, 133, 135, 137–
    38, 139, 144, 148, 149–54
Bush, George W., x, 47, 161–62

capitalism, 85, 88, 106–7, 134–35, 139,
    140–41, 150, 151
Carnegie, Andrew, 39–40
Carter, Jimmy, 102–3, 161
Cheney, Liz, 161
chosen-ness, 137–43
chosen people, 32–33
Christian charity, 33
chronological
    imperialism, 29–30
chronopolitics, defined, 3
Clinton, Bill, 26, 133, 135, 138–39, 140–
    41, 149–54
Clinton, Hillary, 162
Cold War ending/post-Cold War
    American national identity, 134–35
    chosen-ness in, 137–43
    declension in, 137, 144–49
    post-Cold War jeremiad, 137–43,
        138t, 142t, 143t, 149–50
    post-Cold War Other, 135, 148, 149–
        50, 152
    prophecy and, 137, 149–54
    summary of, 154–55
Cold War foreign policy. *See also*
    Soviet Union

American exceptionalism and, 15–
    27, 156–60
anti-communism, 47
data set on, 23–27
enactment of, 25
formulation of, 24
and futurity, 4, 6–8, 25
introduction to, ix, 1, 2, 29
legitimation strategy within, 3
modernization theory and, 79–98
reassertion of, 25–26
reformulation of, 26–27
temporal terms of, 52
Colonial America, 92
Committee on the Present Danger (CPD)
    detente and, 101, 102–3, 104
    futurity of Soviet threat, 110–13,
        111t, 112t
    introduction to, 18–19, 25–26, 28–
        29, 101–2
    legitimation and identity
        performance, 123–31
    NSC 68 history and, 118–23
    present danger, 118–31, 159
    Reagan, Ronald and, 123–31,
        126t, 128t
    securitization and, 103–5
    space-time distance, 113–18,
        114t, 117t
    summary of, 131–32
communism, 52, 59–60, 85, 107, 147,
    150, 152, 156–57
Cotton, John, 40
critical discourse analysis (CDA), 15–27
critical futures perspective, ix, 3–5

declension, 137, 144–49
decolonization, 7–8, 85
democracy
    global future of, x, 147
    liberal democracy, 14–15, 25, 134–
        35, 140–41
    meaning related to futures, 57
    Western liberal democracy, 14–15
democratic peace, 139–41, 143–44,
    147, 154–55
Democratic Review, 36, 38–39
detente, 101, 102–3
dialectical discursive practice, 8–9
divine prophecy, 40

[196] *Index*

divine Providence, 36

Emerson, Ralph Waldo, 39–40
evangelism of fear, 10, 87

foreign policy. *See* Cold War foreign
    policy; space-time in foreign policy
Foreign Policy, 163
Founding Fathers, 33–35, 41
Franklin, Benjamin, 38
freedom
    in future, 81, 82
    global future of, x
    international stability and
       peace, 102–3
    meaning related to futures, 57
    territory of, 4
frontier thesis, 44–45
Fukuyama, Francis, 134
The Future of Underdeveloped Countries
    (Staley), 80–86
futurity
    American exceptionalism and, 12–
      15, 31–45
    American jeremiad and, 136
    Cold War and, 6–8, 25
    data set, 23–27
    foreign policy discourse, 8–10,
      80, 86–93
    futurology of security, 6–8
    geopolitical status, 1–2
    global society and, 2, 55, 76–77, 92–
      93, 141, 158–59
    Great Nation of, 1–2, 8, 18,
      27, 29–30
    indefinite future
      expansion, 43–44
    introduction to, 1–3
    justice, meaning related to, 57
    knowledge of the future, 4
    legitimation, 21–23
    national identity discourse, 8–10
    politics of, 3–5
    postwar future, 53–76, 57t
    post-World War II and, 6–7, 53–76
    progressive future, 41–42, 136, 144,
      148–49, 159
    re-securitization of Soviet
      Union, 106–10
    of Soviet threat, 110–13, 111t, 112t

space-time, 17–21, 19t, 53–76
theoretical framework, 3–15
Western futurism, 4–5
futurology, 6–8, 16

Gallagher, Mike, 161–62
Galston, William, 162–63
geopolitical status. *See also* space-time in
    foreign policy
    futurity and, 1–2
    introduction to, 27–28
    Luce, Henry, 24, 52, 53–58
    policies of, x, 12, 14–15
    post-Cold War jeremiad, 137–43,
      138t, 142t, 143t, 149–50
Gerson, Michael, 161
global domination, 110, 117–18
global leadership, 2, 59, 77, 135, 149–
    50, 166
global society
    American exceptionalism and, 108
    American identity and, 25, 57–58
    evolution of, 132
    future prospects of, 65, 148–49
    futurity and, 2, 55, 76–77, 92–93,
      141, 158–59
    NSC 68 and, 74–75
    Reagan, Ronald and, 128–29
    underdeveloped areas and, 87
Greece, 58–69, 73
Guyot, Andrew, 42

Hoover, Herbert, 57
human dignity, 81–82, 127–28
human liberty, 92, 108

identity. *See* American national identity
ideological square, 22
imaginative geography, 11
imminent threat of Soviet Union, 29,
    101–2, 105
imperialism, 25, 29–30, 129–30
Iraq war, x

Jefferson, Thomas, 34, 38, 41–42
jeremiad. *See* American jeremiad
justice, meaning related to futures, 57

Kant, Immanuel, 139
knowledge of the future, 4

Index [197]

Krugman, Paul, 164, 166

Lake, Anthony, 147
Lapham, Lewis, 1
legitimation, 21–23, 45–49, 123–31
 authorization legitimation, 21–22
 exceptionalism as, 45–49
 moral evaluation legitimation, 22
 mythopoesis legitimation, 22–23
Lerner, Daniel, 80, 93–98, 97t
liberal democracy, 14–15, 25, 134–
 35, 140–41
liminality in American national identity,
 144–45, 146t
Lowell, James Russell, 38
Luce, Henry, 24, 52, 53–58

Manifest Destiny, 25, 43–44, 46–47, 58
market economics, 141–42, 147
Marxist-Leninism, 109, 120, 130–31
material welfare, 81, 82, 90
Mather, Increase, 33
McCarthy, Kevin, 161
Mead, Walter Russell, 164–65
Melville, Herman, 37–38
Metaphor
 ascendancy, 74–75
 building, 74–75, 90–91, 152
 Ego Reference Point, 113, 116–17
 gardening 63–65
 Good Governing is Creating, 74–
 75, 90–91
 integrity, 73–74
 investing, 63–65
 journey, 97–98, 152
 metaphorical distance, 113–14
 powerhouse, 58
 shining city on a hill, 128–29
 temporal, 131–32
 tidal, 130
 Time Passing is Motion, 113
 Time Reference Point, 113
 turning point, 59
 vitality, 73–74, 75
Michta, Andrew, 164
Millikan, Max, 80, 86–93
"A Model of Christian Charity"
 (Winthrop), 32–33
modernization theory (MT)
 Cold War foreign policy and, 79–98

 introduction to, 18–19, 25, 78–79
 Lerner, Daniel, 80, 93–98, 97t
 Millikan, Max, 80, 86–93
 Rostow, Walter, 80, 86–93
 Staley, Eugene, 80–86, 84t
 summary of, 98–100
 underdeveloped areas, 18–19, 80–93,
 89t, 91t, 98–99, 157–58
Monroe, James, 34

national identity. *See* American national
 identity
*National Military Strategy of the United
 States* (1992), 137–38
National Security Council Resolution 20/
 4 (1948), 120
National Security Council Resolution 68,
 24, 52, 65, 69–76, 72t, 118–23
naturalization order, 78–79, 93–98
New World Order, 25, 35, 41–45
New York Times, 2, 161–62, 163, 164
Noonan, Peggy, 164
novus ordo seclorum, 37–38
nuclear war, 109

Obama, Barack, ix, 162
Old World Europe, 40–45, 49
O'Sullivan, John, 38, 39–40, 43,
 44, 46–47
Other. *See also* Self/Other pairings
 Differentiating from Self, 3
 foreign policy and national identity
 discourse, 8–10
 moral evaluation legitimation, 22
 radical Other, 2, 20–21, 25–26, 28–29,
 51, 101–2, 106–7, 109, 132, 133,
 134–35, 137–38, 159
 space-time and, 19–20
 spatial exclusion of Otherness, 10
O'Toole, Finan, 162

Paine, Thomas, 33–35, 58, 127
Partisan Review, 156–57
The Passing of Traditional Society (Lerner),
 80, 93–98, 97t
PATH and JOURNEY schemas, 124
period of peril, 110, 115, 120–21
political imaginaries, 6–7, 106, 157
post-Cold War. *See* Cold War ending/
 post-Cold War

[198] *Index*

post-Cold War Other, 135, 148, 149–50, 152
postcolonial societies, 79, 82, 86–87, 92, 99
post-World War II
  CPD's threat campaign, 132
  foreign policy discourse, 12–15
  futurity and, 6–7, 53–76
  modernization theory and, 79
  Soviet Union and, 7
  space-time construal from, 147
present danger, 118–31, 159. *See also* Committee on the Present Danger
prognostik practice, 7
progressive future, 41–42, 136, 144, 148–49, 159
promised land, 32–33, 154
prophecy, 40, 137, 149–54
A Proposal: Key to an Effective Foreign Policy (Millikan, Rostow), 80, 86–93
Puritan jeremiad, 36, 136
Puritans, 32–34, 36, 40, 47, 140

Raddatz, Martha, 161–62
radical Other, 2, 20–21, 25–26, 28–29, 51, 101–2, 106–7, 109, 132, 133, 134–35, 137–38, 159
Ramsey, David, 35, 37
Rantoul, Robert, 35
Rasmussen, Anders Fogh, 166
Reagan, Ronald, 105, 123–31, 126t, 128t
re-securitization of Soviet Union, 23, 24, 106–18
Romney, Mitt, 165
Rostow, Eugene, 104
Rostow, Walter, 80, 86–93
Rubio, Marco, 161–62

sanctuary, 57–58, 159
Sargent, Daniel, 163, 166
Schumer, Charles, 165
securitization, 103–18
security strategy, 6–8, 74, 137, 152
Self/Other pairings. *See also* Other
  active/passive American Self dyad, 51–52, 133, 144, 148–49, 159
  American Self/periphery Other, 133, 157–58
  American Self/Soviet Union dyad, 158
  contrast between, 19–21, 20t

detente, 101
foreign policy and national identity discourse, 8–10
modernization theory, 78
moral evaluation legitimation, 22
post-Cold War Other, 135, 148, 149–50, 152
re-securitization of Soviet Union, 106–10
space-time and, 19–20
space-times in foreign policy, 19–21, 20t, 51, 52, 157
sociopolitical temporal theme
  Cold War foreign policy discourse, ix
  modernization theory and, 80–86, 84t
  national identity as, 10
  naturalization order, 80, 93–98, 97t
Soviet Union. *See also* Cold War foreign policy; Committee on the Present Danger
  breakup of, 134, 137–38
  Cold War ending, 134–35
  as compelling alternative vision, 25
  defense and investment allocations, 123
  as existential threat, 25, 28–29, 100, 103–4, 106, 134–35
  as expansionist, 64, 68
  false prophet of the future, 2, 18
  fundamental design, 119–20
  futurity of threat, 110–13, 111t, 112t
  geopolitical goals, 119, 120, 122, 139
  imminent threat of, 29, 101–2, 105
  National Security Council Resolution 68 and, 24, 52, 65, 69–76, 72t
  prognostik practice, 7
  programs of expansion, 115–16
  re-securitization of, 23, 24, 106–18
  Self/Other contrast, 19–21, 20t
  underdeveloped areas and, 86–93, 89t, 91t, 157–58
space-time in foreign policy
  American national identity, 10–12
  Committee on the Present Danger, 113–18, 114t, 117t
  defined, 17–21, 19t
  futurity and, 17–21, 19t, 53–76, 57t
  introduction, 51–52
  Luce, Henry, 24, 52, 53–58
  marking time, 117–18

Index [199]

space-time in foreign policy (*cont.*)
   National Security Council Resolution
      68, 24, 52, 65, 69–76, 72*t*
   postwar future, 53–76, 57*t*
   Self/Other pairings, 19–21, 20*t*, 51,
      52, 157
   summary of, 76–77
   Truman, Harry, 24, 52, 58–69
   Truman Doctrine, 58–69, 63*t*,
      67*t*, 76–77
spatial exclusion of Otherness, 10
spatiotemporal practice, 10–12, 56
"Special Message to the Congress
   on Greece and Turkey"
   (Truman), 24, 52
special nation, special destiny belief,
   32–38, 43
Staley, Eugene, 80–86, 84*t*

temporal imperialism, 4
temporality
   of American exceptionalism, 1–3
   of American national identity, 2–
      3, 147
   authorization legitimation, 22
   critical discourse analysis, 15–27
   politics of, 3–5
   of securitization, 103–5
   spatiotemporal practice, 10–12
   theoretical framework, 3–15
temporal location authorization, 66
temporal pluralism, 7, 24
Tharoor, Ishaan, 161–62
Third World societies, 79–80
totalitarianism, 63, 64, 65, 75,
   84, 156–57
Trofimov, Yaroslav, 162–63, 164–65
Trope
   alternative futures, 55–56, 59, 63, 64,
      81, 83–84, 90, 101–2, 106, 128–29,
      145–46, 157–59
   opportunity/challenge, 153, 154
   pivotal moment, 145

Self/Other, 51, 87, 136, 137
shape-the-future, 55–56, 58, 59, 63,
   136, 145–46, 147–48, 159
threat/promise. 151–52, 153, 154
unrealized errand, 145
Truman, Harry, 24, 52, 58–69,
   73, 158–59
Truman Doctrine, 58–69, 63*t*, 67*t*, 76–
   77, 157–58
Trump, Donald, 160–67
Turkey, 58–69, 73
Turner, Fredrick Jackson, 44–45

underdeveloped areas/countries, 18–19,
   80–93, 89*t*, 91*t*, 98–99, 157–58
United States/Britain (European)
   dyad, 51–52
*The United States Magazine and
   Democratic Review*, 38
United States/periphery dyad, 51–52
United States/Soviet Union dyad, 51–52
U.S. foreign policy. *See* Cold War foreign
   policy; space-time in foreign policy
utopias, 3–4, 48, 88

Wall Street Journal, 162–63, 164, 166
Washington, George, 34, 46
Washington Post, 161–62
Wells, H. G., 55–56
western frontier, 42–43, 44–45
Western futurism, 4–5
Whitman, Walt, 37
window of vulnerability, 115
Winthrop, John, 32–33, 136
Winthrop, Robert, 46–47
world environment, 56–57, 69–
   76, 86–87
world making, 3–4, 8
world revolution, 87, 130
World War II. *See* post–World War II

zones of peace, 141–43, 142*t*
zones of turmoil, 141–43, 142*t*